THE SEARCH
FOR UNITY

THE SEARCH FOR UNITY

*Relations between the
Anglican and Roman Catholic Churches
from the 1950s to the 1970s*

William Purdy

With an appreciation by
Professor Sir Henry Chadwick

GEOFFREY
CHAPMAN

Geoffrey Chapman
A Cassell imprint
Wellington House, 125 Strand, London WC2R 0BB
215 Park Avenue South, New York, NY 10003

First published 1996

British Library Cataloguing-in-Publication Data
A catalogue record for this book is available from the British Library.

ISBN 0–225–66710–X

Typeset by Keystroke, Jacaranda Lodge, Wolverhampton
Printed and bound in Great Britain by Redwood Books, Trowbridge, Wilts

Contents

William Purdy: an appreciation

Among the many English participants in the intricate process of serious ecumenical dialogue central to the implementation of the decree of the Second Vatican Council (1965), the name of William Purdy has a place of its own. He brought to the dialogue with the Anglican Communion a number of qualities and capacities which were integral to the prosperity of the conversations. With a first-class degree in history from Cambridge he could move with ease and familiarity in the story of the events which had brought about separation in the sixteenth century. The historian is not able, merely by historical method, to solve the problems of ecumenism, but has a unique capacity to see how and why the problems came to be seen as issues leading to ecclesial division. William Purdy shared with John Henry Newman the instinctive and intuitive power to get behind polemical formulas of the past and to ask what is actually being affirmed or denied. He also shared with Newman what can only be called Englishness. He was a walking refutation of any hazy residual notions that somehow being a Roman Catholic was not quite an English thing to be. He loved cricket and was very much a monarchist without supposing that this committed him to belief in the royal ecclesiastical supremacy (a doctrine in which today it would be hard to find Anglican believers). In addition there were no terrors for him in a Latin or Greek text, and he could cope easily with the Church Fathers or the Schoolmen or the Acts and Canons of the Council of Trent.

His training has also equipped him with great facility in the writing of clear prose, and this was to be important both when he was entrusted with the drafting of a papal statement on the progress of ARCIC and also when he was the Secretary on the Roman Catholic side of the Commission responsible for practical arrangements for meetings and for the incisive sentences of agreed statements. He had behind him experience in teaching theology first at St Edmund's, Ware, then at St

Hugh's, Tollerton, in the diocese of Nottingham, and finally at the Beda in Rome.

He himself began as a student at the English College in Rome where he was a contemporary and good friend of the future Cardinal Heenan. That friendship was important when the future Cardinal Willebrands at the then Secretariat for Christian Unity needed a priest to take responsibility for the Anglican and Methodist conversations with the Vatican's teams of bishops and theologians. A constructive link between the two archbishops played a crucial role in the invitation to him to undertake this work, for which he was particularly well qualified, as shown by a series of articles in *The Tablet*.

Throughout the conversations in ARCIC he was a serene source of confidence and strength. With potentially explosive topics under discussion, the debates were not always free from trouble and anxiety. There could be meetings of the Commission where for successive days there seemed to be deadlock with no escape, and in the morning coffee-breaks walking in the garden one could suddenly be confronted by an archbishop in uncontrollable floods of tears, frustrated by the feeling that the commission was in a gridlock, unable to move forwards, backwards, or sideways. At particular points with a long past history of confrontations and negations, the temperature of discussion could feel unbearably warm – though always filled with mutual charity which, naturally enough, did nothing at all to make things cooler. William Purdy always retained a calm temper, suggesting from time to time a helpful way of analysing the problem causing difficulty. Very characteristic of him would be an *obiter dictum* that the essence of the Ave Maria consisted of two scriptural texts strung together; and why should that be felt as an obstacle in what was more an acclamation than a prayer or a doctrine? He would perceive that behind the statement that Mary was free of the taint of original sin lay the non-controversial proposition, underpinned by St Luke, that divine grace prepared her for the responsibility of being mother of the incarnate Lord. And beyond the affirmation that Mary's honour in the communion of saints is elevation to heavenly glory redeemed by her Son, there lies the conviction that this honour is wholly of a piece with that which God conferred upon her on earth.

One of his major sources of strength to the Commission was the breadth of his vision, and dislike of anything narrow or crude. This width of sympathy was surely related to his authoritative expertise in the visual arts and in art history. For him the eye was as important a medium as the ear for apprehending the wonder of the gospel entrusted to the Church. Words have some inherent inadequacy when treating of divine mysteries. Subjects such as the Church, which at first sight look as if the matter under discussion was an empirical society and no more, turn out to be affirmations of faith. Transubstantiation should not be thought of as physics and chemistry, and if William Purdy had to explain what he understood by the term, something indistinguishable from ARCIC's footnote on this subject would have come. He played an important part in commending this form of statement to the Commission.

William Purdy loved God and loved the Church. All else was secondary in his life and work. He was a deeply loyal priest who saw the conversations between the official representatives of Rome and Canterbury as a momentous opportunity for bringing healing to a painful wound of the past. At the same time he knew, perhaps better than anyone else in the room, that the problems confronting the Commission were more than merely intellectual and could require more than his lifetime to reach their resolution. It has to be enough to ensure that the agreed statements were without significant ambiguities in the sense of papering over cracks, and removed the wreckage of centuries of misrepresentation and misunderstanding.

Henry Chadwick

Acknowledgements

The publishers wish to acknowledge the support of the Secretariat for Christian Unity, which made possible the publication of this book. Jane Williams contributed greatly by shortening the author's text. For historical detail we have relied upon Michael Walsh.

Unhappily, Monsignor Purdy died in November 1994 at the age of 83. He was actively involved in the earlier stages of editing but ill-health prevented him from undertaking any supervision of the final preparation of the manuscript.

William Purdy was born in Derby, where he continued to live when on leave, and he studied for the priesthood at the English College, Rome. He was ordained in 1934 and two years later went on to Christ's College, Cambridge, to read history. He taught in England until 1959 when he was sent back to the staff of the Beda college. Following Archbishop Michael Ramsey's visit to Pope Paul VI in 1966, he was recruited to the staff of the Vatican's Secretariat for Christian Unity as an expert on Anglicanism. He was therefore a natural choice as Catholic secretary to ARCIC. For a quarter of a century he reported – anonymously – on Vatican affairs for the Catholic weekly *The Tablet*; in 1966 he published *The Church on the Move*, a comparative study of the pontificates of Pius XII and John XXIII.

Abbreviations

AAS	*Acta Apostolicae Sedis*
ACC	Anglican Consultative Council
ARCIC	Anglican–Roman Catholic International Commission
ARCM	Anglican–Roman Catholic Commission on Marriage
ASS	*Acta Sanctae Sedis*
BEM	*Baptism, Eucharist, Ministry* (WCC)
CDF (SCDF)	(Sacred) Congregation for the Doctrine of the Faith
CFR	Council for Foreign Relations (C of E)
DS	H. Denzinger, rev. A. Schönmetzer, *Enchiridion Symbolorum*
ECUSA	Episcopal Church in the USA
FR	*Final Report* (of ARCIC)
ITC	International Theological Commission
JPC	Joint Preparatory Committee (of ARCIC)
MCT	*Marriage and the Church's Task*
MDC	*Marriage, Divorce and the Church*
PECUSA	Protestant Episcopal Church of the USA (later ECUSA)
SPCU	Secretariat for Promoting Christian Unity
WCC	World Council of Churches

Setting the scene

Popular preconceptions

In the nineteenth century, many English clerics travelled and took the opportunity to observe Catholic customs. Some were impressed, some not. Archbishop Tait had once complained that the scene in a church in Perugia was 'like the worship of some heathen deity'.

One of his successors, Archbishop Benson, on the other hand, thought the Easter Vigil in Florence edifying enough to be capable of adaptation for the Church of England. Yet this same Archbishop, when invited to send a present to Pope Leo XIII for his Jubilee, wrote to a close friend to say 'I thought I had long since made it clear that I would not approach the Pope ... It is the Pope's business to eat dust and ashes, not mine to decorate him.'[1]

Centuries of British distrust of Catholic countries lay behind this remark. The ghosts of *Praemunire*,[2] the Armada and the fires of Smithfield were not laid, despite a temporary unity between Britain and the Vatican in opposing Napoleonic France. The shocking and stupid treatment of the Irish during the eighteenth and nineteenth centuries had effects on ecumenism well into the next century, particularly after the famine of the 1840s, with increasing Irish Catholic immigration to England. The fierce suspicion of the 'Romanizing' tendencies of the Tractarian movement highlighted the extent of the misunderstanding and mistrust between Catholic and Anglican populations.

1

One step forwards and two steps back

Against this cloudy background, a number of things occurred in the nineteenth century.

First of all, a Catholic Emancipation Bill was passed in England in 1829, though without widespread support from either Anglicans or Catholics.

Then in 1850 the Catholic hierarchy was restored in England which, despite considerable care on the part of Vatican officials, raised a further bout of no-popery. The first Archbishop of Westminster, Nicholas Wiseman, was perhaps less tactful than some of his English colleagues wished, only arriving in England some weeks after delivering his first pastoral letter.

In 1854 came the definition of the Immaculate Conception, a 'Marian dogma' that was later to prove a King Charles's Head for Roman Catholic–Anglican dialogue, but aroused little notice at the time.

Not so, however, the *Syllabus of Errors* of 1864. This was a collection of Plus IX's utterances which became attached to an encyclical, so that its anathemas against a number of governments with which the Vatican had recently concluded concordats took on unintentional weight.[3]

The First Vatican Council met in 1869 and become famous in non-Roman-Catholic minds only for the dogma of papal infallibility, while the statement in *Apostolicae Curae* (1896) that Anglican orders are 'absolutely null and utterly void' sounded like a death-knell for those few in both churches who were trying to make the wilderness bloom. George Bell called *Apostolicae Curae* 'one of the sharpest and most public rebuffs that the Church of Rome can ever have adminstered to a peaceable Christian communion'.

When Pius X succeeded Pope Leo XIII in 1903, the Roman Catholic church felt itself under siege all round. In particular, the anti-clerical policies of the French Government led Pius X to what sounded like a blanket condemnation of 'Modernism'. From the point of view of relations with Anglicanism, the worst effect of the 'Modernist crisis' lay in the setback to Catholic biblical scholarship. Something akin to a new inquisition practically immobilized biblical scholarship, creating a situation which lasted down to the time of Vatican II.

Missionary activity and the First World War

The immense spread of missionary activity in the nineteenth century had led to inevitable contact and conflict between different churches, not just Roman Catholics and Anglicans. Two practical Americans, the Methodist J. R. Mott (1865–1955) and the Episcopalian Bishop C. H. Brent (1862–1929), together with the Swedish Lutheran Archbishop Nathan Soderblom, had seen enough for themselves of the bewilderment caused by conflicting Christian preaching and the scandal of rivalries. They took part in the World Missionary Conference of 1910, and although the war delayed further practical steps towards unity, it also sharpened the appetites of many who were sickened by the sight of supposedly Christian countries at war with each other. In 1927 a Conference on 'Faith and Order' was held at Lausanne, with delegates from 108 churches. This movement was finally to coalesce into the World Council of Churches in 1948.

The beginning of the beginning

The Roman Catholic Church had some scars from the Modernist scare, and was unwilling to get involved in large and miscellaneous gatherings dominated by 'Protestantism'. Shortly after the Lausanne conference came the papal encyclical *Mortalium Animos*.[4] It was destined to achieve notoriety in ecumenical circles, and was almost certainly compiled by members of the Holy Office, but though they were typical of many, they by no means represented the whole Roman Catholic approach to ecumenism.

For example, Cardinal Mercier, with the knowledge of Benedict XV and his successor Pius XI, was working towards a small meeting at Malines, with himself as host to 'one or two theologians from each of the principal dissident Churches, especially the Anglican and Orthodox'.[5] There was a good deal of correspondence between Mercier, George Bell (then archbishop's chaplain at Lambeth) and the Jesuits Fr Michel d'Herbigny and Leslie Wallace. There was no excessive optimism.

In Germany, too, conversations between theologians proved fruitful. In Tübingen, for example, where Lutheran and Catholic theological faculties existed side by side, Dr Simon, professor of the Catholic faculty in the late 1920s, began private ecumenical conversations with his Lutheran colleagues. Similar dialogues were taking place in Bielefeld, promoted by Alfred Bosi, and at Mentingen helped by Max Joseph Metzger. They earned far more favour in Rome than the more disparate meetings represented by Lausanne.

The Anglican Church had felt itself rebuffed by the famous declaration on Anglican orders, but the Lambeth conferences of 1920 and 1930 both stressed ecumenical endeavours. In 1930, the conference recorded 'the signs of a growing movement towards Christian unity in all parts of the world ... [and] expresses its appreciation of the courage and Christian charity of Cardinal Mercier in arranging the Malines Conversations'.

In 1932 an Anglican body, quaintly and revealingly entitled the Archbishop of Canterbury's Council for Foreign Relations, was set up. Its first chairman was Arthur Headlam, Bishop of Gloucester, and its second the great George Bell of Chichester. The Council for Foreign Relations (CFR) had some soul-searching over whether to participate in the 1937 meetings that were part of the process that led to the formation of the World Council of Churches. Rome was opposed to it, and Headlam was inclined to think that the Church of England should not participate in what might help to create a non-Roman-Catholic bloc. He was finally over-ruled by William Temple, who promised, not wholly convincingly, that Rome would be involved as much as possible, at least at the unofficial level.

The Second World War

Pius XI died and was succeeded by Pius XII, who governed the Church until 1958.

In 1940 Cardinal Hinsley formed the Sword of the Spirit movement[6] to give a common witness to a Christian world order. This was one of the many signs of the way in which the war broke down old attitudes.

Other ecumenically important shifts were happening within the Roman Catholic Church. One, partly the achievement of Augustin Bea, who was to achieve later fame as an ecumenist, was the change in attitude to biblical scholarship. The encyclical *Divino Afflante Spiritu* went a considerable way towards reversing the suspicious attitude towards biblical thinking that had characterized the Church since the time of the Modernist scare. After the encyclical, it became much harder to represent Vatican attitudes as the Catholic equivalent of the American Bible Belt.[7]

This, together with the 1947 encyclical *Mediator Dei* on liturgical matters, looked promising in Anglican eyes, but it was bewilderingly coupled with a *monitum* in 1948, which stated:

> Since it appears that ... joint meetings of Catholics and non-Catholics have been held to discuss matters of faith, all are reminded that canon 1325 section 3 forbids these meetings, *without permission*, to laity, clerics and religious ... And since joint acts of worship have taken place ... we repeat the warning that all *communicatio in sacris* is forbidden.

Yet the Vatican knew of the academic conversations mentioned above, and of the meeting organized by Archbishop Jaeger of Paderborn, where Lutheran theologians and Catholic theologians headed by Edmund Schlink discussed theological terminology. It seems that the *monitum* was not intended as an all-out veto on inter-church dialogue.

In this uncertain climate, Herbert Waddams of the CFR made cautious overtures to someone in the Vatican Secretariat of State who was increasingly recognized as not in the familiar mould. This was Giovanni Battista Montini, the future Pope Paul VI. Montini welcomed Waddams warmly, and with this encouragement, and the cautious assessment of the Jesuit Charles Boyer that Anglican–Roman Catholic relations were possible provided dogmatic questions were avoided, Stephen Neill was sent to Rome for a conference.[8] He was followed by the Oxford patristic scholar (and later Canon of St Paul's) Leonard Prestige, who prepared thoroughly, consulting a number of Catholic scholars about how he should proceed. He also got a modified blessing from Archbishop Geoffrey Fisher, who expressed himself keen for information but not for involvement, least of all with the newly-formed World Council of Churches (WCC).

In 1949 Prestige wrote an account of the agreement that he had reached with Boyer about how dialogue should proceed. It included the following points: (1) A pre-established programme with no deviation from it; (2) carefully selected participants, four or five a side; (3) the Roman Catholic side to include two members normally resident in England (the Jesuit Maurice Bévenot was suggested); (4) the primary object was to expound respective views and teachings, perhaps starting with the nature of the Church; (5) the talks should be with Anglicans and not within the ambit of the World Council of Churches.

With the help of Boyer, Prestige also met Montini, whom he got on with extremely well. His visit to Rome was quickly followed by another from Samuel Gurney. The stage was now set for the entrance of the official Roman Catholic–Anglican dialogues.

NOTES

1. Quoted in Bernard and Margaret Pawley, *Rome and Canterbury Through Four Centuries* (Mowbray, 1974), p. 240.
2. A series of statutes passed in England in the fourteenth century to prevent clerics evading the royal courts by appealing directly to the papacy.
3. ASS 3 (1867–69); DS 2890–2980.
4. AAS 20 (1928), pp. 13ff.
5. For a brief account of the Malines conversations, see Ruth Rouse and Stephen Neill (eds), *A History of the Ecumenical Movement 1517–1948* (SPCK, 1954), pp. 298–300.
6. Cf. Michael Walsh, *From Sword to Ploughshare* (CIIR, 1980).
7. AAS 35 (1943); DS 3862–3864.
8. Stephen Neill (1900–84) became interested in ecumenism as Bishop of Tinnevelly in India. In 1947 the Archbishop of Canterbury appointed him his assistant bishop for ecumenical work.

PART

I

1

Conversations

On 4 November 1949, while Prestige was preparing for his journey to Rome, Oliver Tomkins[1] wrote to Christopher Evans:[2] Tomkins had just returned from Paris where he had been talking to Henry Brandreth, the Anglican chaplain. He had also talked to the great Dominican Yves Congar, to whom (Tomkins claimed) he had independently suggested the idea of conversations. Tomkins stressed the nature of the great revival which was going on in French Catholicism: 'partly parochial and liturgical, partly in evangelism, partly biblical, partly ecumenical and overall a living alliance between scholarship and practice'.

This 'great revival' (which had its own troubles) was the outcome of intense self-questioning which had begun in France following the collapse of 1940 and continued through the period of occupation. It had produced the report which led at once to the foundation of the *Mission de France* and the *Mission de Paris* and the worker priests. The movements were not looked on with favour or much understood in Rome[3] but the French hierarchy found the situation too serious to be over-tolerant of curial criticism. In his Lenten pastoral of 1949 Cardinal Suhard had written:

In too many so-called Christian countries, particularly in France, the
Church, in spite of the existence of many ecclesiastical buildings
and many priests, has ceased to exist for the majority of people.
They no longer have the chance of deciding for or against Christ.
A vast accumulation of prejudice has completely distorted the face

of the Church in their eyes. The priesthood is no longer accessible to them. Therefore it is a good thing that priests should become witnesses again, less to conquer than to be a sign. They have been told that to be a witness does not mean to spread propaganda nor even to stir up emotions, but to keep the mystery of God present. This means so to live that one's life would be inexplicable if God did not exist.

All this would find an echo in the minds of many Anglican observers and goes far to explain why Tomkins insisted that the proposed conversations should not be 'another Malines' – not concerned with unity schemes, orders or sacraments. Congar wrote a memo showing his own priorities; he saw the plan as an exchange of opinions about (a) the apostolic effort of evangelizing an indifferent and pagan world; and (b) a theological activity of *ressourcement* in the Bible, in tradition, in the Fathers, and in liturgy. The aim should be 'to know each other better and nourish an immense desire for unity, with a view to a better exercise of our mission to preach the gospel to men'. There should be no controversy at this point. Each side should expound its main lines of progress in biblical studies, in liturgy and in *formules apostoliques* – an expression to be taken practically – and in evangelization and pastoral strategy.

Paris meeting, 14–15 April 1950

The first meeting was arranged for Paris, 14–15 April 1950. The participants were a distinguished lot. On the Anglican side Prestige had collected:

- S. L. GREENSLADE, Lightfoot Professor of Divinity at the University of Durham
- OWEN CHADWICK, then Fellow of Trinity Hall, Cambridge
- THOMAS PARKER, Librarian at Pusey House
- RICHARD HANSON, Vice-Principal at Queen's College, Birmingham (at that time a wholly Anglican establishment)
- REGINALD CANT, lecturer at St Chad's College, Durham
- CHRISTOPHER EVANS, chaplain and Fellow of Corpus Christi College, Oxford
- HENRY BRANDRETH, Anglican chaplain in Paris.

The only possible criticism of this galaxy would have been that it might list towards the more academic side of the balance hoped for by Tomkins and Congar.

The French participants were:

- CHRISTOPHE DUMONT OP
- LAMBERT BEAUDUIN OSB
- LOUIS BOUYER
- CLÉMENT LIALINE, editor of the review *Irénikon*
- JÉROME HAMER OP, then Professor at La Sarte, Belgium; later Cardinal
- ROBERT ROUQUETTE SJ, editor of *Etudes*
- P. YEPLI, a chaplain at the Sorbonne
- MAURICE NEDONCELLE, Professor of theology at Strasbourg

Brandreth reported in advance that Dumont 'had no word of English; Congar, Bouyer and Beauduin very few'.

There were four long sessions – two each day. There seems to have been no detailed record, but it was noted that the Anglicans led off Session 1 with a 'forcible' presentation which however was no shock to the Romans, 'whose independence of judgment and force of intellectual power made a deep impression on the whole Anglican party'.

Session 2 was devoted to discussion of objective history and intellectual honesty. (No doubt they all agreed that these were 'good things'.)

Session 3 was given over to an account of the Mission de France. Who gave it is not clear.

In Session 4 a reciprocal account of evangelistic problems in England was provided. Prestige stayed in Paris after the meeting and made further valuable contacts.

Strasbourg meeting, September 1950

A second meeting took place at Strasbourg the following September, but with the numbers halved and drastic changes of personnel. In the interval two events occurred which were not likely to encourage these faltering ecumenical steps. On 12 August, the encyclical *Humani Generis* was issued, and was seen by many as taking a retrograde attitude towards some current philosophical, theological and biblical work (DS 3875–3899). On 1 November the dogma of the Assumption was defined in the Apostolic Constitution *Munificentissimus Deus* (DS 3900–3909).

In fact there was no Roman Catholic survivor from Paris and only Owen Chadwick and Prestige himself of the Anglicans. Prestige's subsequent report offers no explanation of this. The list of Anglican participants was: Prestige, Chadwick, Ian Ramsey (the distinguished Oxford philosopher, later Bishop of Durham) and H. G. Whiteman of Liddon House.[4]

The Roman Catholics were Charles Journet of Fribourg (the future cardinal described by Prestige as 'prophetic and humorous'), and Jean Manasce OP, a Paris academic, bilingual, who was eulogized by Prestige for his brilliance and versatility. The third member was the Heythrop Jesuit Maurice Bévenot, who – Prestige rather unkindly said – 'was supposed to know all about the Church of England until one of his own colleagues in the conference demonstrated that he knew virtually nothing about it' – but at least he lived near Oxford. He was destined to play a major part in the dialogue which preceded the Anglican–Roman Catholic International Commission (ARCIC).

The fourth member was Charles Boyer. It would be interesting to know why so many fell out after Paris, but certainly they missed a good party at Strasbourg. Prestige was lyrical about the hospitality.

Turning to the work itself, Anglicans concentrated, said Prestige, on showing they have principles of authority, though of a different kind, and the Romans were deeply sympathetic and deeply interested. In the end half the entire conference centred on 'the grounds for assurance about dogmatic truth'.[5]

The 'Anglican position' was summarized in Prestige's words as follows:

[The position] does not involve, as might seem at first sight, that the Church is directly dependent on scholars and enquirers for its authorities for religious truth; scholars produce evidence, but the bishops decide questions of faith, retaining a genuine *magisterium*. This is the great respect for all that the Church has taught and practised, but it is all subject to the aforementioned controls. Moreover in a divided Christendom traditions which are less than universal must always remain in some degree an unsatisfactory guide.

The *Church as institution* is seen as having a hard core of episcopal churches, with a penumbra of others more or less incompletely constituted. At the edge, there are some not constituted at all in any intelligible sense, though they are by no means inorganic or invisible.

Are formal dogmatic definitions open to re-statement or re-interpretation? Anglicans see Roman Catholics as making too sharp a distinction between natural and supernatural knowledge, which for Anglicans is a distinction of degree rather than kind.

Turning to the nature of the act of faith, the classical Roman Catholic analysis was presented. Faith is primarily an act of the intellect, secondarily an act of the will moving the intellect to assent. The object of faith is 'things not seen', the motive, simply the authority of God acting in Christ and in his Church.

Against this, wrote Prestige, the Anglicans saw faith not as assent to propositions but as self-surrender of the total personality to a redeeming God, as an 'encounter': a 'kneeling theology'. It seemed to them that for Roman Catholics, Christ teaches, rules and sanctifies *in* the Church, while for Anglicans the Church is the object of these divine activities.[6] The report said:

> The Roman Catholics appeared at times to hold a doctrine of
> verbal inspiration of dogmatic pronouncements. Their notion of
> tradition seemed (to Anglicans) to open the door to the elevation
> of superstitions into doctrines.

Subsequent discussion seemed to produce an adumbration of what later became famous as the 'hierarchy of truths'. Journet was quoted as admitting that Roman Catholic history showed more *bouleversement* than used to be admitted, while Anglicans 'unexpectedly found more division in relation to doctrine among Roman Catholics than among themselves'.

Prestige sent copies of this report[7] to various people: first to Austin Farrer, who was to have been at the meeting and who obviously wondered when he read it how far the report reflected the discussion. He wrote:

> I suggest that the position you stated, and which is widely held, is a
> modernism due to the desire to present theology as empirical – i.e.,
> as the rational interpretation of irreducible 'facts'. But this is not
> true, for God *speaks* just as much as he *works* ... The Anglican
> fathers believed in the *Word* of God, speaking in the bible, and in
> the hearts ... we are illuminated by the divinely given interpretation
> of the facts as it stands in scripture etc., but also by the extension of
> the same illumination into our own minds through our membership
> in Christ himself.

Prestige answered:

This is very important; it just shows why I wanted you at Strasbourg. What bothers me is to interpret correctly the scriptural interpretation. Unless you have verbal inspiration or a living Voice (and I just cannot take either) *quis interpretabitur ipsos intepretes*? Christian common sense over a period of serious reflection and debate, summed up in the end (when that is really reached) by competent (in every sense) authority.

Farrer replied next day: the old Anglicans had a doctrine of Christ the revealer–interpreter. It placed Christ, the apostles, and the Church of the Fathers in concentric circles of dwindling illumination, with the rest of Christian history perhaps outside that again.

It was a pity perhaps that Prestige did not circulate this correspondence along with his report. It is a greater pity that there seemed to be no Roman Catholic report, but it seems there was nobody to send it to.

A copy of the report was sent to Manasce, who acknowledged it with the brief comment that 'a good many points still could be cleared up if we set about them systematically'. Yet he did not think that the meeting went off on a side-track: 'theological epistemology would lead to better understanding.'

Hampstead meeting, 1–4 January 1952

A year elapsed before arrangements were made for another meeting – partly because Journet dropped out, excusing himself on the grounds of growing deafness and unfamiliarity with English. Prestige and the others courteously dismissed this diffidence, but Journet insisted, and Boyer, being consulted, proposed two English names: George Dwyer and George Smith. These two offered an interesting contrast.[8]

Dwyer was completely fluent in French and Italian. He was gifted with a very sharp mind and a photographic memory, but had found certain aspects of Cambridge life, not least Anglican aspects, antipathetic. He was affable and witty, though of strong opinions. He had been Cardinal Heenan's right-hand man in refounding the Catholic Missionary Society after the war.[9] George Smith, on the other hand, was an older man who had taught at St Edmund's College, Ware, for many years, during some

of which time he was a friend and colleague of R. A. Knox. Affable and
something of a *bon viveur*, he was a traditional theologian, but a clear
thinker and excellent teacher with a limpid and graceful English style.
He had edited the *Clergy Review* until 1951. Both men attended the
Hampstead meeting. Otherwise the personnel was exactly what it had been
at Strasbourg, Journet apart.[10]

The programme was somewhat different – perhaps an attempt to get
at Manasce's more systematic treatment. The general subject was
Revelation. (Alec Vidler, who professed himself very pleased about the
inclusion of English Roman Catholics, observed after reading the report
that it turned out to be a discussion on the *presupposita philosophica* of
Revelation.) During the five sessions a short paper was used from each
side on one of the following topics:

1. Did God reveal to man a reality which was inexpressible or a reality
   expressed in statements which could be passed on? Did Revelation end
   with the death of the last apostles? In what sense?
2. Did Christ establish an institution whose duty is to guard the accurate
   transmission of revealed truth?
3. Is the Church infallibile in the transmission of revealed truth and what
   is the organ of this infallibility. Is there an official teaching body which
   teaches with authority? Is the episcopate this body?
4. Can the Church tolerate the teaching of error within its ranks? Must
   unity of faith among the bishops be maintained and by what means?
5. In what sense can the primitive revelation undergo a development?
   What are the conditions of this development?

It seems there was no transcript of the discussion but Prestige wrote his
own report, which he sent to Anglican correspondents of his own choice
(see below). If the Roman Catholics did anything similar, no evidence of it
has so far come to light. The meeting produced a 'declaration of five points
of contact between us'.

1. Revelation is God making known by supernatural means his character
   and saving action in a form capable of our assimilation and in such wise
   as to communicate to us statements which express truly though analogic-
   ally the realities God intends us to know.
2. Natural theology provides a valid aid towards accurate expression of
   revealed truth.

3. The death of the last apostolic witness to the saving words and acts marks a definitive period. This completes the *depositum fidei* which Christ delivered, to which nothing can be added and which it is the Church's duty to preserve and guard. Christ promises to the Church aid in the fulfilment of this duty. An explication of the Deposit is a possibility – maybe a necessity – of Christian thought.
4. The Church is an extension of the Incarnation. It is continuous, visible, with the triple bond, credal, sacramental and structural, and is not merely the invisible communion of the elect.
5. It is incumbent on the Church to correct error and in the last resort to enforce discipline in order to ensure that the Gospel is truly taught.[11]

One of Prestige's correspondents, A. G. Hebert, commented: 'my own feeling is that the discussion moved along – as it were – on the Roman terrain of abstract systematic theology.' If this was so, was it because the Romans obstinately refused to move off this ground, or because the Anglicans were unable to get them on to any other ground? Prestige himself, writing some weeks afterwards, spoke of the 'fearfully technical and frightfully abstract scholastic philosophy [which] ties them up in a network of thin but collectively binding threads, like Gulliver in Lilliput'.[12] This led him on to a more general judgement on the prospects for Anglican–Roman Catholic relations:

> Perhaps there is real opportunity for a social rapprochement and for interchange of factual information. There is not a greater hope than that of ice in hell for any theological or ecclesiastical coalescence.

The letter ends: 'Sorry to bore you – I love the Romans and hate their ways, just as I do the Americans.'

NOTES

1. Oliver Tomkins was at this time Associate General Secretary of the World Council of Churches and secretary of its Faith and Order Commission. He became Bishop of Bristol from 1959.
2. C. F. Evans: Chaplain, Fellow and Lecturer at Corpus Christi College, Oxford.
3. There is much literature on the 'worker priest' and related movements. A brief account may be found in chapter 10 of the present writer's *The Church on the Move* (London, 1966).
4. Owen Chadwick notes (in *Anglican Initiatives*, ed. E. G. W. Bill (SPCK, 1967), p. 98) that 'there was no evangelical despite Bp. George Bell's insistence to Prestige that there should be'.

5. A fuller account of the discussion is given in the course of a long article by Dom Alberic Stacpoole OSB in *One in Christ*, vol. 23 (1987), pp. 311–17.

6. cf. George Tavard at Huntercombe: below, pp. 109–11.

7. This was presumably the same report that Owen Chadwick saw and which had been sent to Archbishop Fisher. Chadwick 'felt that it was too optimistic, too cheerful; but such was the nature and faith of the men' (*Anglican Initiatives*, p. 98).

8. The present writer knew both intimately for many years.

9. To mention this organization to Anglicans was to produce rumblings about 'proselytism', which was not altogether just. The aim was very much that of the Mission de France, though the method was different. England was seen as a largely secularized country, or better, perhaps, as one which had drifted into non-malicious indifference, and the way to combat this was to go 'knocking on doors' – that is, to get into direct contact with people and start them thinking about the faith they had lost or never had. It was not the way of the traditional Catholic 'mission', which had been to cajole backsliding or lapsed Catholics into revival and increase fervour among the regulars: the CMS missioners addressed themselves to everybody in the allotted area; but they certainly had no aim to seduce practising Anglicans from their allegiance. All this allowed, their very zealous work may not have been the best preparation for ecumenical dialogue at such a tentative period.

10. The meeting at Hampstead in 1952 produced a fascinating argument upon the pastoral nature of authority. Both sides confessed that it must be possible for the Church to exclude members. Both sides confessed that the Church was the mother of sinners and must act with gentleness for the sake of individual souls. The Anglicans insisted that this duty of gentleness must extend (some distance at least) to doctrinal aberrations, that liberty of mind was a virtue to be encouraged, and such encouragement meant (sometimes) a tolerance of error on the part of teachers, provided that they were simple and reverent. They were little confident that 'error' had sharp and visible edges. The Roman Catholics insisted that the individuals in the flock must not be led astray by the errors of a single teacher. For them the duty to silence the teacher of error came high in the duty of authority. Fruitful discussion is possible only on common ground (Owen Chadwick in *Anglican Initiatives*, p. 99).

11. All this may be compared with the treatment of such questions in Vatican II's *De Revelatione*, just over a decade later; see below for the observer Frederick C. Grant's comments and the contrasting ones sent in the Anglican observer's report.

12. Was it the Catholics or the Anglicans who felt like Gulliver? Michael Ramsey was to say to Paul VI some years later – (1966) 'Anglicans know nothing of scholastic philosophy' – rather a sweeping judgement.

Conversations II

However, the Council for Foreign Relations (CFR) as a whole was undaunted by this rather cheerless report. Six months later, 13 June 1952, Waddams returned to the charge. He now surveyed the curial scene more thoughtfully. He even saw the *monitum* of 1948 and the subsequent *instructio* as the products of slowness and caution, and hailed the advance evident in the concession of joint recitation of the Our Father!

The Pope he saw as a *Deus* extra *machina*: without him Rome would be in the grip of a dead-weight bureaucracy. Yet the bureaucracy severely limits the Pope's powers. Things once set in train grind on – like the Assumption definition process.[1]

He saw the formidable Cardinal Ottaviani,[2] and derived the impression that decisions were made in the Holy Office. Ottaviani said he disliked attacks on the Roman Catholic Church such as that made by Karl Barth at Amsterdam, but he was quite satisfied with the report he had received about Roman Catholic–Anglican conversations[3] and had no objection to their continuing.

A few conclusions emerge clearly from these four years (1948–52). The Church of England CFR was very much making the running in improving relations – courageously in view of the Holy Office utterances of 1948. The Roman response, in Rome itself, was on the whole warm. There was a beginning of breaking down stereotypes on both sides; and there was a beginning of quiet but officially recognized theological dialogue set up in a way which showed recognition of lessons learned from Malines.

Milan meeting, 1956

In 1954 Montini went as Archbishop to Milan. This took away perhaps the most valuable Vatican contact, but the new archbishop evidently felt able to compensate by taking an initiative himself. In 1956 he let it be known that he would welcome a group of Anglicans as his guests in Milan.

Bell urged strongly that the invitation be accepted but it does not seem that he had any say in the choice of personnel. Some were chosen, it appears, because they knew some Italian, and Bell said that he thought this unduly limiting. The man chosen to head it was John Moorman, the Franciscan scholar, future Bishop of Ripon and a man outstanding in the history of Anglican–Roman Catholic relations. Unfortunately, circumstances prevented him from going. The list of participants was as follows:

- J. C. DICKINSON of Pembroke College, Cambridge, later lecturer at Birmingham
- C. L. GAGE-BROWN
- COLIN JAMES – now Bishop of Winchester
- COLIN HICKLING – then at Chichester, not ordained
- BERNARD PAWLEY

Boyer was present from the Catholic side and the encounter was assured of success from the start by the presence of Sergio Pignedoli,[4] Montini's right-hand man, who had meals regularly with the visitors. Pignedoli was a man with extraordinary gifts for personal relationships – warm-heared, expansive, quietly humorous. He also had very good English.

C. L. Gage-Brown has left a report of the visit. He says there was no word of controversy, no scheme behind it all but to enlarge information. Montini, who dined with the group three or four times, welcomed criticism and advice. He said once: 'Of course we are the only Church, but we do not think you are all going to Hell!' According to Gage-Brown: 'We said as tactfully as possible that relations with English Roman Catholics were not particularly friendly, and I said that perhaps this could be understood by our persecution of them in the past, to which he replied that such history should be forgotten.'

Meanwhile other events of the early 1950s, such as the definition of the dogma of the Assumption in 1950 and the encyclical *Humani Generis* of the same year, did nothing to kindle ecumenical fires. But encouraging things were coming about. It was in 1952 that the Catholic Ecumenical

Conference was founded for discussing ecumenical questions at annual meetings. It is enough to say that its secretary was the future Cardinal, and President of the Council for Christian Unity J. G. M. Willebrands. In Rome, the Italo-American Igino Cardinale took up the torch of Montini in the Secretariat of State. It was Cardinale who arranged the important visit of George Bell to Rome in 1958, just before the Lambeth Conference, and his audience with Pius XII. This was the last year of Pius' life – he died at Castelgandolfo in the late summer. It was the heyday of the power of the small group in the Roman Curia known as 'the Pentagon' – a power which grew during Pius' long illness and increasing withdrawal. Yet Bell was much encouraged by the audience and by his other impressions, and he probably influenced a report at the next Lambeth Conference which registered perseverance. It was soon to be justified to an extent no one could have dreamed of in 1958.

Meanwhile in 1957 the Hampstead conversations of 1952 were courageously resumed in Rome – the lion's mouth.

Rome meeting, 8–11 April 1957

Prestige had met a sadly early death in 1955 and Alec Vidler, Fellow and Dean of King's College, Cambridge, now headed an entirely new Anglican team:

F. W. DILLISTONE, Dean of Liverpool Cathedral
C. F. EVANS, of Corpus Christi College, Oxford
M. P. C. HANSON, lecturer in Theology at Nottingham and Chancellor of Lincoln
T. R. MILFORD

On the Catholic side similarly, only Boyer survived and his side consisted entirely of Roman residents. They were:

JOSEPH GILL SJ, author of the standard work on the Council of Florence and lecturer at the Oriental Institute in Rome
CONLETH KEARNS OP, lecturer in Scripture at the Domincan University, the Angelicum
AIDAN WILLIAMS OSB
SALVATORE GAROFALO, later Rector Magnificus of the College of Propaganda Fide – and an Italian.

The theme was 'The authority of the Bible' and Kearns set things off by claiming that Anglicans would find that Roman Catholic scholars now enjoyed practically unrestricted exegetical liberty,[5] and Dr Vidler responded by saying that he could have invited Anglican theologians, Anglo-Catholic or Evangelical, to the meeting, who would have been shocked by the freedom exercised by the Roman Catholics.

Selwyn meeting, 22–25 September 1958

Another meeting was organized within eighteen months at Selwyn College, Cambridge where Owen Chadwick (then the nearest thing on either side to an established participant, apart from Boyer) was Master. Again there were considerable changes of personnel. On the Anglican side Norman Sykes, the historian and Dean of Winchester Cathedral, Cheslyn Jones, Principal of Chichester Theological College, and Victor de Waal, Chaplain of Ely Theological College, replaced Dillistone, Evans and Milford. On the Catholic side only the Jesuits, Boyer and Gill, survived from the Roman meeting. Tindall-Atkinson returned and there were three newcomers. Joseph Höfer, ecclesiastical counsellor at the German Embassy to the Holy See in Rome, was perhaps the most interesting acquisition. He was a leading figure in German ecumenism and had succeeded Dr Simon as co-chairman of the famous Braunsharter Conference held twice a year since 1948 between Lutheran and Catholic scholars under the patronage of the Archbishop of Paderborn, Lorenz Jaeger.[6] Höfer spoke English fluently. H. F. Davies taught theology at Oscott, the Midlands seminary near Birmingham, and lectured: at Birmingham University. Alan Clark was vice-rector of the English College in Rome. He was destined to become chairman of ARCIC I (see below, p. 126).

The topic for the Selwyn meeting was 'Liberty and authority', a subject which had been increasingly imposing itself for some time. The opening discussion revealed that the root question was likely to lie in the claim that the Church 'is entitled to impose acceptance of revealed truths which are supernaturally guaranteed free from error'. On the next day it was reported, predictably, that 'to Anglicans it seems that Roman Catholics are determined to adhere to their beliefs about inerrancy and infallibility, however much it is shown that they cannot be reasonably maintained'. ARCIC was to make some progress here. Nearly a quarter of a century later, the Anglican–Roman Catholic International Commission, presenting the Final Report of the first stage of its work (ARCIC I), showed Anglicans after fifteen hard years of dialogue still with reservations about 'infallibility' especially as ascribed to the Pope. But the impasse implied in the sentence just quoted is no longer evident. The sentence is more a description of supposed states of mind than a pronouncement on a problem.

On the quite different problem of *tolerance* presented in Höfer's long paper, and then commented on by Norman Sykes, discussion moved more easily. History presented no homogeneous picture for either side. Sykes pointed out that in the sixteenth and seventeenth centuries Anglicans and Presbyterians had prompted a search for a theological basis. In Rome Pius XII began confronting the problem as he thought of the possibility of an international community in the post-war period. Plenty of papal utterances, especially from the nineteenth century, could be adduced which rejected what the Second Vatican Council was solemnly to declare (after protracted resistance by a minority): that the right of freedom in religious allegiance and worship is rooted in the dignity of the human person, and hence not subject to external coercion. The title of the decree – its first two words – was *Dignitatis Humanae*.[7]

The Roman canonist school, who were usually thinking of Catholic states, had never progressed beyond the idea that toleration has no reason except the avoidance of greater evils.

Pius XII, addressing Italian Catholic jurisconsults in Rome in 1953, showed signs of going beyond this position, even saying 'in determined circumstances, God may give us no mandate, *even no right*, to repress what is erroneous or false'. He argued from the parable of the wheat and the cockle, as Höfer did five years later at Selwyn. The men at Selwyn in 1958 went so far as to agree on the idea of exploring the possibilities of truth in new thinking 'outside the Christian sphere' – for example, in linguistic philosophy.

Tindall-Atkinson's paper on 'Conscience and authority' was gratefully accepted by the Anglicans as admirable. Vidler noted in the meeting a 'thoroughly irenic spirit and willingness to learn', though 'for the most part it was the Roman position which was being called in question and on the defensive; it would have been salutary if the Roman Catholics had been more concerned to probe the Anglican position than they were'.

By the time the group met again at Assisi, in April 1961, some momentous things had happened. CFR correspondence during Pius XII's reign amply shows great interest in and appreciation of Pius' international outlook. Waddams made this positive assessment at Pius' death:

He never ceased to give attention to relations with other Christians. (Instance G. Bell's visit.) During the past fifteen years or more there had been distinct change for the better in relationships and much greater readiness on both sides for Christians to see each other. For this development, which must be a cause of thankfulness to all Christians, the late Pope was in considerable measure responsible.

On 28 October 1958, to general surprise, the conclave elected Angelo Giuseppe Roncalli, the aged Patriarch of Venice, to succeed Pius XII as Bishop of Rome.

NOTES

1. Defined by Pius XII in 1950 (1 November) in *Munificentissimus Deus*.
2. Alfredo Ottaviani, son of a Roman baker, a brilliant canonist and moral theologian, was to become the most outstanding conservative figure in Vatican II.
3. At Strasbourg and Hampstead. This shows that Boyer reported to the Holy Office. It was only two years since the *monitum*.
4. Later made Cardinal.
5. This might sound ironic since it was said only three years before the miserable efforts of scholars associated with the Lateran University (Pope John's old college) to impose a conservative document on Revelation on the fathers of the Council, thereby contradicting the teaching of the Pontifical Biblical Institute whose Rector had been, until a few years before, Cardinal Bea. But in fact the ultimate outcome of that, with the story of the Constitution *Dei Verbum*, really confirms Kearns' judgement, showing the unrepresentative character of the reactionary element in Rome.
6. Later a decisive figure in the foundation of the Secretariat for Promoting Christian Unity. See below, pp. 25–6.
7. An excellent account of this document and its adventures during the Council is given by William J. Wolf, Professor of Theology at the Episcopal (Anglican) Theological School, Cambridge, Massachusetts and an observer at the Council. See Pawley (ed.), *The Second Vatican Council: Studies by Eight Anglican Observers* (Oxford, 1969), pp. 178–201.

Archbishop Fisher's visit to John XXIII

Preparations

Ecumenical stirrings

The Archbishop of Canterbury, Geoffrey Fisher, was by no means without ecumenical aspirations and ideas, but Anglican–Roman Catholic relations were not at the time in the forefront of them. His sympathies lay more with Orthodoxy.

When Cardinal Hinsley was at Westminster relations with Lambeth were very much warmer. The chillier climate which followed gave rise to constant difficulties.

Fisher cannot have been excited by the election of the new Pope John XXIII in 1958.[1] Be that as it may, he telegraphed and then wrote his congratulations through the Apostolic delegation and informed William Godfrey (now Archbishop of Westminster) of the fact. Fisher also wrote to Waddams about a trickier point:

> The *Telegraph* says there is a plenary indulgence for all who listen to the papal coronation on radio or television. Can you give me exact information as to what a plenary indulgence means, and is there the text of a decree which extends its supposed benefit to everybody who happens to turn on the radio at the right time?[2]

The following April (1959) Fisher received a letter from the expansive Bishop of Southwark, Mervyn Stockwood, describing an audience he had

had with John XXIII. Stockwood had attended what seems to have been a *baciamano* – a small group audience in which the Pope speaks a few words and greets each visitor briefly. John with his usual informality gave instructions on the spur of the moment that Stockwood should be winkled out and taken to his private study. The Pope sent a special message by Stockwood to Fisher: 'Two souls can meet in prayer though distance divide', it said. The message seems to have sown the seed of a momentous idea in Fisher's mind, his round trip to Istanbul, Rome and Geneva. But before turning to its historic fruition we must look at other aspects of the early phase of John's pontificate. They were far from homogeneous.

Sir Marcus Cheke, who was British Minister to the Holy See, sent his impressions to the CFR. They were mainly two: (a) it was noticeable that all the new Pope's pronouncements since his enthronement had been much narrower than those of his predecessor; (b) there was a decentralization going on, so that power was returning to the hands of the Curia.[3]

The Second Vatican Council was announced on 25 January 1959. One of its aims was to be an invitation to the separated brethren to search for the unity of Christians which was everywhere so longed for. Augustin Bea carefully followed the discussions and speculations which succeeded the announcement. He was against overstressing the unity theme – an age-old problem which could not be solved in a hurry. He thought particularly of ecclesiological and Church–state problems which had to be tackled before unity issue. Too many things should not be decided in Rome. Each department of the Roman Curia should have at its head an expert in its field – whether Cardinal or not. He welcomed the interest aroused by the Council but feared misrepresentation and excessive speculation.[4]

On 16 November Bea was made a Cardinal. John must have known or quickly learned of the scholarly accomplishments of his predecessor's confessor. According to custom Bea was assigned on elevation to various curial congregations, and to the Pontifical Biblical Commission. This would leave him time for biblical work. But he cannot have taken long to see the opportunities now offered for ecumenical activity.

Foundation of the Secretariat for Promoting Christian Unity

In August 1959 Professor Willebrands, of the Catholic Conference for Ecumenical Questions, went with the editor of the ecumenical journal *Istina*, Christophe Dumont OP (as journalists), to the meeting of the Central Committee of the World Council of Churches on the island of

Rhodes. Dumont had the bright idea of using the occasion for a talk with Orthodox theologians. The press and the WCC chose to interpret this as taking advantage of the WCC to make overtures to the Orthodox and the latter reacted strongly. The Archbishop of Paderborn, Lorenz Jaeger, decided that this clearly showed the need for introducing some co-ordination into Catholic ecumenical enterprise, and on 8 November he wrote to Bea to that effect. Bea and Jaeger then concocted a proposal that was sent to the Pope. In 48 hours the Secretariat for Promoting Christian Unity (SPCU – originally called a 'commission')[5] was born, with Bea as its president.

The official publication of the proposal came on 5 June 1960, in the Motu Proprio *Superno Dei Nutu*, together with other preparatory commissions for the Council. The purpose of the Secretariat was 'to show in a special way our love and benevolence for those who bear the name of Christian but are separated from the apostolic see, so that they can follow the work of the Council and find more easily the way to that unity which Jesus Christ implored of his heavenly Father'.

Willebrands arrived from Holland on 7 July to take up his duties as Secretary of the new office. One of his first excursions was to Edinburgh for the meeting of the executive committee of the WCC, of which he was an observer (no longer a 'journalist'). This was to give him a glimpse of the thorny path ahead.

Bea gave fullest recognition to the 'variety of pioneer enterprises which already existed',[6] and was chiefly exercised about the lack of ecumenical experience he was likely to find among the bishops and theologians at the Council.

Archbishop Fisher's visit to the Pope

Preliminaries

On 3 November 1960 a press release from Lambeth Palace announced Fisher's coming journey.

In Rome the announcement held its own even against the last stages of election fever. *Il Tempo*, a right-wing daily, described it as 'truly sensational' and concluded: 'The imminence of the Council must again turn the minds of all men of goodwill to the hope of the reunion of Christendom.' Both here and in the left-wing, normally anti-clerical *Espresso* (usually well informed) the welcome was positive, though no extravagant quick results were forecast.

The Catholic papers were more lukewarm – most of all the Vatican *Osservatore Romano*. Cardinal Bea wrote to Cardinal Samoré (at the Department for Extraordinary Affairs) complaining that the *Osservatore* report was insensitive to the spirit of trust and respect indispensable to the preliminaries of such a visit, and so much so as to endanger the visit.

This strong reaction had a touch of nervousness in it. There was nobody on the permanent staff of the SPCU who really knew much about the Church of England, so a report was requested from the Jesuit Bernard Leeming, an Oxford man who had taught for many years at the Gregorian University before and during the war and was now doing the same at Heythrop College. It asked for a page about Fisher, another about the history of Anglicanism and a third about the position of Anglicanism today.

Leeming answered in Latin with a strong English flavour. For Englishmen who knew him it was both revealing and entertaining; how much it conveyed in the Secretariat's office is another matter. He wrote:

> I have had some personal relations with Fisher. I once dined with
> him at Christ Church where his son teaches. I told him I had two first
> cousins in the Anglican Church, and he said 'Good, good, so it should
> be, we should mix together (*debemus intermisceri inter nos*)' . . .
>
> He is not much of a theologian but I think a very sincere man,
> more led by feeling than cold reason. He loved his predecessor
> William Temple, whom he had also succeeded as headmaster of
> Repton.

Few reports quite like this can ever have been made to a Vatican department, but there were valuable nuggets in it. Leeming added a postcript suggesting that the Pope might be presented with an essay by Austin P. Bennet, *The Jurisdiction of the Archbishop of Canterbury: An Historico-Juridical Study.*[7]

Two days later there followed another 'postscript', noting that Fisher had travelled a lot. It went on:

> The position of the Archbishop gives possibilities of considerable
> influence. He has direct access to the sovereign, he is usually
> consulted by the Prime Minister, he presides at the Lambeth

Conference and at many Anglican societies. He has considerable influence on educational matters. About things like the abdication of Edward VIII, industry and strikes, he can obtain a hearing where others cannot. But all this should not be exaggerated. Anglicans, whether bishops, clergy or laymen, have not the slightest hesitation in dissenting from his views.

On 24 November Leeming fired off a last postscript. He insisted that Fisher's *first* wish was to visit the Pope.

A rumour had arisen that the project of Fisher's visit to Rome had been hatched at the WCC assembly in St Andrews in the summer – not an idea likely to warm either Vatican or Geneva hearts. On 7 November John Satterthwaite, the Secretary for Europe on the Church of England's Council on Foreign Relations, wrote to Willebrands assuring him that he had written explaining to Visser t'Hooft, the WCC's Secretary General, that the visit was being planned *before* St Andrews and that therefore there was no exploitation of that assembly nor of the WCC. He added the comment that 'the more left-wing element of the WCC is extremely suspicious of any contact with Rome'. Fisher, who was rather proud of his initiative, was much crisper. The Church Assembly, the predecessor of the General Synod of the Church of England, welcomed the visit and Fisher replied. 'There is no more the atmosphere which surrounded Malines', he said, 'we can speak in charity, happiness and confidence. On the continent they do not wish anyone to think the WCC is a place where ecclesiastics get together to hatch plots: [this one] was hatched in the Lambeth study in my own sometimes not infertile mind.'

It would be nice to say that no trace of the atmosphere which had surrounded Malines survived in the Vatican. It would also be untrue.

Willebrands had been able to write to write to Satterthwaite saying he was pleased with the Lambeth communiqué and grateful to Lambeth for taking the initiative in scotching the St Andrews canard. He apologized for the *Osservatore Romano* report and gave assurance of the Pope's 'great respect and friendliness'.

But there was nothing he or anyone else could do at this time to improve the predominant attitude in the Roman Curia. For them, polite paper exchanges at a thousand miles were one thing; top-level visits were another. The SPCU was only a few weeks old and was already seen as up to antics which the old guard viewed with grave disapproval. Prudence dictated drawing heavy purple curtains.

The archbishop of Liverpool, John Heenan, who never trembled at publicity, had written to Willebrands announcing that he had been invited to broadcast with Fisher a discussion on Church unity. Fisher declined, saying that the date proposed was too soon after his visit to Rome and the Archbishop of York, Michael Ramsey, was taking his place. Heenan asked Willebrands if there were any points he would like emphasized. Willebrands replied welcoming the discussion, but strongly recommended that neither should report any supposed quotations from Fisher's audience with the Pope. He also later added:

> I think we will be in a very difficult position on the whole subject of
> press information during the Archbishop of Canterbury's visit,
> because in the Vatican everything is lacking in this line. We will do
> whatever is possible to meet such difficulties.

Fisher in Rome

Fisher arrived from Jerusalem at Ciampino, at the old airport of Rome, on the afternoon of 1 December 1960. He was met by the British Ambassador to Italy, Sir Ashley Clarke,[8] the British Minister to the Holy See, Sir Peter Scarlett, and Canon Wanstall, chaplain at the English Church of All Saints. There were, it seems, no Roman Catholics present. The press were there in strength, but got practically nothing for their pains.

Scarlett told the Archbishop that Cardinal Tardini, Pope John's Secretary of State, had laid down what Fisher rightly thought astonishing conditions to be greeted with:

> (i) There should be no official photograph of me with the Pope.
> To make sure of this, Tardini had sent away the official photographer
> for a fortnight's holiday. So that was off. It had never occurred to me
> that there would or would not be official photographs: but he,
> Tardini, obviously thought it was important.
> (ii) It was stated that I should not see Cardinal Bea, the Head of the
> department recently set up by the Pope to foster relations with other
> Churches. This sounded a preposterous thing, but there it was.[9]
> (iii) There was to be no kind of press release after my meeting with
> the Pope. That was a little odd as I had already drafted one.
> (iv) This Minister was not to invite to meet me at his house any of
> the Vatican officials.

At 6.30 p.m. Fisher attended evensong at the English Church of All Saints and preached a sermon, eagerly awaited and listened to by many. History, he said, has brought it about that the Orthodox Churches have found their greatest strength in their withdrawal into worship, while the Churches of the Roman Communion have found their greatest calling in the strength and authority of their witness to the world. We of the Anglican communion and indeed all the Churches must ever be grateful for what the Church of Rome has done for us all by that strength and authority.

Elaborating on this, he spoke of the dangers it entailed, of involving doctrine with other disputes about prestige, property, authority. He described the English as passionate lovers of freedom, but he spoke too of 'the harsh lessons of history by which the Church of England was taught how to respect in others that freedom which it had won':

> For the first time in 400 years an Archbishop of Canterbury has come to Rome neither to boast nor complain, but only to greet the Pope in the courtesy of Christian brotherhood. I could only have suggested my visit here because the Pope on his side would receive me in a similar spirit.[10]

Thus inoculated and refreshed he set out next morning for the Vatican.

'Your Holiness, we are making history' were the Archbishop's first words to the Pope. The rest of the conversation, needless to say, was not reported, but Fisher at various times dropped remarks about it. 'I did not have to create an atmosphere of friendship, I walked straight into it', he said on his return. 'We talked like two good Christian gentlemen about anything that came into our minds.' He talked much more amply about it after his retirement. Amongst his recollections were the following:

> The Pope read, in English, a passage [from an address of his] which included a reference to 'the time when our separated brethren should return to the Mother Church'. I at once said: 'Your Holiness, not *return*'. He looked puzzled and said 'Not return? Why not?' I said 'None of us can go backwards. We are now running on parallel courses; we are looking forward until in God's good time, our two courses approximate and meet'. He said, after a moment's pause, 'You are right'.
>
> ... Somewhere in our conversation I thanked the Pope for what he had done in setting up the new department under Cardinal Bea.

He then said with a smile and a twinkle 'Yes, and this afternoon you shall see Cardinal Bea'. I realised that Tardini had been overruled by the Pope, revealing a little of the breaking of the barriers and the icy wastes of the Vatican curia.

So ended this notable interview. It had been much longer than any normal courtesy visit – so simple in nature, so historic and rich in results. It remained for the two principals to exchange gifts. The Archbishop gave the Pope a special copy of the Coronation Service, bound in white vellum and bearing a special commemorative inscription. The Pope in return presented the Archbishop with the recently published volumes of the Roman Synod, the addresses delivered by him when Patriarch of Venice and the first volume of the preparatory acts of the Roman Ecumenical Council. He also gave Fisher a medal.

So, at any rate said an official statement later. The reality was more colourful and animated. As Fisher recalled the matter:

As they could not be given to me to carry away, the Pope said he would send them down. The next day I went to our Minister's office where the gifts were to be brought to me by the present Apostolic Delegate to England, dear Cardinale. I said to the Minister: 'Why have we got to go there?' he replied: 'It would be too conspicuous if he came to my own residence. It would be less conspicuous if he comes to my office.' It struck me as odd that it should matter if it were conspicuous or not, but there it was. I got to the office and there I found that Cardinale had arrived twenty minutes before, very secretly, and was upstairs in a room waiting for me. I went up to him and he was grand, as Cardinale has been ever since. We had a lovely time, and he gave me not only the Pope's books but also a portfolio of Raphael's cartoons. The time came when I was to go, and I supposed we should go together. But he said he must let me get away first, before he appeared, and he suggested that I should draw the reporters after me from the Minister's office before he did so. This was a queer and notable thing.

Fisher's press officer, Colonel Robert Hornby, had done much to offset the secrecy campaign. In newspapers secrecy leads to fairy stories. He went to Rome several days before the visit and with the help of Willebrands he held a quiet press briefing in a correspondent's flat.

At the Anglican church hush-hush could not be contrived and in the narrow Via Babuino television cameras made a meal of the Archbishop receiving at the door after his service.

At the Vatican next day Hornby was put into a small room to wait until the great conversation was over and then receive his communiqué. The conversation took much longer than was expected and after an hour Mgr Samoré of the Secretariat of State 'opened the door, put his hand on his heart and said "I cannot speak. I am too full of emotion. I must lie down." I said "We have the world press waiting for this communiqué, you cannot lie down."' Samoré went out (whether to lie down or not will never be known) but eventually came back and supplied the communiqué. The content, needless to say, hardly justified the fuss.

For Fisher, deeply aware of the spiritual yields of his venture, there remained a great content and thankfulness.

Rest of the visit and repercussions

On the afternoon of 2 December Fisher went to meet Bea.[11] Willebrands and Satterthwaite were also present at the 35-minute discussion, of which a report was afterwards made and signed by Willebrands and Bea.

Willebrands began by explaining the structure and scope of the Secretariat for Promoting Christian Unity. This was the only item specified in the press. Fisher then spoke of the situation of the Anglican Church; he described it as less divided even at episcopal level than before. He expressed himself willing to form a small group of experts to inform and advise himself, or even to send, at least now and then, a delegate whom the SPCU could deal with, though not in an official guise – more perhaps as 'assistant' to the resident Anglican chaplain of All Saints. Turning to England, he spoke appreciatively of Anglican good relations with Heenan, lamenting that other bishops were less accessible. He wanted better relations, especially with Westminster, and collaboration on common concerns. He mentioned the 'secret' conversations and said they could remain unofficial but that Church leaders at least should know about them.[12] He expressed regret at the Roman Catholic practice of re-baptizing Anglicans.

Speaking of Church of England observers to the Council, he thought they should be chosen by himself in consultation with Church of England leaders. He concluded that his own flying visit was less important than the establishment of the SPCU.

But the pick of his comment came in the press conference given in the Embassy Residence on the late afternoon of 2nd December.

As correspondent of *The Tablet* I attended the Villa Wolkonska conference. Arriving at the gates I suddenly realized that I had left my press pass at home, when I spotted and was spotted by a minor official who stood within and with whom I had umpired a cricket match in Villa Pamphilj the previous Sunday. He siezed the telephone and said 'Fr Purdy is here for the press conference; he's forgotten his pass but I'm sending him up. H.E. knows all about it' – this last a flagrant but effective lie.

I was swept in and up the drive and made what I quickly realized was a theatrical entrance. The press were all sitting upright and expectant, like a sixth form waiting for the headmaster. The one or two who knew me grinned and waved, the rest looked at me with a wild surmise. I was clearly a tailor-made Vatican spy. I sat down meekly but was soon sighted by the embassy press attache and by the Archbishop's press officer, Colonel Bob Hornby, who in later years was to become a warm friend. Eventually Hornby summoned up his martial spirit and advanced on me. 'Excuse me', he said, 'but should you be here?' I told him I was Rome correspondent of *The Tablet*. Far from mollifying him, this seemed to make matters worse.

But the entrance of the Archbishop began what was easily the most bracing press conference of my experience. I cannot improve on the short account I gave to *the Tablet*. The Sunday's match had brought cricket metaphors to the surface, and, remarking on the shortage of information, I went on:

The bowling was consequently keen, but Dr Fisher scored briskly off the opening overs:

'Would you say that so-and-so could be read into your visit?' led off some unfortunate. This half-volley was treated on its merits:

'Anything *could* be read into it; people spend their time reading into things what they want to see.'

'During your fifty-five minutes with the Holy Father. ... ' began the *Daily Express* correspondent ...

'Come, come, the *Daily Express* doesn't usually minimise things – it was one hour and five minutes.'

Did he foresee any relaxation of coolness following the meeting?

'I don't know – good example is sometimes taken.'

Was he received at the Vatican with any *particular* ceremony?
  '*Particular*? I don't know – you'd better ask the Vatican.
I've never called on the Pope before.'

Had he any comments to offer on Pope John's personality?
  'Certainly not, he might retaliate by offering some on mine.'

  This sort of thing put everybody in high good humour, but
Dr Fisher had several more positive things to say. He was rather
impatient with drawn-out questions about the quantity and manner
of osculations: 'We greeted each other as two high ecclesiastics
normally do in the West.'
  The Archbishop spoke at some length about his visit to the
Brazilian College (his reception there had evidently delighted him)
and his talk with Cardinal Bea and Mons. Willebrands. He described
the SPCU over which Cardinal Bea presides as 'an extremely useful
organ, a natural channel of information of a sort that had never
existed before', but denied that it had disclosed anything about plans
for possible observers to the coming Council.
  Dr Fisher admitted that when he set out on his tour Jerusalem
was 'the biggest thing in his mind' and that he had in fact been
tremendously moved by his experience in the cradle of Christianity.
Asked about English reactions to the visit to the Pope, he said firmly
that on the whole it had been excellent. There was a small extreme
Protestant minority that had feared he might 'sell the pass' but he
invited people to look at his sermon of the night before to see
whether he had.

The Catholic *Il Quotidiano* in a dignified paragraph summed up the
better Roman feeling:

There will not be lacking discordant voices, unwarranted pessimism.
We prefer to record the event as in a page of goodwill which looks
to God, to the Redeemer, to the Gospel, to the Church, to the
salvation of the human race. If non-Catholics, English or other, have
their own views of the event, if they do not see beyond the particular
aspects of it, if indeed it produce no tangible effect, we know that
above the vicissitudes of time and space God watches over all,
echoing the Redeemer's wish *Ut sint unum* . . . The Christian world is
in movement. God grant it be towards better things.

On Sunday 4 December Patrick O'Donovan of the *Observer*, pointing out that Ottaviani and Tardini regarded ecumenicalism (sic) with 'practised suspicion', speculated (modestly as it was to prove) 'It is just conceivable that Canterbury might one day attend Midnight Mass in a chair of honour in Westminster Cathedral and Westminster do the same at a Coronation'.

On the same night Michael Ramsey and John Heenan made the promised appearance on television. Ramsey proclaimed 'the end of bigotry' and said that both sides had much to be ashamed of: Heenan stressed the scope for co-operation in an unbelieving world.

A rather more practical reaction came from the *Manchester Guardian Weekly*, which printed three long articles on inter-church relations in Liverpool, Birmingham and Gloucestershire, in which Christopher Driver gave some of the cold facts, including examples of aggressive bigotry, particularly in country life. His Liverpool article was based on an interview with Heenan:[13]

The less acceptable face of the press appeared in more comments from abroad on Fisher's resignation, which drew his characteristic fire: 'I always find it difficult to make a public denial of stories so absurd that no intelligent person could give them credence.' He specified two 'wildly untrue' reports. The first, from a transatlantic source, said 'My retirement was due to the fact that, having met the Pope, I desire to submit myself to the Roman obedience. To that I can only say that it is just as likely, no more no less, than the Pope having met me desires to become an Anglican.'

The second complaint was that the 'continental press in considerable volume attributes my forthcoming retirement to controversies in this country following my visit to the Pope'. His reply was that there was no controversy but almost unanimous approval, and that good results beyond expectation were already clearly visible.

On the whole Fisher earned much good-natured and admiring comment from all but extremists. The Convocation of York, meeting in mid-January, expressed through Bishop Harland of Durham a 'grievous sense of loss at the Archbishop's resignation' (which was tendered on 17 January 1961), and 'affection, regard and gratitude ... [T]he dominant force of his life was his ardent desire for the unity of Christ's church', and the visit was 'a gesture only he could have made'; it sprang from his heart and kindled action and hope. Fisher was similarly congratulated for his 'courageously imaginative tour' by Kenneth Black at the Dublin meeting of the British Council of Churches in April.

Praise for him on his retirement was almost unanimous and tributes included a 'strikingly cordial' one from Cardinal Godfrey of Westminster.

NOTES

1. The standard life of John XXIII in English is Peter Hebblethwaite, *John XXIII: Pope of the Council* (London, 1984).
2. Note from the archives of the Council for Foreign Relations.
3. It had been doing so increasingly during Pius' last long illness, but not far beyond the walls of the Vatican.
4. S. Schmidt SJ, *Il Cardinale dell'Unità* (Rome, 1987)
5. Ironically, it was Tardini who advised the change of title from 'Commission' to 'Secretariat' on the grounds that if (as he thought likely) nothing came of it, it would be easier for it quietly to disappear. In the event, being simply a Secretariat helped and continued to help the SPCU to maintain its freedom of action.
   The title was again changed to the Pontifical Council for Christian Unity in 1988.
6. It was not clear how far he was aware that these included the Anglican–Roman Catholic talks of the 1950s described above, though it is unlikely that his fellow Jesuit Boyer did not inform him of them. They were later referred to during Fisher's conversations with Bea and Willebrands in Rome, 2 December 1960.
7. *Analecta Gregoriana*, CVIII B, no. 6 (Rome, 1958).
8. '[A]n old Repton boy, a great friend of mine', said Fisher.
9. See p. 32, and note 11 below.
10. The last Archbishop of Canterbury to visit Rome had been Thomas Arundel during Richard II's reign in 1397. He came to ask the help of Boniface II in a Church–state quarrel.
11. The present account derives from the memorandum in the SPCU archives.
12. This refers to Strasbourg, Hampstead, etc.
13. Cf. Cardinal J. C. Heenan: *A Crown of Thorns*, p. 270.

The Fisher visit II

Fisher's visit to Rome was an epoch-making event which faced the Secretariat for Promoting Christian Unity at a moment when it was undergoing its baptism.

Anglican relations were important in the SPCU's view, but they were not the only ones. The 'ecumenical movement' centred in the World Council of Churches, and its Secretary General, W. A. Visser t'Hooft, could not be ignored. Bea had sounded out John XXIII about this and the Pope had said that 'the time was not ripe'. Bea characteristically concluded that it 'needed to be ripened'.

In the September before Fisher's visit Bea spent a day at Gazzada, in northern Italy, with a meeting of the European Catholic Conference for Ecumenical Questions of which Willebrands was the moving spirit.

The next day Bea went to Milan for a highly secret meeting with Visser t'Hooft. They discussed both the sending of Roman Catholic observers to the WCC New Delhi Conference of the following year, and the possibility of non-Roman-Catholic observers at Vatican II.

After Fisher's visit, the preparatory work for the Second Vatican Council began and the SPCU held its first plenary meeting, at which Bea laid down very firmly what the role of the SPCU was to be in this preparation.[1]

When talking with Bea in Rome,[2] Fisher had spoken of sending a permanent personal representative to Rome. In 1961 the *Church Times* announced the nomination of Bernard Pawley. Although there had been no prior consultation with the SPCU, Pawley was received without fuss.

About that time the question arose of having official Catholic observers at the WCC New Delhi conference. It had been agreed that the choice was the SPCU's task through the Holy Office. Having sent the names Bea received a solemn letter from the Holy Office saying that its Cardinal members had decided that the chosen ones should go only as journalists. Schmidt, who was Bea's secretary, recalls the cardinal reading the letter, folding it and saying tersely 'questo non va' (this won't do).

He replied at length to Ottaviani, who gave way, adding 'Your Eminence, I am glad to have taken this thorn out of your heart'.

There were to be a fair number of such tussles over the next twenty-odd years.

The Catholic observers were received at the New Delhi conference 'with great joy'. Bea's victory on the matter was of course of the highest importance in clearing the way for observers at Vatican II, which was now a little over a year away.

In England the *Sunday Times* greeted the New Delhi conference with a 'clarion call': 'Let the bigots skulk in their caves; the time has come to do open battle against the forces of disunity.'

A few days later the Bishop of Kensington wrote suggesting a *joint* week of prayer, fasting and penitence for the bitterness of the past. Cardinal Heenan supported this.

The pioneers at Assisi

The Vidler–Boyer group, coming together again at Assisi on 4–7 April 1961, must have felt that since their last meeting the cards had been shuffled in their favour. The theme was 'Faith', and the main focus of the discussion was the relation between faith and intellect.

The Catholic team was exactly that of Selwyn. Of the Anglicans, only Vidler and Cheslyn Jones survived, but two men came in who were destined for a long stint in Anglican–Roman Catholic dialogue, Howard Root of Emanuel College, Cambridge, and Henry Chadwick of Christ Church, Oxford.

One novel feature of the meeting was that a Catholic newcomer, Alan Clark, gave a paper on 'Faith according to Anglicans'. At the end Vidler wrote that Anglicans still felt the Roman Catholics over-intellectualized the nature of faith, while Roman Catholics felt that Anglicans underrated the intellectual element.

The new Archbishop

In 1961, the appointment of Michael Ramsey to Canterbury was announced. Reaction to the announcement naturally acquired what was coming to be called an 'ecumenical dimension'. *The Times* saw the succession of a scholar as apt, since problems of inter-church relations were now primarily theological, calling for the service of subtle, patient and scholarly minds. Donald Coggan, who was to move from Bradford to York, 'will be a leader of marked administrative ability'. The leader concluded skittishly 'Whether from Trollope or from other sources Mr Macmillan has acquired a touch in making church appointments'. Fisher was doubtless to thank for the fact that the Italian press took considerably more notice of the Canterbury succession than it had ever done before.

The question arose whether there should be Roman Catholic representation at Ramsey's enthronement on 27 July. Heenan wrote to Willebrands, after some thought, declaring that the time was not yet ripe for accepting such an invitation 'without risking a scandal'. 'The faithful', he said, 'are still puzzled by the changed relations between Catholics and Protestants'; writing from Liverpool he could, as the phrase is, say that again.[3]

At the beginning of June the Abbot of Bec in Normandy wrote to Willebrands proposing to offer Anglicans the use of a room in the abbey (which had become the Mecca of Francophile Anglicans) for the celebration of the Anglican eucharist. Today such a request would certainly seem a harmless one, but 1961 was rather different. Willebrands wrote indicating Heenan's disquiet about the possible results of such a move. Once it became known (Heenan thought) that Anglicans were having such celebrations in a Catholic monastery the attitude of the English hierarchy would be compromised. He ended by advising, in the name of the SPCU, that the French bishops concerned should make contact with Heenan.

The episode neatly illustrated the complexities of ecclesiastical courting at the time. The English had long been suspicious that some French sat very lightly indeed to Roman directives. On the other hand Heenan's phrase about 'compromising the attitude of the English hierarchy' was rather misleading. That 'attitude' was by no means as homogeneous as it seemed. It was certainly solid in sticking to the existing rules, and sometimes exceeding them, as when the bishop of Clifton, Joseph Rudderham, forbade a Catholic to speak at a public meeting planned for the following January's Week of Prayer.

Heenan was not I think particularly attracted to Anglicans, though in public he always spoke them fair; but he was conscientious in his ecumenical efforts, which he thought should include but not be confined to Anglican–Roman Catholic relations.

Anglo–Roman tensions

It was in 1961 also that the SPCU turned its attention to the question of the canonization of the English martyrs of the Reformation period. It needed little thought to see that it might be a delicate matter for ecumenism in England. The SPCU decided, mistakenly as they may well have thought afterwards, to consult the new Anglican man in Rome, Bernard Pawley. He produced a most unhappy memorandum beginning with a sententious excursus on the limits of Anglican enthusiasm for saints in general. He went on to give an account of the martyrs' history which showed how wise he would have been to consult a historian or two first:

> It was as political spies first and not only as Roman priests that they were executed. Now, I am not sufficiently an historian to be able to say whether Edmund Campion and other proposed saints were themselves actively engaged in hostile activity of this sort, *though it is on general grounds most highly probable that they were.* [Italics mine]

The SPCU sent this to three English correspondents: Bishop Thomas Holland at Portsmouth, Francis Davis at Oscott, Birmingham, and Maurice Bévenot, the Jesuit. Holland and Davis came down on Pawley's memo most heavily, and even Bévenot, though an inopportunist about the canonization, pointed out that Pawley's 'history' was open to serious objection. It was an object lesson in how not to conduct ecumenical dialogue and fortunately the Secretariat decided to bury it – if publicized, it could have stirred up trouble at a vital moment.[4]

Bea also wrote to Heenan, who sensibly did not offer any comment; at least none is recorded. In his television conversation with Ramsey, *Meeting Point*, Heenan had shown that he was wearing Pole's ring, and Ramsey had said it was

> a reminder of a period of history in which we've both got things to be ashamed of. I shudder when I think of our persecution of your

co-religionists in the reign of Queen Elizabeth and, well, the name Bloody Mary doesn't leave you wholly at ease ... It's the entanglement of religion and secular and nationalistic, and sometimes materialistic, movements that has betrayed us.

The chairman of the discussion, Kenneth Harris, had raised the question whether popular English belief in the Pope as a foreign power did not still survive, and both bishops had dismissed this, insisting that the only difference today was about the Pope's ecclesiastical authority.

But Ramsey remained unhappy about the canonization.

Another illustration of the difficulties of coping with the island race struck the SPCU in February 1961. They received a long and enthusiastic report from the Servite Gerard Corr, who entirely on his own initiative had made an extensive visitation of Anglican VIPs. Even if his report had been more impressive, his intervention would have appealed neither to the SPCU nor to Heenan. On 26 February Willebrands wrote to Corr, sharply discouraging these freebooters, 'because of the extreme sensitivity of England at present'. There was to be no courting of Anglican bishops or theologians without first getting advice from Heenan.

NOTES

1. A fuller treatment is given in S. Schmidt, *Il Cardinale dell'Unità* (Rome, 1987), p. 6.
2. Schmidt, ibid., p. 368.
3. Willebrands was able, even ten years later, to have a taste of the Merseyside religious climate for himself (see below, pp. 137, 139–40).
4. The canonization took place in 1970 (see pp. 137–40) without any of the uproar that Pawley and Bévenot had predicted. In the meantime in 1967 Professor Patrick McGrath, then of Bristol University, produced his admirably impartial and thorough *Papists and Puritans Under Elizabeth I* (London, 1967), which left neither Catholics nor Protestants with excuses for contentious simplifications.

Ecumenical lines cross

The ups and downs of 1961 no doubt persuaded Willebrands that it was high time he visited England for himself. He intimated his intention and was invited to lunch with Ramsey on 17 September. Both he and the Church of England Information Office carefully avoided publicity over the visit, which was a great success.

In March 1962, six months before the Second Vatican Council, Willebrands was in England again. Meanwhile the Catholic Church in England had established an ecumenical committee of five bishops with Heenan as their chairman. Its members were: J. P. Murphy (Cardiff), Joseph Rudderham (Clifton), Thomas Holland (Portsmouth) and David Cashman (Arundel and Brighton).

Heenan wrote: 'One of the first actions of the new committee was to announce a national conference on ecumenicsm to which every bishop and major religious superior was asked to send a priest.' It was arranged at the Jesuit College, then at Heythrop: 'I asked Cardinal Bea to be the chief speaker.' Willebrands was able to discuss Bea's projected visit, and to sound out Derek Worlock before talking to Ramsey about rumours that French clergy had invited Anglicans to celebrate and even concelebrate the eucharist. When Willebrands finally put the matter to Ramsey the Archbishop replied that the Church of England would unhesitatingly condemn such a practice but that it seemed that the rumours were false.[1]

On the subject of observers to the Council Ramsey said that he would be delighted to send them, one from the Church of England, one from the Episcopal Church of the United States and one from missionary lands.

Preparation for the Heythrop Conference

Writing in his autobiography twelve years later, Heenan said of Bea's visit to Heythrop.

> I invited him as the greatest living authority on Catholic ecumenism but also because I wanted him to meet the bishops in a relaxed conference atmosphere. For reasons already given, foreign cardinals are not highly regarded in English Catholic circles as authorities on the religious situation in this country. I hoped that personal acquaintance with Cardinal Bea would reassure the Archbishop of Westminster and my other brethren.
>
> > (*Crown of Thorns*, p. 325)

Misgivings about inviting Bea to Heythrop were not wholly unreasonable. Some bishops blamed him for the slow progress of the canonization of the English martyrs. This was 1962. The infant SPCU was overwhelmingly preoccupied with the final preparations for the Council, only five weeks away, and especially with ensuring the presence of the observers. Bea was as yet far less than the world figure he was shortly to become. On the other hand, he was by no means lacking in tact. What he did, having apologized disarmingly for his English, was to read them a general paper on 'The priest's responsibilities for unity'. This could hardly have cast him in the role of a foreign busybody teaching his grandmotherly English audience to suck eggs. He made sufficient impression at Heythrop to be invited to give the final summing up, which he did in Latin.

It was also natural enough for Bea during his long stay in London to go to Lambeth as well as Westminster. There is no record of his conversation with Godfrey, but that with Ramsey followed predictable lines: a rather one-sided list of insular squabbles, which might well have seemed burdensome to Bea but which was redeemed by Ramsey's suggestion of a joint episcopal commission to talk them out (a proposal to be taken up four or five years later by the Joint Preparatory Commission). For the moment Bea's main interest was in impressing on Ramsey as president of the Anglican communion what a splendid and welcome idea was that of having observers at the Council. Here there was no difference of opinion.

The Heythrop Conference

In spite of misgivings about inviting Cardinal Bea to give a paper, the Heythrop Conference was an historic event, well organized. In a 7,000-word report on the conference to his fellow bishops in England and Wales, Heenan felt able to state:

> Those who had come to the conference out of obedience to their superiors without any great attraction for ecumenism soon became enthusiastic. This was largely due to the presence of Cardinal Bea. If hitherto any had thought his judgement unsound on English religious affairs they now discovered the Cardinal to be a well-informed man of balanced views, great learning and evident piety. In many ways the conference was more like a retreat than a course of study.

There were six bishops and 70 priests – both diocesan and religious – present, and all were encouraged to speak openly with promise of anonymity.

There were six study groups, five of which reported, through their secretaries, at the end of the meeting. Heenan moved around among the groups, simply to test the reactions to the six papers, intervening hardly at all. Nearly all the groups' suggestions had to do with some aspect of education. Catholic education itself was seen as inadequate and sometimes negative. Too few priests had any access to university education either individually or through seminaries. Hence few opportunities existed of getting to know what serious non-Roman-Catholic Christians really believed and thought, or what foreign Roman Catholic scholars of weight were thinking. One result of this was a gap between the clergy and educated laity.

Bernard Leeming SJ gave a verdict that was rather different from Heenan's: 'The pompous reports of the secretaries', he wrote to Bévenot, 'masked the utter ignorance of the majority.' But they were judging the conference from different standpoints and with different objectives. Leeming looked at ecumenism from the standpoint of the theologian and the experienced ecumenist. Heenan's approach, on the other hand, was pastoral.

Yet in one vital respect Heenan divined the ecumenical need. He saw it as a challenge to prayer, to spiritual renewal. This at least united him with Ramsey. Heenan's impatience to 'get on with it' in England ran him into difficulties – not all of his own making.

Oxford meeting, 1962

The group which had last met in April 1961 was hoping to arrange another meeting at St Edmund Hall, Oxford. The Master, J. N. D. Kelly, had been invited to take over the Anglican leadership from Alec Vidler, who complained of staleness. Meanwhile Cardinal Heenan had written to ask Boyer to cancel the Oxford meeting, since he wished to organize one himself. There ensued a comedy of errors, which demonstrated both Heenan's inexperience in ecumenical conventions, and the extent to which the conversations had actually been seen as 'unofficial'. It seemed extraordinary that neither Willebrands, nor Heenan, the English bishop chiefly concerned with ecumenism, had been informed of the Oxford meeting or of what had been going on for over twelve years.

In the event, no great harm was done. The group from the 1950s met at St Edmund Hall on 16–19 July 1962 with several new faces. The theme was 'The eucharistic sacrifice'. The Anglican rapporteur Cheslyn Jones complained that the debate might have profited by more going back to sources, whereas Scholastic and Reformation issues dominated and discussion was kept to small points.

The Worth Conference

The dialogue laid on by Heenan took place at the Benedictine priory at Worth in Sussex. He proposed the subject 'The Eucharist'. He also wanted new faces, especially younger ones, and although, as we have seen, he disclaimed any objection to foreigners, he did not invite any. The teams were eight a side. The chairman on the Anglican side was Canon Henry Balmforth of Exeter.

For once, the Catholics outnumbered the Anglicans in academics. This was still of course some weeks before the opening of Vatican II, and from that point of view the outstanding feature of the conference was the impression made on the Anglicans by the unexpected Catholic attitude to Scripture. No detailed reports seem to have been made, but Balmforth and G. L. Phillips sent reports to Lambeth, Bévenot to Heenan.

Phillips said much about personalities. Bévenot he found 'detached, quiet, rather conventional', Gervase Mathew 'rather wickedly pro-Anglican on almost every issue'. But it was the Scripture men L. Johnson (Ushaw) and Tom Worden (Upholland) who really shook him up; 'their papers', he wrote, 'would not have disgraced a Nineham pupil.'[2] Balmforth echoed this judgement and Ramsey, acknowledging the report, said that he too had been 'quite startled by the radical character of some of the biblical studies that go on in monasteries and seminaries'.

Tom McGoldrick, a Cambridge graduate, chaplain at Liverpool University, was for those days an advanced liturgical reformist, a secretary of the Vernacular Society. All this may have cast a shadow over the Anglican belief that it was no use talking to Catholics except those from across the Channel. An account of the meeting with Bévenot's impressions was sent to Heenan on 10 September. With an eye on episcopal consumption, it was fairly bland.

Owen Chadwick describes this meeting as a turning point in the dialogue (*Anglican Initiatives*, p. 99). 'There was a wide difference of outlook between an arrangement made by a French Jesuit and an arrangement made by an English archbishop', he wrote.

Bévenot said that the Scripture papers by Johnson and Worden were judged to have

> made a deep impression on our Anglican brethren who recognised in them the best scholarship of the day and the same methods they were themselves accustomed to. (Perhaps they had expected obscurantist fundamentalism!)[3]

In a rather more frank covering note, he bemoaned that

> we had not among us a professional dogmatic theologian – there were moments when we felt that our recollections of our theological studies were not precise enough to meet adequately such questions as 'What are the different Catholic theories of the Mass today?'[4]

In his last paragraph Bévenot put a match to a rocket by advocating continuity of personnel in dialogue. Heenan was all for 'dialogue' spread widely (and inevitably thinly) up and down the country, but saw little use in continuity of personnel. He thought this simply generated a kind of social club and probably feared that Catholics, especially academic ones, might come out of such theological huddles with dubious ideas and attitudes. Bévenot bravely replied that he just could not understand this argument, and Heenan came back with a much longer outburst. Its main points were:

1. What matters is wider and wider mutual acquaintance, not 'a few academic friendships'. (The truth was that both were necessary.)
2. The 'social club' argument now appears with true colours flying. A great deal of the ecumenical dialogue has been between Anglicans and foreign Roman Catholics, and has done little beyond isolating the Roman Catholic Church in this country. Willebrands and his friends have been meeting Anglicans for years. They are on Christian name terms and have lovely holidays in various parts of the world. But I cannot see that this has the slightest effect on the Catholic Church in this country.
3. Höfer had written to him about the Oxford meeting 'presuming that Boyer had sent me a full report ... I do not know even the names of those who took part. I do not even know if young Father Küng was one of those who spoke on behalf of the Church.'
4. The Worth dialogue was good but was only with the 'Catholics' in the Church of England.
5. The result of the Heythrop conference and others similar should be to produce more and more priests able to take part in dialogue.

Bévenot replied patiently and thoroughly to all this. He distinguished 'getting friendly' from getting to know what others think. He pointed out that the Worth Anglicans, like the Oxford ones, were nominated from Lambeth. (This was not quite true of the Oxford ones, though they were probably approved there.) The Catholics at Oxford were not 'continental' but nearly all English (too much so for the CFR). They nourished no ambition to 'exclude the hierarchy'. Of the statement about Willebrands and his work he simply made mincemeat.[5]

At Worth, Bévenot said, he had raised the point about the absence of evangelicals, but the answer was that their presence would have made for Anglicans wasting time disputing among themselves. Of multilateral dialogues as favoured by the Archbishop, he said that their value was difficult to assess.

When he replied to this, Heenan had cooled down somewhat. He was evidently anxious not to lose Bévenot's co-operation. He admitted he was hazy about whom Boyer and Co. represented, suggesting even – one can only think whimsically – the Holy Office. He also conceded that 'it would be hopeless to leave it to me or to any other bishop to deal with arrangements and personnel' but thought a committee might be formed under the bishops.

Bévenot had so far kept his end up in this tussle, but it was telling on him. He was a gentle scholar, ill-equipped for the rough and tumble of ecclesiastical politics, and he turned to the tougher and more experienced Leeming with a *cri de coeur*. Leeming was only partly encouraging. He believed that the scope of dialogue was long-term (how right he was), and that it might gradually improve Catholic standing in schools and universities. But he was clearly doubtful whether the nature and scope of dialogue was really appreciated, and unless Bévenot could have assurance about this he would be better employed on Cyprian or *The Heythrop Journal*.

Rehearsing the problem of selection, Leeming warned that 'the perfect team is impossible: we must face the fact that we have few scholars compared with the Anglicans'. He had a good word for the 'fifties' group, though he knew Boyer's reputation among Catholic ecumenists was one of extreme intransigence. He had some sympathy with Heenan's view about 'clubs' but they have the strength of, for example, a communist cell.

Twenty-four hours later he felt he had not warned Bévenot strongly enough against becoming Heenan's sole agent. He listed rather violently what he regarded as Heenan's shortcomings, saying he would do better to commit the business to Thomas Holland and concluding quaintly 'this of course is not against Heenan, only a most friendly warning to you'.

Bévenot digested all this and passed it on with due modesty, in terms more suitable for episcopal ears, with concrete suggestions of his own. He stressed that he thought the Archbishop over-sanguine about providing several good dialogue teams. Anglicans were not only rich in scholarship but also experienced in dialogue. We are only beginners. With a swift and endearing change of heart reminiscent of the last scene in a Shakespearean Comedy, Heenan replied 'I want to say at once that I agree with everything you have said. You modestly apologize at the end for offering me so little, but you have told me precisely what I wanted to know. I shall give a copy of your letter to each of the Bishops' Committee.'

Thus an eventful year drew to an end on the threshold of Vatican II.

NOTES

1. At a later date it would have been impossible to say that they were all false.
2. Dennis Nineham; a Cambridge scripture student, lecturer and writer.
3. Fr Robert Murray SJ, the eminent Syriac and biblical scholar, recalls some impressions: 'I was still a mere boy in Jesuit thinking in those days. I found the Worth meeting a very happy one ... I thought Fr Hebert breathed real holiness (though hardly strong

scholarship). Among my happiest memories is seeing how John Fenton and Tom Warden made great friends. They were always walking up and down the terraces together.' (From a letter to the author.)

4. Bévenot had circularized his men in July with a list of Roman Catholic and Anglican books on eucharistic sacrifice, with two columns beside them headed respectively:

   A. I am acquainted with it and could brush it up.

   B. I could get it up if necessary.

   Few scored much in either column.

5. Two months earlier the Archbishop had written to the Prior of Worth: 'You will probably be surprised to know that I have absolutely no experience of ecumenical dialogue. I have never attended one.'

6

Further English
conversations

The Oxford group met again in 1964, 20–23 July, with two sessions of the Vatican Council behind them and with some new faces. The Council's decree on ecumenism was not published until 21 November, but it was now really a foregone conclusion, and it already allowed dialogue to breathe a freer air. The two years since they last met had been years of revolution. A revolution which was still going on, which nobody yet fully understood but which nobody could ignore, least of all men who had been in dialogue in a spirit of hope since 1950.

They lodged at Queen's College, Oxford, whose chaplain, David Jenkins, now joined the Anglican team. The others were Bishop Francis Taylor of Sheffield, S. L. Greenslade, Regius Professor of ecclesiastical history at Oxford, Henry Chadwick, Regius Professor of Divinity at Oxford, Cheslyn Jones and Howard Root. The Catholic team was much changed. Bévenot was still chairman, but H. F. Davies was the only other survivor from 1962. L. Johnson of Ushaw had been at Worth. Michael Richards came from St Edmund's College, Ware; and there was a Jesuit from Louvain, P. J. Dejaifve, and a Dominican from Holland, C. F. Pauvels. They had some links with the Council. Bévenot, who succeeded Boyer as chairman, attended the Council as guide and interpreter to the Anglican observers. So did H. F. Davies. Howard Root became an observer.

The chosen theme was that which had created the chief drama in the first two Council Sessions – 'Scripture and Tradition'. The revised decree

De Revelatione was not promulgated until 1965 but enough was known about it to make clear how new it would be.

Six papers were presented:

CHESLYN JONES: 'Scripture and Tradition: a New Testament perspective';

MICHAEL RICHARDS: 'Richard Hooker on Scripture and Tradition';

H. DAVIES: 'Newman on Scripture and Tradition';

S. L. GREENSLADE: Issues raised by the formation of the canon of scripture';

L. JOHNSTON: 'The Bible and the role of Tradition';

D. JENKINS: 'The notion of Scripture as an authoritative norm in the light of biblical research and criticism'.

The last title promised an approach to a real problem, but the paper did not please the chairman, J. N. D. Kelly.

He described it as 'lengthy, *ex tempore* . . . rambling, repetitious'.

His general conclusion was that discussion ranged widely but was finally monopolized by questions of authority and the magisterium of the Church, where Anglican and Roman Catholic views were more clearly divided. Roman Catholics might, he thought, have taken Anglicans up more aggressively here and got them to explain how far and in what sense they considered it possible for the Church to make authoritative pronouncements.

Later on that year Kelly wrote to Satterthwaite saying he was discouraged about increasing refusals of invitations to meet. Nevertheless another meeting took place at Heythrop in 1966, by which time Archbishop Ramsey had made a visit to Rome and preparations for the opening of official dialogue between the Anglican communion and the Roman Catholic Church were beginning. There were many new faces: on the Catholic side Charles Davis, whose reputation as a theologian had soared during the Council period but who was to leave the priesthood and the Catholic Church before the end of the year. Bernard Leeming (see p. 27) stood in for H. F. Davies, who was ill. Höfer returned and Dejaifve and Johnston continued.

On the Anglican side, F. W. Dillistone and Howard Root returned (the latter had been at Assisi in 1961 and subsequently observer at Vatican II). Leslie Houlden, chaplain and Fellow of Trinity College, Oxford, stood in for Kenneth Woolcombe of Edinburgh Theological College (later Bishop of Oxford), while Henry Chadwick and Cheslyn Jones continued. The theme was 'The Atonement', which ARCIC did not deal with until the Commission's second phase in the 1980s. J. N. D. Kelly reported in a brief letter to Ramsey, going into no detail. The atmosphere, he again said, was 'wonderfully fresh and inspiring'.

The last of these meetings – ten to them in seventeen years, beginning under the shadow of the *monitum* – came when the Joint Preparatory Commission (JPC) had already met and was at work. It was inevitable that the question should at last arise whether the meetings were now needed and it was put to Ramsey through the CFR early in July. His answer was clear: 'I should be sorry if the informal conferences organized by Dr Kelly ceased on account of the Joint Preparatory Commission.'

In spite of this encouragement, the group met for the last time at Queens College, Oxford, on 24–27 July 1967. Except for Mgr Höfer, it consisted entirely of men from Great Britain. There were three newcomers on the Roman Catholic side: Robert Murray SJ from Heythrop College, Fr Cuthbert Rand from the seminary at Ushaw and Fr Richard Stewart from the seminary at Wonersh. All three were later to take part in official dialogues, and Richard Stewart was to have a distinguished though sadly shortened career, first as secretary of the Ecumenical Commission, then as consultant and later staff member of the SPCU. Yet no one present at Oxford was a member of the official Joint Preparatory Commission, since Canon Root, who should have been at Oxford, was absent because of illness. The theme was 'The Church', with obvious particular reference to Vatican II's Constitution *Lumen Gentium*.

Kelly reported a wide range of agreement, with (of course) reservations about papal power, though Roman Catholic elucidation of the Constitution 'reduced the obnoxiousness of some of its features'. The Anglican co-chairman ended with a striking passage:

> I was struck by the high quality of the younger Roman theologians, especially Murray and Stewart (Mgr Höfer of course stands in a class by himself: immensely learned and acute and wonderfully pro-Anglican.) Their thinking is very deep and well-informed. If this generation prevails in the Roman Catholic Church, Anglicanism, so long as it keeps true to itself, has nothing to fear.

Fifty-five people engaged in Anglican–Roman Catholic dialogue between 1950 and 1967 – fourteen more if one includes the Worth meeting.

Some of this number took part five or six times, some only once. (This offers a striking contrast with the constancy of the JPC and ARCIC.) The large majority of the Anglican participants were from the universities of Oxford or Cambridge. This was true of only half a dozen or so of the Roman Catholics, though of course the latter included a varying number of distinguished foreigners.

Only two of the 55 became members of the JPC (Richards and Root), and three became members of the first ARCIC group (ARCIC I): Root, Henry Chadwick and Bishop Clark. With all possible emphasis on the differing character of the two groups, it nonetheless seems astonishing that one remembers no allusion to this seventeen years' work in the subsequent official conversations. That nothing at all could have been learned from them, and no time saved, seems implausible.

PART

II

7

Preparations for the Second Vatican Council

Observers

The idea of having non-Roman-Catholic observers at a general council was not new and had been under consideration for Vatican II for nearly two years – almost since the opening of the offices of the Secretariat for Promoting Christian Unity offices in fact. Bea had included it in the proposed statute for the Secretariat which he prepared for John XXIII and the Pope gave it strong support. The Bull *Humanae Salutis*, convoking the Council, assigned to the SPCU responsibility for inviting observers, and identified the motive for having them as the interest and prayers which were being devoted to the Council by other Christians.

Willebrands took elaborate preliminary soundings, and these occupied him with some help from others, for most of 1962. The targets were, in the East, the historic Patriarchates and the ancient Oriental (or pre-Chalcedonian) Churches; in the West, the 'world Christian communions', as they are today styled. For Anglicans this meant the Anglican Communion, a federation of autonomous churches subscribing to the Chicago–Lambeth Quadrilateral.[1] It was heavily dominated by British-born bishops, except, of course, for the Protestant Episcopal Church in the USA (PECUSA) as it was then still called.

In 1853 W. A. Muhlenberg had suggested that PECUSA might modify its constitution so as to allow it to become the nucleus of a kind of Protestant constellation, and finally in 1886 the Chicago–Lambeth Quadrilateral came to birth under the ecumenical midwifery of W. R. Huntingdon. Similarly at Edinburgh it was an Episcopal bishop, Charles Brent – a missionary in the Philippines – who promoted the birth of the Faith and Order movement.

At the period we are dealing with, PECUSA, which had three and a half million baptized and two million communicants, was governed by a General Convention which met every three years. In November 1961, a year after Fisher's visit, the Presiding Bishop Lichtenberger visited Pope John XXIII. He told the press that John had explicitly promised him that observers would be invited to the Council; and the Pope had even said that his own original idea had been 'active participants', but he had had to give this up because of 'a variety of complications'. The *Osservatore Romano* communiqué on this audience said nothing at all about observers.

Considerable thought and discussion at the SPCU had gone into the 'whys and wherefores' of having observers. Willebrands' proposal, destined to be decisive in its effect, was that there should be regular meetings between them and the members of the Secretariat.

At a plenary meeting of the SPCU Cardinal Heenan opened on a cautionary note. We should not criticize our institutions in front of these observers. Moreover, we should avoid the danger of offering courtesies which, if they were ever reciprocated, we should be obliged to refuse. Thus, for example, we could hardly invite the Archbishop of Canterbury to be present at the opening ceremony in full pontificals.

Martin of Rouen thought that to invite bishops would be an embarrassment for them and for the Council: expert theologians would be the most suitable observers. (This on the whole turned out to be true.) Franz Thyssen, a long time associate of Willebrands in the Catholic Conference for Ecumenical Questions, was in favour of observers with ecumenical experience.

Finally, the practical details were consigned to the SPCU, which generally meant Willebrands.

There were to be two translators each for English, French and German. They were to be theologians with ecumenical experience and their role was comprehensively seen as that of guardian angels.

Anglican observers

A formal invitation signed by Bea and Willebrands went to Lambeth to send three observers to Vatican II and the names were requested by 1 August.

In the absence of Ramsey, Satterthwaite sent the names and promised that they would be announced at the Church Assembly. The names were:

The Bishop of Ripon, J. H. MOORMAN, the distinguished authority on the Franciscans.

FREDERICK C. GRANT, Professor (Emeritus) of biblical theology in Union Theological Seminary, New York.

HAROLD DE SOYSA, Principal of Divinity School, Colombo, later Bishop of Colombo.

Ramsey wrote confirming this and warning that substitutes might be necessary if the Council went on for a lengthy period: there were to be several before the end of the fourth session in 1965.

Writing his thanks, Willebrands expressed pleasure, as he was to do several times, that the Anglicans were the first to respond to the invitation. He later informed Pawley that he, at the request of the Archbishop, would be either a fourth observer or a guest of the SPCU.

Observers' reactions

It is not intended here to give an account of the Second Vatican Council. Countless books in many languages have done so. It is the ecumenical aspect of the Council that concerns us chiefly here, and hence the reactions of the observers, particularly the Anglicans, are of central interest.

There were forty or so observers who entered St Peter's with the Council fathers on the opening day. Neither then nor at any time afterwards did they complain of the facilities given them. They had first-rate places in the basilica, and both in and out of it they were treated as privileged guests.

But not all the contrivance of hospitality, the provision of 'guardian angels' to translate and explain, could wholly dispel the bewilderment and suspicions, especially of the Protestants. They were partly fascinated, partly repelled by the elaborate costume, ornament and ceremonial which they very indiscriminately dubbed 'baroque'. (Much of it was about to disappear.) J. H. Moorman – doyen of the Anglican observers – wrote that 'one observer remarked cynically "It is of course more pleasant to feel the warmth of fraternal embrace than the acrid heat of inquisitorial flames, but the purpose is the same"' (*Vatican II Observed*, p. 29).

Albert Outler, the brilliant Professor from Southern Methodist University, wrote:

> Even deeper went our doubts that Rome rightly understood the Gospel: God's utter sovereignty, the sheer gratuity of his mercy and pardon, the all-sufficiency of Christ's mediation and grace, the primacy of faith, the untrammelled authority of holy scripture, etc. Rome's reliance, we thought, was on the *opus operatum* – the human management of God's grace. Rome's piety, we thought, was a syndrome of merit and masochism – the gaining of God's favour by dint of human effort. But I was deeply impressed by the self-conscious effort of a great Church attempting an experiment in self-examination and renewal. From the beginning I was convinced that Pope John's slogan *aggiornamento* was seriously meant and should be taken seriously. Whether the effort succeeded or failed, it would in either case be edifying to watch and record.

The observers often found it hard to rid themselves of the mentality of the visiting examiner – particularly on reading the Council texts, to which they had full access. The Anglicans particularly, most of whom disliked being thought of as Protestants and liked to consider themselves the real heirs of the uncorrupted tradition of the early Church, were prone to the attitude. If the Church of England, in particular, saw the Catholic idea of ecumenism as nothing but the Great Return, their own concept of it sometimes looked like nothing by the Great Catchup. Those Church of England men who, as we have seen, had in the 1950s and early 1960s made heroic efforts to get to know Catholicism, were hardly represented.

When reporting to the Council's not-very-sympathetic Secretary General, Pericle Felici, it was natural enough that Willebrands should stress the politer comments of the Council's observers. He could quote the very gracious words of the Armenian Karekin Sarkissian, an Oxford graduate of great charm and wisdom (now Patriarch of the Catholicosate of Cilicia):

> We expected to be received with great courtesy. We are received with heart and we are happy. When we met the Pope we realized the Lord is using him to do great things. We first thought some aspects of the unity problem impossible. Now we believe all is possible.

Halfway through the first session rumours were floated in the more mischief-making press raising doubts about the religious and ecumenical spirit governing contacts with the observers. Reactions were prompt. The great Oscar Cullmann[2] gave a press conference on Saturday 12 October at which he stressed the responsibility of the observers as representatives of their Church, but added:

> our presence here does not turn this into a Council of union in the manner of Florence or Lyons [an obvious point made by Bea before the Council]. We attend, as the Council does, to the question of Catholic reform, but not, I hope, in a pharisaical way forgetting our own limitations and needs.

The dynamics of the meetings had their difficulties: Latin spoken in many different accents was one; but Cullmann stressed above all the value of wider contacts in the refreshment bars, and hospitality from bishops, cardinals, institutes and colleges. On that same Saturday the Pope was giving an audience to journalists. As these made their way up Bernini's Scala Regia to their appointment, they were involved in a traffic block with bishops streaming out – prematurely. They had met to 'approve' the prepared lists of members of the various commissions. Cardinal Liénart of Lille and Cardinal Frings of Cologne had proposed proroguing the assembly to scrutinize the prepared lists of names for various commissions before approving them. This step made it clear that the Council was to be no 'rubber-stamping' operation. If you were there as the bishops came out you sensed their exhilaration, the feeling that 'it moves, therefore it lives'. You sensed it no less in the tremendous cheer that met John XXIII as he joined the journalists. Here was a brief and dramatic step of great practical consequence but no less of symbolic significance.

NOTES

1. The Chicago Declaration of 1886, confirmed at the Lambeth Conference of 1888, is known as the Chicago–Lambeth Quadrilateral. It is a foundation text for Anglican reunion, setting out four elements as the essential features of a united church: Scripture, the Nicene Creed, Baptism and Eucharist, and the historical Episcopate.
2. Born Strasbourg 1902; Professor at Strasbourg, Basel, Paris; New Testament scholar, theologian and ecumenist.

First session:
death of John XXIII

Start of the Council

The Council began in October 1962 with a debate on liturgy which was relatively uncontroversial.[1] The principles which lay behind it were certainly in harmony with Congar's realism. Those who had to preach the gospel and promote and regulate worship in a vast variety of situations, cultures and languages, who had come to Rome expecting a 'pastoral' council, were unlikely to disagree in any numbers about necessary changes in liturgy. Changes had been going on for some time. Those envisaged in the Constitution opened up further possibilities which awaited practical realization, though they were not destined to wait for long.

The liturgy debate also drew attention to procedural defects in the *aula*, not all of which were easily remedied. Freedom of speech must include freedom to bore. At this stage of the Council there were very few good and realistic ideas for curbing loquacity without curbing freedom. Cardinal Ottaviani, who had his own ideas of how to simplify discussion, fluently and passionately attacked any idea of change in the Mass. The president, Cardinal Alfrink of Utrecht, first reminded him politely that he had overrun his time by five minutes, gave him two more and cut him off. Ottaviani would have been superhuman if he had not been upset – he was so totally unused to anything but being kow-towed to.

The incident cast light on another aspect of liturgical reform. The Constitution clearly looked forward to the increasing use of the vernacular.

This simply could not be managed from Rome and necessarily meant more initiative for episcopal conferences. (The point was seized in one of the reports sent back to Lambeth by the Anglican observers.)

The Anglican observer Bishop Moorman of Ripon said, rather mischievously, 'I could not help thinking that if the Church of Rome went on improving the Missal and Breviary long enough they would one day triumphantly invent the Book of Common Prayer'. But Dr Massey Shepherd, Professor of Liturgy at Berkeley, California, pointed out that the Book of Common Prayer

> is in fact a museum piece, which for all its clarity and beauty does not reflect the literary or spoken English that is now one of the international languages of mankind. Roman Catholic translators today must work with a very different set of categories – whatever the jarring results may be to Anglican sensibilities, so long attuned to an archaic vernacular, which even Anglicans themselves find increasingly needs interpretation and simplification.

The next item on the programme was the schema *De Revelatione*. The Anglican observer Frederick C. Grant, a former Professor of biblical theology at Union Theological Seminary, New York, put the contrast succinctly:

> Whereas the schema on Liturgy reflected modern expert thinking and real pastoral concern, the one on Revelation was criticized from the outset as antiquated in outlook and presuppositions and anything but pastoral in spirit and aim.

Pope John intervened. The schema was scrapped and a new one drawn up in collaboration between the Theological Commission and the SPCU. This was a brilliantly appropriate move, not least because Bea was easily the outstanding biblical scholar in the Council.[2]

The observers' report sent to Lambeth was rather sketchy and bad-tempered, ending:

> tradition cannot be used to justify *additions* to the faith (mainly the Marian dogmas and the Petrine texts) which 'fly in the face of all modern principles and methods of investigation'. These traditions are on a par with the Donation of Constantine and with the assurance of

Roman guides that St Peter said his daily mass at an altar in Santa Pudenziana. There is no possibility of union with the Anglican Communion until Rome frees itself of this Holy Mistletoe.

By the time the Council moved on (very much with the air of taking a breather) to a schema on social communications (which the report to Lambeth stupefyingly described as 'excellent') the main lines of the Council's future were looking a great deal clearer. When Ottaviani presented the schema on the Church (after a vain attempt to put it off in favour of one on Our Lady) it needed no clairvoyance to predict a stormy reception for it. Ottaviani even anticipated some of the criticisms, but more in a spirit of defiance than of discussion. Any criticisms of it by observers paled beside the blow-lamp eloquence of the Bishop of Bruges, Emil Josef de Smedt, which was the sharpest cannonade in another mass attack. It was joined in a quieter tone by the Archbishop of Milan, Montini, who had so far said little or nothing in the Council but now came down in favour of reorganizing the document according to the goals set by John XXIII, and focusing on the collegiality and sacramentality of the episcopate. He was reported to have said privately 'Christ would not have seen the role of the bishops, the role of the Christian people, the relations of papacy and episcopate in this way'. On 6 December the Pope announced a new 'co-ordinating commission,' which must have appeased northern critics without raising extravagant hope in the bosoms of experienced Romans.

The Pope's doctors allowed him only a brief appearance at the proroguing ceremony. His comments were eagerly awaited. He said:

> It will be easily understood that, in so vast a gathering, some time should have been needed to reach agreement on things which, *salva caritate*, offered cause for dispute. These disagreements are not in the least to be wondered at (*minime mirandae*) but have a little disturbed people's minds. They are all part of the design of providence, that truth should be put in its true light and that to the whole of human society there should be manifest that holy liberty of the sons of God which reigns in the Church.

It was plain enough what had offered cause for dispute, and who had illuminated truth and liberty. The last sentence was accompanied by John's characteristic gesture of emphasis, the little repeated nod.

It was the last time he spoke to the Council he had summoned. But two months later he addressed them by letter: *Mirabilis Ille* was its title.

> If we concerned ourselves only with Catholic business, lingering behind the ramparts of the Church, would not this way of going on ignore (it has always seemed to us) the lesson of the divine Redeemer, who died not only for our sins but for those of the whole world, who was the true light enlightening every man that cometh into the world? All flesh shall see God's salvation; there are no human preferences with God.

Death and succession

Reactions to the death

None who were present in Rome during John XXIII's last days will ever forget the experience. (He died 3 June 1963.) After 25 years I can still picture a Jewish journalist, a woman, who stood staring up at the lighted window as I left for home not long before midnight; when I returned at mid-morning she still stood on much the same spot as if she had never moved.

There were memorial services everywhere, though what Catholics found more moving was to have their bank manager or grocer eloquent in sympathy. In Lambeth Palace chapel Michael Ramsey celebrated a requiem before a distinguished congregation. It was not the first celebrated there but the first for the head of another Church. Roman Catholics decided that only laymen might attend, while the Protestant Truth Society roundly denounced 'this blasphemous service' as a denial of Holy Scripture and alien to the Church of England.

The new Pope

On 21 June the Archbishop of Milan, Giovanni Battista Montini, was elected to succeed John XXIII.

Montini had wept earlier on as he joined the procession into the conclave. The press of the time was fond of repeating an alleged question of John XXIII's to a Milanese visitor: 'How is your Hamletic cardinal getting on?'[3] But however sparing of speech, Montini could be eloquent, and he was when his predecessor died. He said in his cathedral the next day:

> Why do they mourn his death everywhere in the world? What marvel of spiritual convergence produces this thing without precedent in history? Everyone of us has felt the attraction of that personality, has grasped that the sympathy that enveloped him was not a delusion or a fashionable whim; it was a secret revealing itself, a mystery which absorbed us, the mystery of two words, which, united in magic power, dazzled our eyes – the words truth and charity.

There were plenty of obvious contrasts between the two men, but there was one thing John and he had very much in common – a distaste for the pomposities and clichés of Vaticanese. There was a story that he once sent back a draft report in the Secretariat of State with the marginal comment: 'too many barques of Peter, too many fishers of souls'. His first papal remark in the vernacular was 'Sento fino alla sofferenza i miei limiti' ('I feel my limitations to the point of suffering'), and no one who knew him took this for ritual modesty.

Everybody was delighted with his choice of name, which they rightly related to the apostle of the gentiles and not to the rather mixed bag of five Popes Paul. He was arguably less fond of words than of significant gestures and one of these was, when he made his first appearance at his window for the Sunday Angelus, to bring a cardinal with him. It was the Archbishop of Malines, Leo Josef Suenens.

What was the world to expect of the new Pope, especially of his attitude to the Council? Probably no bishop had been more assiduous in keeping his own diocese informed of what was going on, or helping them to understand it. During the first session he had written, from 13 October onwards, a weekly letter to be printed in the diocesan newspaper *L'Italia*. But few even of those who read Italian read the Milanese diocesan newspaper.[4]

Had they done so, they would have seen the fastidious and antithetical cast of his mind. Further subtleties came out in some of his earliest speeches to the Curia.

> '[The Council's] extraordinary and complex dimensions were discerned more fully by the Curia than by any other sector of the Church or of public opinion. The Curia's concern was such as to

show at times a certain stupor and apprehension ... ' Speaking of 'the sudden splendid decision of the one who called the Catholic Church to the Council and opened doors and hearts to the separated brothers for a sincere reconciliation', he went on 'we are certain that the Curia will never be suspected of any differences from the Pope', 'conformity' must be 'rigorously universal'.

This was a scarcely veiled allusion to the habit, often displayed in the Council, of claiming the Pope's support when convenient and ignoring him when not.

The whole was a masterly exercise in sugaring the pill, but those who wished could and did swallow the sugar and either (if obtuse) failed to notice the pill or (if brighter) spat it out.

NOTES

1. For all this cf. Peter Hebblethwaite, *John XXIII*.
2. Cardinal Garrone (later Prefect of the Congregation for Education), writing as an eye-witness of this 'collaboration', said 'It is painful to talk of it. The best one can say is that the SPCU was not welcomed by some members of the Theological Commission. Certainly Cardinal Bea in those days suffered some of the hardest trials of his life. Many of us shared his travail and fought with him. I must say in all sincerity that I have had many occasions to admire this man: his serenity in the midst of storm, his flawless humility, his calm and firmness of judgement and, I would dare to say, his strength of mind in forgiving want of respect, that another would not have tolerated.' (See Schmidt, p. 459.)
3. It has been claimed that the phrase was never John's but Tardini's.
4. Summary in *The Tablet* (13 September 1963).

9

Second session:
Decree on Ecumenism

A new beginning

29 September 1963

Paul VI's opening speech to the Council was eagerly awaited. The Pope wanted the Council Fathers to be fully aware that Christ was their starting point, Christ the road they must travel, Christ their final goal. The objectives of the Council he summarized thus: 'The knowledge or, if you like, the awareness of the Church', its reform, the search for Christian unity, and the dialogue of the Church with the modern world. It was clear that the Constitution on the Church was to be the centrepiece of the next phase.

> For this reason, the principal concern of this session of the Council
> will be to examine the intimate nature of the Church and to express in
> human language, so far as that is possible, a definition which will best
> reveal the Church's real, fundamental constitution and manifest her
> manifold mission of salvation. This theological doctrine has the
> possibility of magnificent developments which merit the attentive
> consideration of our separated brothers also and which, as we ardently
> hope, may make the path towards common agreement easier.

Turning to Christian unity, he addressed the observers directly in a passage destined to be often quoted:

If we are in any way to be blamed for that separation we humbly beg God's forgiveness and ask pardon too of our brethren who feel themselves to have been injured by us. For our part we willingly forgive the injuries which the Catholic Church has suffered ... We look with reverence upon the true religious patrimony which we share in common and which has been preserved and in part even well developed among our separated brethren.

On 29 September Willebrands asked the observers for some reactions to the Pope's address. Among the replies were 'some notes and comments by Anglican observers' – though the style suggests a single writer. There was praise for the tone of the speech. Paul's style – the administrator, scholar and mystic – was contrasted with John's – the prophet and visionary reformer, imbued with warm human love for his flock and for others. The Christocentric emphasis was approved. The difference was noted between Paul's conception of the relation of the Pope to the bishops and 'the centuries of conflict and struggles for power between papacy and ecumenical councils'.

Yet even here there were negatives: 'the Pope speaks of the Church as temporal today and eternal tomorrow. [This seems] a manifestation of another Roman error – identifying the Church with the Kingdom. The late Pope John used to fall into the same error.'

If the Curia was constantly going back to Trent, this kind of language seemed to hark back to the Thirty nine Articles which were just as much in need of *aggiornamento*,[1] as useless as a starting point for dialogue as the anathemas of Trent.

Fairweather's analyses

The *De Ecclesia* debate continued into the third session. Professor Eugene Fairweather, Keble Professor of Divinity at Trinity College, Toronto, gave an account of the final text.[2] 'Any responsible effort to bring about the renewal of the Church', he said, 'must be based on a reasonably clear idea of what the Church is and what it is called to do.'

The word 'reasonably' is important. There was no question of dogmatic definition, but there was clarification, restoration, capable of still further development. The transformation of Roman Catholic ecclesiology was largely what Congar would call a *ressourcement*. The elements of it were not sheer novelties – they had in recent centuries been obscured both in official statements and in conventional teaching and practice.

Fairweather proceeds to analyse *Lumen Gentium* from this point of view:

> [They] are thus compelled at once to reverence the Church as the gift and sign of God's grace and to accept more than simply human and political standards for the conduct of its life and the accomplishment of its mission.

He describes fully the Church's relation to, and participation in, the Kingdom of God, but judges that 'any tendency to identify the earthly Church with the Kingdom of God in its perfection is carefully excluded',[3] and quotes *Lumen Gentium*: 'the Church is at the same time holy and always in need of being purified and incessantly pursues the path of holiness and renewal.' This last, after all, had been the proclaimed purpose of calling the Council.

Turning to chapter II on the People of God, he says,

> it seems fair to cite the doctrine of these paragraphs as a particularly striking example of the shift in modern Roman Catholic ecclesiology from a narrowly institutional to a communal and missionary mode of thought . . . primarily sacramental . . . the way has been opened for an unprecedentedly positive appraisal of the Roman Catholic communion.

A rearrangement of the ecclesial furniture was still necessary, and chapter II, which dealt with the new vision, showed sign of battle among its drafters. Along with chapter IV, on the laity, it manifested 'the Council's firm resolve to make its fine theological word count towards the reshaping of ecclesiastical institutions'.

Fairweather's essay, with those of Massey Shepherd and Grant, are clear evidence of what was gained by drawing observers and subsequently dialogue partners from the whole field of the Anglican communion.

The Decree on Ecumenism

Ecumenism had been approached in the earlier days of the 70 schemata (by this time reduced to seventeen) from several directions. The Congregation for the Uniate Oriental Churches had introduced a schema on unity at the end of the first session.[4] The Theological Commission had proposed to put a chapter on Protestants in the constitution on the Church.[5] The Secretariat was working on its own schema. The Council voted on 1 December 1962 to lump these together in one decree.

The Oriental Congregation, with fast friends in the Curia, insisted that nothing was to be changed in their draft. A joint commission with them worked inharmoniously and Bea wrote to Cicognani complaining bluntly of the Oriental Congregation's attitude: 'We cannot waste time collaborating in this way ... You should make them toe the line laid down by the Co-ordinating Commission.' Nor were the meetings of the SPCU to draft other chapters of the schema one grand sweet song.

Bishop Thomas Holland of Portsmouth, England, doubted whether it was a good moment for spraying encomiums too freely on Protestants – even on Anglicans: we should remember the *Honest to God* affair and the utterances of some Cambridge theologians. Congar was to make a similar criticism between the second and third sessions, wondering whether 'dissidents are not presented too rosily. What is said applies only to the best – such as those we meet in dialogue.' Willebrands replied that 'we are talking about Churches (including the Roman Catholic Church) as they should be – in doctrine, structure and so on – not about chequered realities'.[6]

The schema was presented to the Council on 18 November 1963. It contained five chapters: (1) Principles: (2) Practice: (3) Separated Churches: (a) Eastern; (b) Western; (4) Jewish relations; (5) Religious freedom. The Council quickly decided to take the first three chapters first and separately.

The later stages of the debate on the lengthy schema *De Ecclesia* had plunged the Council into new depths of boredom. Sardonic stories circulated, like the one about the bishop who announced he would give three reasons why he proposed to speak briefly. An eminent member of the Curia said in my hearing that bishops who had to listen to these speeches should be dispensed from meditation and spiritual reading for the rest of their lives.

Out of this depression came a shrewd move by the moderators. They devised five pilot propositions on which to take a straw vote which could be a guide to revising the parts of the schema on collegiality and married deacons. The effect of the resounding vote in favour of the pilot propositions was to brace the Council for the second half of the session, and the schema on ecumenism benefited from this. Of the 41 speeches on the schema in general, only eight were really unfavourable.

Anglican criticisms

On 19 November the Anglican observers offered the SPCU their comments on chapter I of the schema, most of them critical:

- They welcomed the new spirit and approach, which acknowledged that 'fruitful actions' could come from non-Roman Churches.
- They recognized humility in the draft but wanted rather more of it – such, for example, as the Church of England has for the Methodists.
- They said that there could be no final verdict on this schema until they had the final text of *De Ecclesia*. If that held to universal papal jurisdiction it would be the end of dialogue (a mistaken forecast).
- The distinction between *ecclesiae* and *communitates* was welcomed: 'we of course would be "Church".'
- The expression 'separated brethren' would pass if it was used generally and reciprocally: if used only by Rome of other Churches it is 'totally unacceptable'.
- The biblical basis of Roman ecclesiology was rejected.
- The Anglican Church (Church of England) could not recognize itself as having as risen in the sixteenth century (*a saeculo 16 exorta*). It had an unbroken existence since the Celts.
- There was need for re-examination of terminology. 'The Roman Church interprets *fides* as a set of propositions whereas its real meaning ... is' [not – notice – 'we interpret it as'].
- They accepted that the chapter on the Jews should be separate, but added the curious comment that this would reduce Roman Catholic ecumenism to a general gesture of benevolence.
- The schema said either too much or too little. It was markedly inadequate; there was too much vagueness, and no detailed attention to crucial questions.

It is interesting to compare these remarks with some of the 'Protestant' comments. Oscar Cullmann said

> Could it not be said that the origin of these schisms, which are themselves negative and regrettable things, was a positive element, a diversity of charisms which is of the Holy Spirit. The great fault *of all of us* was to have allowed these to degenerate into schisms: this was a sin against the Holy Spirit.

He added:

we must not let it be thought that we are divided only by reciprocal faults. We acknowledge the moving confession of these, but we are also separated by profound questions of faith.

The French Protestant pastor Herbert Roux, talking to French Roman Catholic bishops, emphasized the scheme's link between unity and renewal.

The Methodist observer, Dr Robert Cushman, seeing the major problem as the Roman Catholic claim to absolute plenitude of unity, grace and holiness, said gracefully 'my intention is not to lecture or instruct but to illuminate this problem'.

Illumination comes from dialogue, and it was the Protestant commentators who most often, at this stage at least, saw the difficulties of doing something so unprecedented as drafting a decree on ecumenism.

At the end of the session the Anglican observers sent reports home to headquarters at the CFR. The Bishop of Ripon stated again their objection to being described as having arisen in the sixteenth century. The *Ecclesia Anglicana*, he said, 'was the church of the English people which had a continuous history from the days of Augustine and Aidan'. It was 'reformed in the sixteenth century but could not be said to have originated then'. Bishop Moorman was a champion of dialogue, but this assertion seemed to prejudge certain questions which were themselves to become matters of dialogue.

Canon Root stressed the importance of Heenan's Council speech welcoming the schema, but Heenan still seemed worried about dialogue not 'carried on normally within the region of those taking part in it'. (The logical implication of this for England was that there should be better dispositions, more mutual trust and more preparation. Moreover Catholic–Anglican dialogue could not be confined to Englishmen: this was what some Englishmen on both sides, for different reasons, found not entirely easy to accept. Others were very glad that it could not.)

Signs of change

Earlier in 1963 a number of lesser but significant events had pointed to a spread of the thaw in Britain. The future Bishop of Kingston and later of Birmingham, Hugh Montefiore, who was then a Cambridge don, visited Rome during March.

Heenan, who was to succeed Godfrey at Westminster on 5 April, had to write to Willebrands reassuring him that 'there is no need for anxiety among Anglicans over the future of the dialogue. Nobody over here has any intention of excluding [from the English dialogue] Roman Catholic theologians from the continent.[7] Our only problem is to find speakers truly representative of Roman Catholic thought.' But who was truly representative?

A few weeks later an up-and-coming continental theologian appeared in London and gave two lectures. Hans Küng addressed 'crowded audiences' at King's College in the Strand.

The Tablet, not then thought of as very *avant garde*, remarked: 'He has been described as the most notorious German theologian since Martin Luther.' Surprisingly, they went on to report:

He was continually aware that he was theologising not in a void, not in a specifically Catholic context, but in a context shared by both Catholics and Protestants, so that we felt that we were listening not so much to someone seeking to deepen the Church's own awareness of the truth committed to her care, but to someone seeking to present this truth in a form which, while valid and perfectly orthodox, would nevertheless be easier for his Protestant partners in the dialogue to accept.

Küng's book *Konzil und Wiedervereinigung* (*The Council and Reunion*) had appeared in English in 1961, and re-reading it today one is flabbergasted that anyone could ever have objected to it.

Heenan had accepted that the ultimate objective of dialogue was 'reunion of all Christians in the one Church of Christ', an expression which suspicious Anglicans thought meant one thing in Heenan's mind and (perhaps) another in the schema.

The CFR meanwhile had been soliciting a rather wider range of reactions to the Council's work from Englishmen of distinction who had not been involved in the Council. One of these came from a man destined to play a leading role in the future dialogue, Henry Chadwick, then at Christ Church, Oxford, who wrote 'The spirit that informs these documents is of course one of profound Christian charity and goodwill. That entitled *De ecumenismo* is deeply moving to read.'

J. N. D. Kelly offered this comment: 'From the Anglican point of view the document is remarkably encouraging in its content and even more in its friendly spirit.' Yet he saw the language as 'studiously vague', for example, about 'ecclesial elements'. 'One notices with regret the assumption throughout that the Roman faith itself stands in no need of modification.'

It is the use of the word 'faith' here that gives pause. It seems to ignore the celebrated distinction between faith and the way it is expressed made in John XXIII's opening speech. One might quote also this remark of R. H. F. McKenzie SJ, the Canadian biblical scholar, introducing the decree on Revelation:

> The New Testament writings do not claim to be – in fact they obviously are not – a complete and balanced inventory of the early Church's belief. Nevertheless they lay down what cannot be changed; the rule of faith as it is recorded, to which the Church is always bound and which she can develop and expand but never falsify.[8]

By 'modification' did Dr Kelly mean this, or more?

In the essay on the Decree on Ecumenism in the Pawley volume, Canon Howard Root recognized how many statements criticized as 'vague' or 'showing tension' are really 'open-ended', providing a stimulus to dialogue.

NOTES

1. Cf. Ian Ramsey, *Lambeth Conference Report* (1968).
2. Contributed the essay on the Church in Pawley (ed.), *The Second Vatican Council*, pp. 54–84.
3. Yet the observer Skydsgaard had written 'in this document the Church always takes precedence over the Kingdom of God'.
4. This body, created in 1862 and part of the missionary congregation of Propaganda Fide, became autonomous in 1917 and had its powers notably widened in 1938. For the Churches of the Oriental rite it took over the tasks of several congregations, and in certain territories it had exclusive authority.
5. Franz Thyssen argued that to treat all Protestant traditions in the space of a conciliar decree would lead either to unwieldiness or to caricature. His view was carried. Cf. Abbott, *Documents*, pp. 361–2, note 71.
6. The difficulty of maintaining this distinction was to be long with us.
7. The publishers Sheed and Ward had for many years been doing a fairly strong trade in translations of French and German theologians.
8. In Abbott, *Documents*, p. 109.

10

The Council's last phase

The SPCU presented the revised text of the Decree on Ecumenism to the Council on 6 October 1964, having worked through more than 700 pages of suggestions. Even then, the voting was not a single vote on the whole, but votes taken paragraph by paragraph; and even the 98 per cent votes in favour were permitted to include suggestions for betterment. They were simply put in order, accepted or rejected with the reason why, and attached eventually as a supplement to the draft decree.

As the third session approached (late summer of 1964), observers of Rome and of the Council were accumulating impressions of Paul VI's first year. These varied considerably according to the dispositions of the onlooker. Many of the contrasts aired were superficial. Rome, which had lived with the papacy for so long, and non-Catholic England, which had cut itself off from the papacy four hundred years earlier, each had a different set of clichés about the papacy. The Roman set was the more complicated; whether Catholic or anti-clerical, it subtly combined a kind of proprietary affection with a tolerant cynicism which had its own valuation of 'Vaticanese'.

The clichés had been first shaken by John XXIII. A further shaking, certainly in Rome, came with the impact of Paul's visit to the Holy Land in January 1964. The announcement of it on the last day of the Council's second session, which was closing not without feelings of doubt and discouragement, lifted the assembly up. The Pope's journey to the sources of the Gospel, the discarding even of the mitre, were almost a proclamation against triumphalism. The brilliant photographic coverage of the event and the intimacy yet immense spread of television transformed the figure of the new Pope overnight.

Paul described his journey as 'like the movement of a plough through old hard-beaten earth'. The scenes in Rome on the night of his return showed how much the Romans appreciated this. It was a first generous deposit in a bank of goodwill with which he would face the second half of the Council.

This pilgrimage in itself was important ecumenically; more directly so the meeting with the Ecumenical Patriarch Athenagoras, who had been greatly struck by the warmth of Paul's reply to his election greetings and printed it with a large photograph in the Patriarchate's official bulletin.

Athenagoras reacted very promptly to Paul's announcement of the pilgrimage. In Bea's words, 'Barely two days later on 6 December he invited all the heads of Churches to go to Jerusalem to pray together with the Pope at a brotherly meeting in the places consecrated by the redemption of mankind'. Obviously it was not to be a meeting for discussion, for which the time was not yet ripe, but a brotherly meeting to pray together.

To anyone with a spark of historical imagination the prospect of this pilgrimage and this encounter was exciting. It caused some flutters in England.

The travel firm Inter-Church Travel approached Bea, proposing an Anglican pilgrimage for the occasion. The letter was signed by their chairman Robert Mortimer, Bishop of Exeter. Nobody directly concerned with Anglican–Roman relations was consulted, though Pawley subsequently endorsed the approach. Ramsey was annoyed about the Anglican pilgrimage and wrote ticking off Mortimer about it. He was strongly against any ideas of a summit, wanting to meet the Pope in his own time and place.

Athenagoras would have been glad to have him (and others) there to strengthen his position against those Orthodox leaders who were cool about the Jerusalem enterprise. The Pope saw the difficulties and would not have wanted anybody there except as a pilgrim like himself.

Ramsey got out of the mild comedy of errors[1] rather neatly. He put out a press release insisting that Anglicans wanted to be friendly with everybody, including the Orthodox. It also announced a new Archbishop's Commission for Anglican–Roman Catholic relations in Britain, under the chairmanship of J. N. D. Kelly of St Edmund Hall, Oxford. He shrewdly sent a copy of this to Heenan and mentioned the goings on about the 'summit'. The Vatican, he added, had been kind enough to let him see a copy of the schedule, so full as to rule out any further involvements.

On the feast of the Epiphany, Ramsey exchanged telegrams with the Pope in Jerusalem, where the Anglican Communion was represented by the Anglican Archbishop in Jerusalem.[2]

Perhaps Paul VI was still thinking of this episode when in his Holy Saturday sermon in St John Lateran he greeted the whole Anglican Church, 'while with sincere charity and equal hope we look forward one day to seeing it honourably re-established in the universal fold of Christ'. The passage was misreported to the Archbishop via the CFR; 'united once more within the one true Church' had an exclamation mark added to emphasize the less subtle interpretation.[3] The Apostolic Delegate commented that 'this was the first time Anglicanism had been given special treatment and put in a special category all of its own'.

A few days later Willebrands set out for England armed with a letter written by Paul VI. It pointed out that by custom the Pope was not allowed to *invite* visitors to see him, but ... Ramsey's comment was that he had long wanted to go and that the Anglican Metropolitans (who were due in London in a few days) wanted him to go.

Willebrands informed Ramsey about the progress of the Decree on Ecumenism, and the permanent shape of the SPCU after the Council. The Pope, he said, wanted conversations with the whole Anglican communion, which would help in getting round difficulties raised by various local hierarchies. Discussion turned to relations of the Anglican–Roman Catholic dialogue with the WCC. It was pointed out that the Toronto meeting had said clearly that the WCC is not there to negotiate union between Churches – these can only do that on their own initiative. The WCC wants only to put them in contact and promote discussion of unity problems. Willebrands added that there was no desire to keep the WCC in the dark, but Ramsey and he were heartily in favour of bilateral dialogue.

A report came from the Bishop of Uganda, Leslie Brown, about the Uganda missionaries (thirteen Roman Catholics and thirteen Anglicans) who at Namugongo had been 'joined in the unity of genuine martyrdom'. The Catholic martyrs were to be canonized in October and Brown intended to be present, as a guest of the SPCU. The SPCU, forwarding the material to the Secretariat of State, asked that the Pope might in his address mention the Anglicans who had been put to death.

The third session

The third session of the Council began more briskly and encouragingly. The draft Declaration on the Jews received strong support from all sides. Chapter III of the Constitution on the Church, which had met so much resistance, was finally voted as a whole, or rather as two parts, the doctrinal (18–23) and the practical. Above all the decree on Divine Revelation, now unrecognizably different from the ecumenical stumbling-block of two years earlier, was brought to the floor and well received, with, however, some *juxta modum* votes which were considered before the promulgation on 18 November 1965.

Then things began to go wrong. At the end of a tiring session, the intransigence of extreme, reactionary speeches caused mainly irritation in the Council itself, whilst for outsiders it obscured the fact that there was no great battle of equal forces going on. Every vote, at whatever stage, produced overwhelming majorities in favour of schemata. Yet on 16 November 1964, Willebrands was summoned to the Secretariat of State and learned on the way from two of his staff that *De Ecumenismo* was not to be promulgated.

Cardinal Suenens confirmed the next day that the Pope had told the moderators confidentially that the decree could not be promulgated. On learning this Bea told Willebrands to go back to the Secretariat of State and tell Cardinal dell'Acqua, the *sostituto* or second in command, that non-promulgation would be a disaster for the whole ecumenical movement and for the authority of the Council. 'Even the Pope cannot change now.' Willebrands did this, and the next day was summoned again by dell'Acqua. 'The Pope thanks you for your note', he said, 'and I am to tell you not to worry (*non impressionarsi*). He asks for understanding of his position and responsibility. He wants not only to know the mind of the Council but to be sure in his own conscience. He begs you to help him.'

Dell'Acqua then showed the series of suggested amendments. As things were, Willebrands could hardly do more than glance through them. He stressed at once (and many were to stress afterwards) that it was not the content of the amendments which mattered[4] but the impression created by this last-minute intervention. Willebrands insisted on taking the proposals home to study them. Bea pressed him to accept anything that was inessential so as to quiet the Pope's scruples and get the text printed.

Willebrands took his note to dell'Acqua, who was satisfied and prepared to send it to the Pope. Willebrands insisted that the order to print must be given at once or it would be too late. Dell'Acqua telephoned Archbishop Pericle Felici, the Council's Secretary to this effect. Felici, however, insisted that the changes must be distributed to the Council next morning, so that the Fathers might have time to consider them before the vote on Friday. This was only possible by having them typed, duplicated and distributed separately. Willebrands heroically promised to have 2,400 copies ready for 11 a.m. on the morrow, Thursday.

Meanwhile the Pope's mind had been active and dell'Acqua telephoned Willebrands to have the text ready for the Pope at 9 a.m. the next morning for the final answer. Willebrands presented himself at 8.30 a.m. Very shortly dell'Acqua was summoned to the Pope's presence and went out saying 'I'll be back in five minutes'. He came back after 40 minutes during which Willebrands desperately calculated the diminishing possibility of producing 2,400 copies before 11 a.m.

In this maddening interval there had been a discussion (with the help of a Latinist brought in from the staff) about the relative merits of *realitas*, *substantia* and *veritas* in the passage about non-Roman eucharists. Further, the Pope, who had originally left an option about whether Protestants 'seek' or 'find' God in the Holy Scriptures, now thought 'find' was too absolute and insisted on 'seek' (*quaerere*). Further still he disliked (this to his credit no doubt), the description of the changes as *mutationes ab auctoritata suprema approbatae* (changes approved by the highest authority) and wanted a phrase which would engage his authority without naming him directly. They hammered out *suggestiones benevolas auctoritative expressas* (friendly suggestions expressed authoritatively). Finally Paul sent down a shattering note to Willebrands giving a 'personal opinion':

> The decree as a whole risks immobilizing the dynamism, the movement towards unity, and confirming the separated brethren in their positions. It is indulgent towards irenicism while at the same time condemning it. It will be little help in promoting the ecumenical movement.

Willebrands' memo, in the first person, must here be quoted:

> I read the note and shrugged my shoulders. I regret that the Pope thinks this, but I believe that it is only what he thinks at this moment

under the influence of fear and the impression that he is being pressurized. After the end of this session I shall have occasion to answer the note.

He rushed back to the office and set things to work and the copies were ready for distribution shortly after 11 a.m. Felici read them out and said that they would be in the printed text to be voted next day.

The copies could hardly have arrived a worse moment. All morning there had been manoeuvres, whispered consultations, about the immediate future of the *Declaration on Religious Liberty*.

As late as the previous March the SPCU had been in favour of maintaining this as part of the Decree on Ecumenism. The theme had been discussed at the first meeting with Visser t'Hooft in 1960 (see p. 37 *supra*).[5] It was a genuinely new development in Catholic thinking and many who approved of it were not agreed (or clear in their minds) about how it should be stated.

The draft presented by Bishop de Smedt on 15 November 1964, also so much revised that its opponents successfully petitioned that it was effectively a new document needing time for study before it could be voted on. Technically, according to the Council *Ordo*, they were within their rights,[6] but no one was starry-eyed about their motive. Five hundred signatures were collected for a petition to the Pope that a vote be taken 'before the end of this session, lest the confidence of the world, both Christian and non-Christian, be lost'.

The Pope decided in favour of the rules, and it was not until the following year that the Declaration was passed by 2,308 votes to 70, with eight spoiled papers.

The atmosphere of Thursday 19 November, when the papal stop-press amendments to the Decree on Ecumenism were distributed, was described by Willebrands as 'tense and exasperated'. Several well-disposed bishops came to Willebrands asking 'Should we vote for the Decree on Ecumenism?' He gave them all the same answer:

Take the long view. The decree is the result of long and serious work. Its substance is untouched. Its importance is for the future. Its non-promulgation would give the SPCU a blow from which it would be hard to recover; its prestige would be lowered enormously. The decree remains for us fully acceptable and will be point of departure for future work. You must absolutely vote *placet* without reservations. Moreoever to promulgate the document *De Ecclesiis Orientalibus* without *De Ecumenismo* would be the end of Oriental ecumenism.

The same afternoon, Oscar Cullmann asked permission to speak of the 'nineteen changes'. His main point was the one already made – that the impression made was far worse than anything in the changes themselves. This was particularly true of changing 'find' (*inveniunt*) to 'seek' (*quaerunt*), when speaking of Protestants' relationship to God in the Scriptures. While 'seek' was perhaps more Protestant than 'find' the change seemed to suggest otherwise. 'Those in the Council might understand, but others will not.'

Willebrands thanked Cullmann and agreed with him but hoped the observers would not protest publicly. 'Stick by us, we belong together, we have need of each other. That is why I ask your prayers.'

Incredibly (remember it was still the evening before the vote) Willebrands was told 'the Pope has re-read the changes and suggests [*not* orders] three more':

1. Suppress the references to the 'seamless robe' in para. 13;
2. 'in the East there *are* many particular or local churches': change *are* (*exstare*) to *flourish* (*florere*) in para. 14;
3. change *substantia* to *veritas* in para. 22.

Willebrands accepted 2, but turned down the others.

On the following day, 'to his relief', the Decree was voted by 2,154 to 64. An historic moment, but in what sense historic? Much of the content is not of the stuff of high drama. Yet where previously there had seemed to be a blank wall, doors were not only uncovered but unlocked, to the great dismay of the small hard core who expected to find the doors opening to Pandora's box or a nest of demons.

The Anglican observes Howard Root commented:

Whatever an Anglican observer might wish to say about his own impressions, the future remains open. But it is open too in other churches. Anglicans are no less wedded to certain words and concepts than are Roman Catholics and they are in no less need of a theological *aggiornamento*. Perhaps, despite all differences, Anglicans need exhortation even more than Roman Catholics. Anglican immobilism and triumphalism are not less a hindrance to final unity than Roman Catholic counterparts. (Root, 'Second Vatican Council', in Pawley (ed.), pp. 145–6.)

The Methodist observer Albert Outler distinguished between the *drama* of the Council and the *progress* of the Council. The drama had filled the stage at the end of the third session.

The end of the Council

The fourth session showed little drama, while the steady if tedious business of voting began to bring out the progress. The Religious Liberty declaration reached harbour.

Of the new material which occupied the session, the most ambitious and most difficult was that contained in the schema on 'The Church in the World of Our Time'. This was in essence an attempt to proceed from the self-examination and restatement of *De Ecclesia* (the *ad intra*) to the sympathetic consideration of contemporary human and social problems in a spirit of service (the *ad extra*).

Some were unhappy with the phrase 'our time' – partly because 'our time' would date quickly, and partly because some were still attached to the 'all time' attitude of the Syllabus of 1864. Some were unhappy with the phrase 'the world': one speaker pointed out that the various biblical uses of the word filled six columns of a standard reference book.

Some felt that the very designation 'pastoral constitution' was unfortunate. While 'pastoral' emphasized the tone of service, of sympathy, above all of desire for dialogue, 'constitution' inappropriately suggested the absolute, the definitive.

The most serious criticism, applicable even to the first, most general part, was that it took insufficent account of the vast variety evident in the world. It was focused mainly on the world of Western capitalism.

Yet the schema, expressed a change of tone – a change likely to be of great value in ecumenical relations.

There was much rather vague repetition of the word 'culture', but the most striking speech in the debate was made by Michele Pellegrino, Professor at Turin and about to become Archbishop of that city. He had been for some years a respected participant in the Oxford Conference of Patristic Studies, organized since 1951 by F. L. Cross, and so was likely to be listened to by Anglicans. He called for the text to give explicit recognition to the historical sciences, and to make explicit mention of ecclesiastics in the proclamation on freedom of research:

> a few years ago I found a religious living in involuntary exile for having expressed opinions which today we find in papal and conciliar documents; this was not a unique case ... If each one knows that he is permitted to express his opinion with wholesome freedom, he will act within the Church.

Pellegrino also took questions at the last press conference of the Council. To a question uppermost in his listeners' minds he answered 'The Curia will have to obey the Council like everybody else'. 'There was some tittering', it was reported. The scepticism of the titterers had its tinge of prophecy. Hard days and years lay before those who were to translate the Council into hard fact, not least its ecumenical aspirations. But those who remembered recent history had a sharp and encouraging experience to leave Rome with. On the last Saturday, in the Basilica of St Paul where the Council had been proclaimed, members and observers gathered with the Pope in a 'liturgy of the Word' offered for Christian Unity. It was entirely the Pope's idea. He sat unattended while Scripture passages were read (some by observers), psalms and a hymn sung, and prayers recited. The hymn *Nun Danket* was familiar to everybody.

NOTES

1. It was an example of the kind of crossing of lines which was to afflict ecumenical activity for many years but was generally amenable to good will and good humour.
2. The Anglicans had their ecumenical pilgrimage in the good ship *Acropolis* at the beginning of the following April, sailing from Cannes to Civitavecchia, led by Mervyn Stockwood, Bishop of Southwark, with a complement of 290 Church of England, 70 Roman Catholics, 55 Protestants and ten Orthodox. It was recommended by the Apostolic Delegate, Cardinale, who specified that the whole purpose of the exercise was a visit to the Vatican and an audience with the Pope. This exercise in ecumenism without tears had in fact been preceded in 1962 and 1963 by a pilgrimage to the Holy Land.
3. The significant reassurance of *onoratamente* was made more explicit in 1970 in the much more widely noticed passage added to his sermon at the canonization of the English martyrs.
4. They can all be seen clearly in notes to the text as printed in Abbott.
5. See also Schmidt, op. cit., pp. 662–4, who quotes a remark of Peter Pavan, one of the chief architects of the declaration: 'It is certain that without the active presence of Cardinal Bea we should never have had the Declaration on Religious Liberty.' Schmidt adds 'This shows

how important were certain speeches of Bea in influencing public opinion in favour of the declaration, particularly one made in the Rome Capitol in December 1963'.

6. Heenan was no opponent of the Declaration on Religious Liberty but he revealed at a lecture in London that, had it come to a vote in the third session, he would have voted against it on precisely these grounds. See *The Tablet* (29 May 1965).

11

Archbishop Ramsey's visit to Rome

During the third session of Vatican II a not insignificant event took place across the Atlantic. To the 61st General Convention of the Episcopal (i.e. Anglican) Church in the USA (then still called Protestant) three Roman Catholic Observers were invited. They were Robert F. Coerva, vice principal of Kewick Seminary; Carl Gaertisen; and Dom Columba Cary-Elwes. The last, a very English Benedictine, had gone from Ampleforth to help found the Benedictine Priory of St Louis and was its prior.

Episcopalian observers had considerably strengthened the Anglican contingent during the second half of Vatican II. The compliment was now returned and these observers at the General Convention were looked after by Peter Day, Ecumenical Officer and an observer at Vatican II, and Arthur Vogel, lecturer in theology at Nashotah House, later Bishop of West Missouri and a valued member of ARCIC I and ARCIC II.

A report by these observers to the SPCU provided the first extended account of PECUSA to be found in the SPCU records. It also recorded some general impressions of the Convention:

1. Doctrinal discussions did not grip the majority of participants.
2. Papal infallibility seemed to be a 'fatal obstacle' to rapprochement with Rome, though there was a conviction that the Convention was 'preserved in inerrancy'.[1]
3. Concepts of authority in general struck these observers as 'rather hazy'.

89

4. The laity had a great say in the convention – rather more than anything they were theologically equipped for.
5. There was much concern among the observers about the problem of Anglican orders (ecumenical concern presumably).

Cary-Elwes was honoured with an invitation to address the Convention: so was Martin Luther King.

A speech by the famous Bishop Pike, in which he described the doctrine of the Trinity as a product of a bygone philosophy and irrelevant to our age, was energetically repudiated by the majority.

A few months later the British Council of Churches proposed inviting Roman Catholic observers to their conference. They were opposed by Maurice Wood, who was then teaching at the evangelical Anglican college of Oak Hill, and later to be Bishop of Norwich. In 1964 the British Council of Churches in its conference at Nottingham had passed overwhelmingly the following resolution:

> United in our urgent desire for One Church Renewed for Mission, this
> Conference invites the members of the British Council of Churches, in
> appropriate groupings such as nations, to covenant together to work
> and pray for the inauguration of union by a date agreed amonst them.
> We dare to hope that this date should not be later than Easter Day
> 1980.

Wood's objection to inviting Roman Catholic observers was that their presence would hold back the union scheme convenated for and hoped for in 1980.

It was not easy to see why they should do so, except as skeletons at the feast emphasizing by their presence the necessarily partial character of the 1980 aspiration. The objection was rejected by no less a person than the leading English Baptist Ernest Payne, and received only four supporting votes.

In the same month the convocations of Canterbury and York voted, also overwhelmingly, to go ahead with the Anglican–Methodist unity scheme, first prompted by Archbishop Fisher's Cambridge sermon of 1946 and launched in conversations ten years later.

Back in Rome, the first Week of Prayer for Unity since Vatican II tested the water, and gave some support to those who had tittered at the final conciliar press conference (see above, p. 84).

The American Paulist fathers of the church of Santa Susanna planned to have a joint service, which would be reciprocated at the American Episcopal church in Via Nazionale. They approached the Cardinal Vicar, Cunial, and the application eventually reached Ottaviani in the Holy Office. The answer was that they could invite Protestants to Santa Susanna to a Catholic service, but there was to be no going to the Episcopalian church and no joint service at either place.

Preparations and difficulties

At the beginning of 1965, the Revd John Findlow took up residence in Rome as the Archbishop of Canterbury's representative.

Findlow's first audience with Paul VI (who expressed surprise at his fluency in Italian) seems to have included the first recorded reference to a possible visit to Rome by Ramsey as 'President of the Anglican Communion'. As early as 1 December 1964, according to a letter from Ramsey's secretary John Andrew to Satterthwaite in Rome, the Archbishop had wondered if there was anything to be said for his 'coming to Rome this month to see the Pontiff before Christmas'. He was evidently advised against this; but in the following June he gave an interview to the *Economist* repeating his intention, even suggesting slightly skittishly what would happen to Roman Catholic bishops in the event of reunion: 'They would regard themselves as superfluous.' In April 1965 he sent Easter greetings to the Pope and looked forward to meeting him 'after the Council'. This last proviso was repeated in November by John Satterthwaite of the CFR, when he came to Rome to announce formally (though confidentially) the Archbishop's intention of making a visit. It would begin on 21 March 1966, and would last no more than 48 hours.

It was agreed that Ramsey and his entourage would be the guests of the Holy See.

In December Ramsey wrote to the Pope thanking him for the gift of a facsimile copy of the Codex Vaticanus and for the constant kindness, opportunities, help and encouragement which had been given to the observers at the Council. The Pope replied stressing (as he always did) the important contribution made by the observers to Vatican II.

On 10 December the prospect was far enough advanced for John Findlow to write to Lambeth:

in Rome great importance is attached to what is called *bella figura* . . .
after the magnifical [*sic*] events in Rome and Constantinople it is up
to us now to put on a good show . . . What we must work for is
something in the nature of what would best be described as a 'splash'.

When Satterthwaite had gone to Rome in November to announce
Ramsey's intended visit, enormous, perhaps excessive stress had been
placed on secrecy. Only the Pope was to be told, said Satterthwaite.
Willebrands asked what was being done about informing Cardinal
Heenan and the Apostolic Delegate in London. The reply was that the
news should be kept absolutely secret and that it would be given to the
Cardinal and Delegate in England 'at the proper time'. Staff members of
the SPCU were not told, and even dell'Acqua, the *sostituto* in the
Secretariat of State, kept it to himself. Unfortunately nobody seemed to
think it necessary or appropriate to inform the Pope of this pact of
silence, and when Heenan came to Rome on other business a few days
later, the Pope told him the 'news' and the fat was in the fire.

More fat was added in December, by the Bishop of Winchester,
Faulkner Allison, who was in charge of Anglican–Roman Catholic
relations in England. He went to Rome to explain to Willebrands and the
Pope the project for opening an Anglican Centre in Rome, but did not
inform Heenan until he got home.

On 3 January, Heenan wrote what is best described by the colloquialism
'a stinker' to Willebrands, complaining of these improprieties, and adding
as another example the SPCU's neglect of his offer of an English priest for
its staff. He concluded with a truly awful sentence: 'Our great fear is that
the Secretariat will continue to come between us and our Anglican fellow-
countrymen.'

Bea decided to answer this himself. Taking first the Ramsey visit, he
pointed out that the insistence on secrecy had come from the 'Anglican
fellow-countrymen' and added 'Of course the Holy Father was free to
speak to whomever he wished.'

The last sentence of Heenan's letter had clearly upset Willebrands and
probably Bea too. Bea wrote that the words were 'most painful and I think
unfair to me'. 'We never "came between" and have not the slightest intention to do so in the future, but we hope to continue our efforts to bring
both together.' Bea ended diplomatically but also justly: 'I will not finish
this letter without expressing my sincerest thanks to your eminence for the
many examples of collaboration between you and the Secretariat and me

personally, and I am sure this collaboration may grow in confidence and effectiveness.'

In the perspective of today this incident looks like a storm in a teacup, but it illustrates several difficulties of that moment, which was a moment of resolve but still weighed down with the past.

The placing of dialogue on an international level did not have to be read as either a belittling of English Catholicism or as a puffing up of Anglicanism into a rival world religion. (There was a whiff of this suspicion in the Roman Catholic memorandum sent to the SPCU from England in advance of Ramsey's visit.) International dialogue was one way of defusing the history-laden English situation. Ramsey grasped this. But it was also an acknowledgement of hard fact. The Anglican Communion was, through its constituent and largely autonomous Churches, present in every place where English was spoken and a few where it hardly was. Though some of these churches were still only emerging from the missionary stage, and were mostly ruled by English or English-trained bishops, all of them in varying degrees were becoming conscious of their separate existence and impatient of inheriting English historical problems. This of course was most marked in the USA.

In the several-sided business of smoothing Ramsey's path to Rome, considerable credit was earned by the Apostolic Delegate, Igino Cardinale. An Italian from the Ciociaria district between Rome and Naples, who had had many years of his education in America, he spent years in the Secretariat of State under Pius XII, John XXIII and Paul VI, before going to London. Apostolic delegates, as distinct from nuncios, have no diplomatic status or function and are simply there to keep the Holy See informed of internal ecclesiastical matters in their territory. Cardinale, who while in Rome had been sympathetic and helpful to the SPCU, now managed both to avoid upsetting Catholics and to cultivate non-Catholics of consequence. He sent regular and usually discerning accounts of events and opinion in England to the Vatican Secretariat of State, with copies to the SPCU where this was appropriate.

On 4 January, ironically the very day after Heenan had written his letter to Willebrands, Ramsey had a conversation with Cardinale about the visit, and left copious notes on fourteen points. Here are the main ones:

1. The suggestion of a Common Declaration was made for the first time by Cardinale, as coming from the Pope. Ramsey gave it a cautious assent.
2. The Pope wanted liturgical consultation and theological discussion.[2]

3. Cardinale favoured a joint service in S. Gregorio[3] and a call to prayer in England.
4. Ramsey wanted also practical matters discussed and Cardinale agreed, instancing mixed marriages.
5. Cardinale said he expected there would be a formal reception not a dinner.
6. Ramsey had come round to Heenan's proposal of the English College as a lodging. He thought a representative of the English hierarchy should be there.

There should be an exchange of presents. (This was normal for such high-level encounters.) The Pope, he reported, wanted an entirely private interview, but an interpreter would be required: Findlow was the obvious choice with his great command of Italian. The Pope was ready to make a 'return' visit to the Archbishop on some 'English' ground in Rome (Cardinale thought of the British Embassy to Italy). Nothing was to come of this but it did bring up in the conversation the question of a papal visit to England. Rumours had suggested that the Pope was about to visit Liverpool. Cardinale reported that the Pope had been greatly vexed about this gossip and had directed him to see Heenan about silencing such rumours.

Cardinale asked the Archbishop whether he should inform Heenan of their conversation. Ramsey agreed but said 'You must remain in control'.

Not a word was said, it seems, about the conversations which had been going on since 1950, which strikes the impartial observer as somewhat ungrateful.

In advance of the official announcement of Ramsey's visit, Cardinale sent excellent, comprehensive notes to Willebrands about Ramsey and Anglicanism with suggestions about handling the visit. This dispatch shrewdly included a telling passage on papacy from Ramsey's own book *The Gospel and the Catholic Church* (p. 65 and Appendix). Cardinale managed to draft all this in collaboration with Heenan, or at least to his satisfaction, while giving it no aggressive flavour at all.

Heenan, however, who had been a friend of Cicognani, the papal Secretary of State, for nearly forty years, was determined that the latter should have no excessively rosy ideas about Anglicanism and went out to Rome to make sure of this.[4]

Heenan pressed successfully to get Ramsey lodged at the English College in Rome. Originally a hostel for pilgrims, it had been converted by Cardinal Allen in the sixteenth century into a college for recusant priests. Forty-four of its alumni had been put to death for this activity, their executions gruesomely portrayed around the walls of the upper gallery of the college chapel – where fortunately only the ultra-curious were likely to see them. The college had a reputation for hospitality and had housed many distinguished non-Catholic Englishmen including Milton.

Having given Heenan ample notice of his intentions Willebrands set out for London to discuss the visit, taking with him the undersecretary Jean François Arrighi, a founder member of the SPCU staff who was well-versed in Vatican outlook procedure and protocol. The visitors were lodged at Lambeth Palace, Willebrands being the first Roman Catholic archbishop to stay there since Pole.

The first 'business' call was to the Apostolic Delegate, Igino Cardinale. On the next two days, they had two sessions with Ramsey and his advisors and two visits to Westminster for discussions with Heenan. Willebrands had brought a draft programme for the visit to Rome; with this Ramsey expressed himself substantially very satisfied.

For the private conversation between Pope and Archbishop seven items were proposed. Four were simply positive:

- Satisfaction at liturgical renewal in both Churches; this should lead to collaboration for better translations;
- a joint world-wide commission for dialogue;
- the ecumenical importance of the *spirituality* of Newman;
- the open and comprehensive character of Vatican II's *De Ecclesia*, *De Libertate Religiosa* and *De Ecumenismo*.

The other three items concerned standard Anglican complaints of Catholic practice: 'indiscriminate' conditional re-baptism of converts; mixed marriage discipline; and the attitude to Anglican orders, which should be reconsidered in a wider and more up-to-date theological context than that of 1896.

Meanwhile preparations went ahead in Rome. These centred mainly on the proposed Common Declaration by Pope and Archishop which was to be the culmination of the visit. The essence of this was to be a declaration of intent, prepared in seven languages.

The meeting

Primate and Archbishop met in the Sistine Chapel, though the climax came in the service in St Paul's. No English Catholic voice was raised in readings – at that time a common defect of Vatican-organized ceremonial. Paul VI alone raised the occasion above the tentative when with characteristic symbolic effect he took off his ring and placed it on the Archbishop's hand.[5]

The centrepiece of the visit was the private talk in the Vatican, of which the media learned nothing. The Archbishop began with praise for Vatican II as a spiritual renewal for others besides Roman Catholics and especially for Anglicans. There was desire in England for ecumenical development on the spiritual plane, for example in common retreats and occasional public prayers.

Told of the common concern for liturgical renewal, the Pope said he would very much like Anglican observers at the *Concilium Liturgicum* which was engaged in putting into effect the Council's Constitution. (They came, along with others, and the effect on general liturgical advance was great.)

Ramsey now introduced the subject of dialogue. The Pope was wholly in favour, pointing out that there was already Roman Catholic dialogue with the World Council of Churches (first met at Bossey, 22–24 May 1969) and the Lutheran World Federation (first met at Augsburg, 25 August 1965). Again no allusion was made to the dialogues going on since 1950.

Ramsey wanted a joint commission which would be international, drawing from many provinces of both Churches. The Pope replied by sketching something like the Joint Preparatory Commission which was to meet before the end of the year (see below), and wondered whether the different strands in Anglicanism might call for more members. A number of about eight a side was enough, thought Ramsey. The Pope turned to Willebrands and told him to go ahead with the task.

Ramsey then took up firmly the chief Anglican difficulties about Roman practice. The first was the re-baptism of converts from Anglicanism. Paul pointed out that this was not at all the rule – that there was no justification for re-baptism except where there was serious doubt that it had been properly administered. The Pope promised to write to Heenan about it.

A more serious and intractable irritant was about mixed marriages (cf. Chapter 24). In March 1966 the Vatican, with strangely insensitive timing, had issued a new Instruction which left Anglican difficulties unresolved.

Ramsey had come to Rome with strong feelings on this. Paul VI could do little more than point out that the Instruction was world-wide in its scope and therefore had to cover a great variety of situations and that Anglicans could refer their particular difficulties to Rome.

Paul's last word was to recommend to particular attention three of the Council's documents, the Constitution on the Church and the Decrees on Ecumenism and Religious Liberty.

Apart from this audience, the Archbishop's excursion into the 'Vatican's majestic halls' was restricted to a visit to the library conducted by the librarian, Cardinal Tisserant, who told him 'I work in here three days a week'. Ramsey's reply was 'Lucky man'.

The visitor's last act was to give a press-conference at the English College. He handled it deftly, exuding good humour and crisp confidence. The faithful Colonel Hornby at his side must have remembered Fisher in 1960 and drawn all the contrasts.

An hour or two later the Archbishop left the college for the airport, still in his Holbein cap. In a couple of days he had roused the inmates of that very Counter-Reformation institution to affectionate enthusiasm: as they cheered him off deafeningly he took off his cap, tossed it in the air and caught it. He had just given them his blessing.

The press was waiting for him again at Heathrow and one of them asked if he had gone to Rome cap in hand. He said 'You may notice in the pictures of me and the Pope that I had my cap on'.

The British legation to the Holy See sent the Foreign Office a full and sympathetic account of the visit. The diplomatic corps to the Holy See had not been invited as such to the Sistine chapel: but the British Ambassador to the Quirinal, as well as those of Australia, Canada and the USA, together with the British Minister to the Holy See, Michael Williams, and his First Secretary Donald Cape, attended less as diplomats than as members of their respective churches. At St Paul's, at the insistence of their doyen, the diplomatic corps of the Holy See was present in force.

The aftermath

Repercussions came thick and fast. Willebrands wrote to Heenan proposing himself for a visit to London in early May to discuss adding an Englishman to the SPCU staff, and a few weeks later I was invited to lunch with Willebrands and offered the job. My first appearance in the CFR files is in a letter of John Findlow to Satterthwaite, reporting a conversation he had just had with Willebrands:

> Willebrands himself raised the question of Bill Purdy as a Secretariat appointment (communicated to and then approved by Uncle Carmel[6] of course) and told me that I can be very happy about a middle-of-the-road man who has more than one foot in Rome and yet retains a quarter pied-à-terre in Uncle Carmel's set up [An acrobatic stance, but perhaps describing vaguely my compromise candidature.]

I had accepted this move with hesitation. That I have never regretted it speaks volumes for the generosity of many Catholics and Anglicans.

NOTES

1. Bishop Moorman, after four sessions of Vatican II, judged that since the 'enormous distaste' of the 1870 definition only one infallible definition had been made 'and it is now unlikely that there will ever be another'. Papal infallibility, therefore, was little more than an academic question (*Vatican Observed*). His colleagues of ARCIC were not able to reach this point, though they no longer saw the obstacle as 'fatal'.
2. Both of these were already taking place, but theological discussion was now to be moved on to another plane.
3. This church on the Coelian Hill occupied part of the site of Gregory the Great's home from which he had dispatched Augustine to England in 597. It was used for the joint public service of prayer during Archbishop Runcie's visit in 1989.
4. In Heenan's student days, Cicognani, then a young man making his way, had spent much time at the Venerable English College villa at Palazzola the Alban Hills, perfecting his English.
5. It was the ring he had worn as Archbishop of Milan. When Ramsey got back to London he showed the ring to the crowding press and said 'I think I shall wear it a lot'. And he did. Archbishop Runcie also wore it on his visit to Rome in 1989.
6. This was the received fashion in Lambeth for referring to the Archbishop of Westminster.

12

Anglican–Roman Catholic Joint Preparatory Commission

One of the chief points of difference between the earlier dialogues and those which began in January 1967 was that the latter were planned as a whole, in accordance with an official mandate from the highest authorities of the respective communions. This mandate was reflected upon and enlarged in three meetings within less than a year by the body known as the Joint Preparatory Commission (JPC).

It will be part of our aim to see how far this commission's report, the Malta Report, influenced the work of ARCIC I. But first we should look at the composition of the JPC and at how this was arrived at, its mood and its methods of work. The members were:

ANGLICAN DELEGATES

The Bishop of Ripon, the Rt Revd J. R. H. Moorman	Senior Anglican observer at the Second Vatican Council
The Revd Canon James Atkinson	Lecturer in theology, Hull University
The Revd Canon Eric Kemp, later Bishop of Chichester	Lecturer in theology and medieval history, Exeter College, Oxford
The Revd Professor Howard Root	Professor of theology, Southampton Univesity

The Bishop of Llandaff, the Rt
Revd W. G. H. Simon

Formerly Warden, St Michael's
College, Llandaff

The Revd Dr Massey H. Shepherd

Professor of liturgics, Church
Divinity School of the Pacific,
California

The Revd Professor Eugene R.
Fairweather

Professor of dogmatic theology,
Trinity College, Toronto

The Bishop of Colombo, the Rt
Revd C. H. W. de Soysa

Formerly Principal of the Divinity
School, Colombo, Ceylon

The Bishop of Pretoria, the Rt
Revd E. G. Knapp-Fisher

Formerly Principal of Cuddesdon
Theological College, Oxford

Secretaries[1]

The Revd Canon John Findlow

Archbishop of Canterbury's
representative at the Vatican

The Revd Canon John R.
Satterthwaite

General Secretary of the Church
of England's Council for
Foreign Relations

ROMAN CATHOLIC DELEGATES

The Rt Revd Charles Helmsing,
Bishop of Kansas City

Chairman of the United States
Roman Catholic Bishops'
Commission for Relations
with the Protestant Episcopal
Church

The Rt Revd William Gomes

Titular Bishop of Porlais,
Auxiliary to the Archbishop
of Bombay

The Rt Revd Langton D. Fox

Titular Bishop of Maura and
Auxiliary to the Bishop of
Menevia, Wales

The Revd Louis Bouyer

Priest of the Oratory; French
ecumenist

The Revd George Tavard

Assumptionist; Professor and head
of the department of theology
at Mount Mercy College,
Pittsburg

The Revd M. Richards

Professor of theology at St
Edmund's College, Ware

The Revd John Keating	Secretary of the English section of the Canadian Roman Catholic Bishops' Commission on Ecumenism
The Revd Adrian Hastings	Professor at Kipalapala Seminary, Tabora, Tanzania
The Rt Revd Mgr J. G. M. Willebrands	Titular Bishop of Mauriana and Secretary of the Secretariat for Promoting Christian Unity, Vatican

Secretary[1]

The Very Revd Canon W. A. Purdy	Secretariat for Promoting Christian Unity

The official dialogue was to be between the Roman Catholic Church and the Anglican Communion of, at that time, 26 autonomous churches. Nevertheless, of the eleven Anglican members seven (effectively eight since Canon Root had lived in England from the age of sixteen) were British, only four Roman Catholics were. There were similarities and differences between the two teams: There were four bishops a side. Of the Anglican team, nine out of eleven, that is all except the secretaries, were either active lecturers in theology at universities or equivalent institutions, or former heads of theological colleges. This was true of only six Roman Catholics. Five Anglicans and five or six Roman Catholics had been part of the Vatican Council as members, consultors or observers. (In addition the present writer had been in Rome throughout the Council and followed it closely, though outside the *aula* assembly, as journalist, broadcaster, and in frequent 'conversations' with bishops.) These members obviously owed their selection in greater or lesser part to their Council connections.

There were hiccups about membership. Harry McAdoo, Bishop of Ferns, Ossory and Leighlin, was originally invited, but along with other Church of Ireland bishops he did not feel that the politico-religious situation in Ireland at that moment justified his taking part, though eight months later it was judged to have eased enough to allow him to join and thereby embark on a lengthy stint of ecumenical service (1966–81). On the Roman Catholic side, one chosen member was objected to by the Holy Office, to which all names had to be submitted. The objection was firmly and successfully resisted.

This was frankly told to the Anglicans by Willebrands at the first important meeting with Anglicans that I attended, to make plans for the coming meeting at Gazzada. It was my first occasion to admire his candour and calm resolve and I could see that the Anglicans present did the same, though for those who had witnessed the Council the impression was not new.

About this time the Anglican Centre in the Palazzo Doria was opened. This was an enterprise with few if any precedents, certainly none in Rome. Its warden was John Findlow, now styled Archbishop of Canterbury's representative in Rome, and it housed him and his family, together with a chapel, a library – mainly of Anglican works – an office, a reading room and reception rooms. Potentially it struck at one of the chief burdens of four centuries of separation – ignorance.

A few days after the opening of the Anglican Centre, the fortieth anniversary of the Malines conversations was celebrated in that city, and a commemorative plaque was unveiled in the cathedral by Cardinal Suenens and the Bishop of Winchester, Dr Faulkner Allison. We have seen how subsequent conversations had been anxious to avoid 'another Malines', but none who noted the event can have failed to admire those pioneers of 1926 or failed to be thankful and hopeful that the work was being taken up again at a time so marvellously more favourable.

Gazzada

The Joint Preparatory Commission began at Gazzada on 9 January 1967. Introductory papers had been agreed on from either side on two titles: 'Why is dialogue possible now?' and 'Where should dialogue begin?' The first question was treated by Bishop Willebrands and Bishop Moorman.

Willebrands concentrated on the changed climate in the Roman Catholic Church since the encyclical *Mortalium Animos*. The changes he pointed to were biblical renewal (including co-operation in the translation and diffusion of the Bible), liturgical renewal and common realization that Church and world were being estranged by social disintegration – factors which Yves Congar had pointed to before the Paris meeting of 1950. The common factor in these Catholic changes was Vatican II.

John Moorman also looked at the Council (he had been the doyen of the observers) but more from the standpoint of ecumenical strategy. The separation of 453 years ago he saw as a 'failure of negotiation – Anglicans had not intended schism',[2] and he had been happy to note that the revision of *De Ecumenismo* had changed the original *se sejunxerunt* (cut themselves off) to *sejunctae sunt* (been cut off). He noted instances of 'Great Return' language as late as 1964, but *Lumen Gentium* and *De Ecumenismo* had dropped it.

On their side the Anglicans had always recognized that no planning for unity can omit Rome, something which, George Bell in 1948 had claimed, no Protestant could understand or admit. Moorman traced the advance of hopefulness from the first Lambeth Conference of 1867 down to the famous 'Appeal' of 1920. This hopefulness was checked by the failure of Malines and by *Mortalium Animos* but was still alive in 1958 (the conversations of 1950–1967 surely deserved honourable mention here but did not get it). Turning to the present and future, he saw three possibilities for Anglicanism:

- To 'plunge further and further' into non-Roman Catholic schemes of union.
- To concentrate on drawing the Anglican Communion into greater self-consciousness, on lines set out at Toronto in 1963 and illustrated in the programme Mutual Responsibility and Interdependence.
- To stand firm with the Great Latin Church of the West against Protestant mergers.

This was a personal point of view which, besides being unrepresentative, raised some difficulties. George Bell's 1948 judgement of the intransigence of Protestants (a name not all Anglicans wanted to repudiate) was now something of an anachronism: Protestant observers had been present in plenty at Vatican II and at times had shown rather better understanding of it (with more humility) than Anglicans.

The SPCU had already instituted dialogue with the Lutheran World Federation and was about to do so with the World Methodist Council, while near to Bishop Moorman sat Eric Kemp (now Bishop of Chichester) who was the moving spirit of the Anglican–Methodist scheme which stemmed from Archibishop Fisher. The SPCU could hardly see Moorman's first and third possibilities as mutually exclusive.

However, the main point was that Anglicans and Romans were gathered together with a great sense of urgency, and hence the pressing question was the second: 'Where should dialogue begin?' Michael Richards tackled this very bravely at the short notice occasioned by Charles Davis's withdrawal.[3]

He suggested that perhaps the prior question was where should dialogue lead? Its purpose could not be exclusively theological. We should be seeking together to clarify and illuminate faith, but also and no less to live the mystery of the Church better. He neatly recalled Wiseman (not thought of as an ecumenist) saying at Oscott in 1841 'We must say to one another, we have all fallen short'. He suggested four themes linked with the doctrine of the Church:

1. The Church as *Communion* – of the redeemed, the saved, made one in their Head (Christ). A *new* people, new and distinct in being created and bound by new forces: the Eucharist, the universal priesthood, an authority not dominating but serving communion.
2. The Church as *witness to Christ*. The function of theology: the relation of faith to the Church, the relation of the teaching office to the sources of the inspired word, historic life, present context.
3. The *pastoral office* of the Church. The relation of the local to the universal; the best relationship of the Church to the State.
4. What is the *uniqueness* of the Church? This would be a stumbling block in dialogue: on the first three ideals agreement might be easier though on the second point it was very necessary to register the convergences which were evident and possible from Vatican II.

Recalling William Temple's words, 'I believe in the Holy Catholic Church and sincerely regret that it does not at present exist', he said that the continuing existence of the Church is the heart of God's plan of salvation – but where is it? Roman Catholics must be trying all the time to see how they have obscured the mystery in which they believe.

The longest and most substantial of the four Gazzada papers was that of Eugene Fairweather. He proposed to isolate the 'crucial substantive issues' – the 'points of serious conflict' over four centuries – but first to state (a) the indispensable condition of dialogue, and (b) the position from which Anglicans approached it.

(a) His indispensable condition was entirely in harmony with *De Ecumenismo*, often repeated but easily slid away from: self-criticism by the yardstick of preaching and living the Gospel. He though that this had begun in both Churches.

(b) the Anglicans' starting point on its positive side he very much identified with the Chicago–Lambeth Quadrilateral (see p. 61, note 1), which however entailed the negative side – i.e., rejection of later definitions of faith and order by Western councils and by the Roman ones which were seen as *ultra vires*. Consistently with this, the Anglican Church itself has never 'felt entitled to define and impose dogmas of its own and has hence gained the description of comprehensiveness'.

Towards the medieval Western and modern Roman Catholic dogmas, which they reject, he distinguished three different Anglican attitudes:

1. to reject them as dogmas but esteem them as acceptable expressions of sound theology;
2. to reject them as dogmas and regard them as uncongenial in method and idiom;
3. to reject them as dogmas and also as misinterpretation of the Gospel.

> My first proposal is that we should build our dialogue on what has already been accomplished and proceed to a common study of the themes which I have labelled 'Revelation and Tradition' and 'The Nature and Structure of the Church'.

The paper was properly well received, but the formidable list of matters he assembled under the two main heads proved a strong temptation to the more articulate, under too tolerant chairmanship, to launch into dialogue before charting it. In succeeding years, it became clear that progress was best achieved by small groups.

Two sub-commissions were soon formed according to the division commissioned in the Common Declaration, one for 'theological matters' and one for 'practical proposals'. The first produced a plan for exchange of papers at the next meeting on the general theme of 'The Word', more fully 'The Authority of the Word of God and its relation to the Church'. The allocation of the papers was as follows:

- *What is the Word?*
  - Paper by   Father Tavard
  - To open discussion   Bishop Simon
- *How is the Word received by man?*
  - Paper by   Canon Atkinson
  - To open discussion   Father Hastings
- *How does the Word call the Church into being?*
  - Paper by   Professor Fairweather
  - To open discussion   Father Keating

- *How does the Church proclaim the Word?*
Paper by	Father Richards
To open discussion	Bishop Knapp-Fisher
- *What should be the minimum structure and essential life of the local Church?*
Paper by	Canon Kemp
To open discussion	Bishop Fox
- *How do the local Churches form the unity of the Universal Church?*
Paper by	Father Bouyer
To open discussion	Dr Shepherd
- *To what extent can or should there be diversity in a united Church?*
Papers by	(a) Bishop Willebrands
	(b) Bishop Moorman and Professor Root

The sub-commission on practical issues came up smartly with seven draft proposals, which eventually appeared, after modification, in the JPC's full report. They covered a wide field:

1. That the bishops of both Churches should meet more often both socially and for discussion of problems which they have in common.
2. That the clergy of both Churches should meet, for example in deanery chapters, for the discovering and study of their common heritage and responsibility in Christ.
3. That local groups should be formed in which clergy and laity together meet for prayers, for common study of the Bible and of each other's beliefs and ways of worship, and for Christian witness in social, charitable and educational fields, and any other areas where common action seems possible.
4. That ecumenical co-operation should be fostered at universities and colleges, for Christian witness and service, with the support of the respective chaplains.
5. That Christian unity and mission should be furthered by the joint use of churches and ancillary buildings wherever possible.
6. That stress should be laid upon the urgent need to work for common texts in those prayers and formulae which are in use in both Churches.
7. That a greater measure of collaboration should be urged in seminary and theological college training and in faculties and departments of theology in universities.

A third task of the meeting, and by no means the easiest, was to compile a press release, since it was clear that 'secret' dialogue would be self-defeating. It began with an arresting sentence:

After four hundred years of separation between the Roman Catholic and Anglican Churches, official representatives from both Churches have taken the first steps towards restoring full unity.[4]

A pattern of shared prayer was followed which was to persist until the end of ARCIC I. Each team celebrated its own Eucharist each day and also attended that of the other team. In the evening a form of common prayer (sometimes evensong with hymns) was followed. Although for some this sharpened the sense of division and no doubt some wished the Roman Catholic regulations about liturgical sharing and communion less strict, the latter were observed with complete fidelity, then and for fifteen years afterwards. At Gazzada this did not go uncontested. A very long discussion on it (which rather tried Louis Bouyer's patience) was prompted by our evangelical member James Atkinson.[5]

There were two matters on which dissatisfaction appeared, rather on the Anglican than on the Roman Catholic side. The first was about the representative character of the Anglican team. Much as Atkinson was liked, it was felt that he hardly represented the evangelical wing of Anglicanism and both the chairman, Moorman, and Eugene Fairweather wrote to Ramsey asking that a 'liberal evangelical' should be added. Several names were suggested, including two whom we have met in pre-ARCIC conversations: F. W. Dillistone and S. L. Greenslade. Ramsey answered that 'it was supposed that Massey Shepherd answered to that description, but no one can be blamed for not exactly answering to the labels hitherto attached to them'. It was doubtful whether anyone at Gazzada would have accepted that label for Massey Shepherd even if he had carried it on his coat; 'he is such a sacramentalist and has become so pro-Roman', wrote Fairweather (an attitude largely due to his sojourn at the Vatican Council). In the event, A. T. Mollegen from Virginia Theological Seminary was appointed.

The second difficulty, felt most acutely by the Anglican co-chairman but also by others, was about the World Council of Churches observer. There was a deal of talking in corners about this and Bishop Moorman wrote in his report to Ramsey:

This commission was by no means certain that they wanted to be observed ... we should be sorry if someone were approached [who might prove] a real embarrassment. If a WCC man is to come we felt that (a) we should have some choice in who it is to be, and (b) we should be able to lay down some conditions as to the part he is to play in our deliberations.

Ramsey replied:

I do not know how you 'gather' that strong pressure was put on me to allow a WCC observer. The plan to have an observer was initiated by myself and Mons. Willebrands. I think *he* can secure that the next observer from the WCC is a person who will be helpful and not make difficulties.[6]

For the rest of the JPC meetings we had Dr Harding Meyer, and throughout ARCIC Dr Gunter Gassman, both of whom performed their function impeccably.

Ecumenical excursions

The next meeting was held in England at the end of August. The months between were not ecumenically barren. They were a busy time at the SPCU as also for its peripatetic staff. I, for instance, had scarcely drawn breath after Gazzada before I was packed off to the USA for four weeks to find out what I could about Roman Catholic–Episcopalian relations there. (I cannot think that I was yet equipped to contribute anything to them.)

In Boston I attended as observer a conference of an organization for stimulating North Americans to help their less fortunate brothers in Latin America. It was held in the Hilton Hotel on a scale (in every sense) that left a European country cousin slightly dizzy, and spiced by the Cardinal Archbishop of Boston's diatribe against the ungrateful criticisms of the *avant-garde* priest Fr Ivan Illich.

In Chicago I found James Atkinson lecturing, and was much helped by him and by the head of Seabury Western Theological Seminary and by my host Mgr John Quinn. In Nashotah House near Milwaukee, a historic Anglican site with some buildings surviving from its foundation, I got to know Arthur Vogel (later Bishop of Missouri), who was to be a fellow member of ARCIC I.

I was lucky enough to arrive in Toronto on the day the Canadian Anglican bishops were meeting there, and in the evening found myself on a platform with Eugene Fairweather in a large crowded room, expected to talk about Gazzada without going substantially beyond the press release. I remember admiring how Fairweather managed to sound wise and informed while keeping to this narrow path.[7]

I returned to Rome feeling slightly less of an innocent abroad. I have described the journey briefly for the benefit of any reader who may still think that the SPCU ever imagined that its work could be done solely from desks within sight of St Peter's.

A mere list of happenings of 1967 illustrates the range and often historic character of the Secretariat's activities.[8] Besides holding its own plenary meeting 19–28 April, bringing together 21 bishop members from as many different countries,[9] it organized a conference of national and regional ecumenical officers from 29 May to 3 June. Both of these were almost indispensable as forums of exchange if the Secretariat was to give guidance which was useful yet flexible, adaptable to local conditions.

Apart from the Anglican Commission just dealt with, it had joint commission meetings with the World Methodist Council and the Lutheran World Federation and a Joint Working Group with the WCC, which produced a working paper on ecumenical dialogue. It had observers or participants at the British National Ecumenical Conference at Heythrop and at the Evangelical Anglican Conference at Keele; it played a considerable part in organizing the visit of Pope Paul VI to Istanbul and that of Patriarch Athenagoras to the Vatican and it continued vigorous co-operation with the United Bible Societies.

Huntercombe

The Anglican–Roman Catholic Joint Preparatory Commission which met for the second time at the delightful Huntercombe Manor in Buckinghamshire had acquired four new members. The Bishop of Ossory, Ferns and Leighlin, Dr Harry McAdoo (later Archbishop of Dublin), now felt able to join. He was a specialist in classical, seventeenth-century Anglicanism. The other three were A. T. Mollegan from Virginia (see p. 107); Bishop Christopher Butler OSB, who as Abbot of Downside had been a considerable figure in Vatican II and was now an auxiliary bishop of Westminster; and Fr Camillus Hay OFM from Melbourne – the SPCU had been anxious to bring in an Australian.

The first two papers – one by George Tavard, a Frenchman very familiar with the course of Vatican II but of independent judgement, the other by James Atkinson, a Reformation-orientated Anglican – considered the Word in the widest and richest sense: that which is given through Scripture, and through the experience of God, i.e. God's handling of the human race. Tavard traced the shifting balance of those elements through history, concluding that no one approach is ever adequate or comprehensive.

Atkinson was if anything more critical of the Liberal Protestant approach than the 'deductive theology' of the Roman tradition, speaking of the proud Titanism of 'coming of age' theology.

Professor Fairweather set out rather less apocalyptically to trace the organic connection between Word and Church as a living process in which authentic variation and development, inseparable from life, must be distinguished from the unauthentic

Fr Richards, examining 'how the Church proclaims the Word', began to uncover issues of authority, magisterium, apostolic succession, schism within or from the Church, and finally, the nature and limits of papal jurisdiction.

The question 'How do local Churches form the unity of the Universal Church?' brought forth two papers and the longest discussion of the meeting. This was not surprising, but it did take the commission beyond its mandate of setting the terms of dialogue and plunged us into the thick of it.

The last pair of papers were given the title 'To what extent can or should there be diversity in a united Church? Freedom and authority'. The first was written by Bishop Willebrands, the second a collaboration by Bishop Moorman and Canon Root on Anglican 'comprehensiveness'.

Discussion of these two papers raised points likely to be helpful for reporting on the strategy of dialogue, some of which appear in the Malta Report. Comprehensiveness should have limits which allowed it to be a defence against sectarianism without exposing it to incoherence. The notion of a 'hierarchy of truths', which had been hailed by observers when introduced into Vatican II but not yet explored much farther, came into consideration.

The last two days were devoted to thinking about the next and last JPC meeting which was beginning to feel uncomfortably close. A sub-commission under Bishop Butler had already been working on this and now reported. It had been exploring the notion of 'communion by stages', first brought up by Bishop McAdoo.

Some vagueness and some scepticism persisted about the concept of stages – the more so as it was seen by some to raise the question of orders, which hardly anybody saw as yet opportune. The decision was taken that Bishops McAdoo and Butler, with the assistance of Canon Root and Fr Richards, should present fuller proposals at the next meeting and that at the same time a note should be presented on 'Approaching the problem of Anglican Orders'.[10]

Malta

The third meeting of the JPC took place at Mount St Joseph, Malta from 31 December 1967 to 3 January 1968. Bishop McAdoo read the first of the two commissioned papers on 'Unity, an approach by stages'. This was his summary of the four elements in Stage 1:

1. Mutual recognition that each Church holds the essential Christian faith, neither being tied to a positive acceptance of all the beliefs held by the other.
2. The removal of the obstacle to ecumenism caused by mixed marriage legislation.
3. Joint examination of (a) the missionary situation; (b) sharing of buildings; (c) theological education; and (d) the possibility of joint pronouncements.
4. Joint action to ensure (a) an agreed text for common prayer forms; (b) an agreed three-part lectionary for Eucharistic lessons from the Old Testament, the Epistles and Gospels; and (c) arrangements for common worship and interchange of preachers.

Discussing Stage 2 he looked at existing stages of 'partial intercommunion' – Roman Catholic–Orthodox and Anglican–Old Catholic – for possible parallels. In the first of these he recognized that 'acceptance of the Petrine claims and Mariological dogmas is not essential'.

Moving on he came to the question of Orders, or better, to a reconciliation of ministries coming after a re-examination of Anglican Orders in the light of post-Vatican II theologies of the Church, ministries and sacraments.

Bishop Butler began with the urgency of the search for unity in the world situation – 'an unprecedented situation calling for unprecedented measures', which however must be seen, by both sides, as theologically justified. He then rehearsed firstly 'existing theological agreements between us' and then 'doctrinal divergences'.

Moving into the area of McAdoo's Stage 2, he saw no possible stage before *communicatio in sacris*. Here he deployed the familiar argument that hasty sanctioning of intercommunion had not been found to hasten reconciliation. He insisted on the particular obstacle of *Apostolicae Curae*.

He concluded 'we wish to emphasise that in our view there is no automatic implication in Stage 1 of subsequently accepting Stage 2, still less, that Stage 2 will inevitably lead on to Stage 3, i.e., full communion. Unity, to the extent to which it comes about, will be the work of the Holy Spirit.'

This ending seemed to be in a different key from that in which the paper had begun. 'Unprecedented measures' had faded into cautious, rather grudging reactions to problems long discussed.

Discussion and publication

The pressure which had brought the JPC together three times in a year and induced it to complete its task was partly caused by the imminence of the tenth Lambeth Conference which would bring 462 bishops of the Anglican communion to London towards the end of July. That such a document as the Malta Report should not fall under the attention of this rare (ten-yearly) gathering was unthinkable.

The misadventures of the document over the year 1968 revealed the gulf between the Secretariat's (and still more the JPC's) conception of the nature and importance of its task and that of the Secretariat of State and the Congregation for the Doctrine of the Faith, and the contrast of both mind and feeling which they brought to reading the report.

First, the sequence of facts. The report, dated 2 January, was submitted 'for their consideration to His Holiness Pope Paul VI and His Grace the Archbishop of Canterbury'.

The Secretariat for Christian Unity naturally examined the document before sending it through the bureaucratic process which surrounded the Pope. It was sent to the Secretariat of State with a covering letter by Cardinal Bea on 15 February. By the end of March nothing had stirred. Bishop Langton Fox of Menevia wrote to Willebrands, politely 'wondering whether anything could be done to expedite matters'. He was followed by Bishop

Butler saying 'it would be unfortunate if it came to be thought that the Church is preventing publication'. The following day Archbishop Ramsey wrote to the Pope, combining pleasure at the promised presence of Roman observers at the coming Lambeth Conference with gentle pressure for publication, saying that his own metropolitans had now seen the report (in fact it had been sent to them so long before that by 1 April all comments had come in except from Japan: they were in varying degrees favourable, except for a doubt from Uganda). In the first week of April, the SPCU was informed from the Secretariat of State that the document had been 'lost'. On 5 April I myself took by hand a duplicate with copies of the relevant correspondent, including the letters of anxious enquiry from England.

By the middle of May these had produced no reaction. Desperation was beginning to show. Bishop Moorman came to Rome and accompanied Willebrands to a papal audience. Moorman found the Pope 'very tired and extremely vague about the report' and Willebrands then suggested that Ramsey write direct to the Pope again, asking for publication over the signatures of the co-chairmen and pointing out that the Anglican metropolitans had seen it.

On 13 May Cardinal Bea addressed a letter to the powerful Monsignor Benelli in the Secretariat of State. Bea recalled the sequence of events, and pointed to the risk of leaks, even of irregular or unilateral publication. He suggested ways of stressing that the report engaged only the Commission. On 16 May Ramsey himself was thinking of coming to Rome.

I myself felt a touch of desperation, compounded by the feeling that one of my superiors was aspiring to have the *text* of the report altered. This pointed once more to the utter inability to understand the Anglo-Saxon conception of a commission's report to its masters. The latter can do what they like with it – adopt it, reject it, comment on it favourably or not, sack the commission, appoint another, but to alter the text, especially unilaterally, was Gilbertian.

It transpired that on the day Bea wrote to Benelli, 13 May, the consultors of the Congregation for the Doctrine of the Faith met to examine the Malta Report. Their full complement was 32 (nineteen of whom were Italians) but only twenty opinions were recorded. It is difficult after this time to know how many of those present had ever met an Anglican. Almost certainly very few.

Analysis of the opinions is most interesting and hardly fits the Hollywood or grand opera image of a chorus of hooded inquisitors with thumbs down. Exactly half of the twenty spoke favourably of the content: unfavourable views were not homogeneous.[11]

On the separate question of publication there was more solidity, in the Holy Office tradition – only two really favoured it. It was sufficiently clear by this time that, short of direct papal intervention, all prospect of ordinary publication in time for the Lambeth Conference had disappeared. As pressure from England mounted, a compromise was arrived at by which the report was printed in pamphlet form and distributed to the members of the Lambeth Conference accompanied by a letter signed by Cardinal Bea and Bishop Willebrands which amounted to an official reaction to the report (see *Final Report* of ARCIC, p. 1 and Alan Clark and Colin Davey, *Anglican–Roman Catholic Dialogue: The Work of the Joint Preparatory Commission*, p. 25). This showed an estimate of the loyalty and carefulness of the Anglican bishops which was triumphantly justified.

NOTES

1. I have included the secretaries, since they were free to take part in discussion and drafting – though one Anglican bishop was at first a bit restive about this.
2. He did not however claim that they were 'utterly guiltless' as Benson had in 1887 (cf. p. 1 above). In fact he had the honour of being the first to regret that no Anglican had yet publicly echoed Paul VI's confession of blame in the matter.
3. Charles Davis, a Westminster priest, had come to prominence as a *peritus* during Vatican II. He was now writing and teaching at Heythrop and editing the *Clergy Review* and was an obvious choice for the Joint Preparatory Commission. His departure was sudden but not silent; it saddened his friends and caused a great stir far beyond England.
4. The sentence was strongly proposed by Bishop Moorman and unanimously accepted.
5. More will be said of this very attractive man later on.
6. There was an anomaly in that while the Anglicans Churches were members of the WCC, the Roman Catholic Church was not, yet had a close relation with the WCC through a joint working group. This had produced a long joint report in 1965 which (among much else) had stated the usefulness, function and limits of exchange of observers – including those for bilateral dialogues: see SPCU Information Service no. 1 (1967).
7. At the Paulist Ecumenical Centre in Toronto I was given a welcome part of which remains unique in my experience. I concelebrated with the community, and the chief celebrant, pausing in the middle of his sermon about the money changers in the temple, invited me to take over from him. Perhaps he thought I was a specialist on the subject.
8. They can all be found reported in the SPCU Information Service no. 3 (1970).
9. Paul VI addressed this 'first full and official audience' of the SPCU in a long speech which it is striking to go back to. In a famous passage he recognized that the Pope '... is the greatest obstacle in the path of ecumenism'.
10. In the wake of Archbishop's Ramsey's visit to Rome, Archbishop Heenan had publicly stated his agreement with the idea of a re-examination of the question.
11. A digest of the discussion, with the opinions identified only by numbers, not names, exists in the SPCU archives.

13

Lambeth conference, 1968

Roman Catholic presence

Lambeth 1968 was not really comparable to Vatican II, being shorter and not legislative, but the influence of the Council was acknowledged. It was notable mainly for the presence, for the first time, of consultants and observers from other Christian Churches. In fact the conference had to move from Lambeth Palace to Church House, because of the numbers.

There were eight Roman Catholic observers (effectively seven since two of them alternated). They were:

• The Rt Revd Thomas Holland	Bishop of Salford and President of the Roman Catholic Ecumenical Commission for England and Wales
• The Rt Revd Christopher Butler	Auxiliary Bishop of Westminster and a Member of the Anglican–Roman Catholic JPC
• The Rt Revd Remi de Roo	Bishop of Victoria, Vancouver Island, Canada
• The Rt Revd William Gomes	Bishop of Poona, India and a member of the Anglican–Roman Catholic JPC

- The Rt Revd Peter Butelezi   Apostolic Administrator of
                                    Umzimkulu, South Africa
- The Revd John Coventry sᴊ   Director of Studies at Heythrop
                                    College and Secretary to the
                                    Roman Catholic Ecumenical
                                    Commission of England and
                                    Wales
- The Revd Herbert Ryan sᴊ   Professor of historical theology
                                    at Woodstock College,
                                    Maryland, USA
- The Revd Canon W. A. Purdy   Staff member of the SPCU.

In addition, Bishop Willebrands attended the opening ceremony at Canterbury and Westminster Abbey, and the opening meeting at which he read the Holy Father's message to the Conference. He was also present, together with Mgr Arrighi, for the last week and for the closing ceremony of the Conference. Roman Catholics who attended for part of the time as special guests were Canon Dessain of Louvain and the Prior of Bec.

The JPC was represented by three Roman Catholic observers and four Anglican consultants. Three consultants had taken part in the 1950–67 conversations, namely, Professors H. Chadwick and Howard Root and Dr Jenkins. Besides Professor Chadwick, three others of the contributors to *Preparatory Essays*[1] had also taken part in the conversations. These were F. W. Dillistone and J. L. Houlden, both of Oxford, and Canon R. P. C. Hanson of the University of Nottingham. Among the 29 authors of the essays there were three Americans: Charles C. West of Princeton, Dr Gibson Winter of the University of Chicago and Dr Kitagawa, a Japanese-American; there was one Canadian: Gregory Baum; one Greek: Dr Nissiotis; and one Sri Lankan. The rest were British, with Oxford and Cambridge strongly represented.

This was given as one reason for not providing formal schemata, as they would have had an undesirable 'Western bias'. Whether this bias was really corrected was open to question.[2] Nor was it clear how much the rather formidable collection of preparatory essays had been read.

The conference was divided into three sections: Renewal in Faith; Renewal in Ministry; and Renewal in Unity. Each of these was divided into sub-commissions – 32 in all. Each section had to work during the first week to produce an 800-word draft which was hastily considered in a short section meeting at the end of the week, then conflated into first-draft reports after the weekend in time for the plenary debate of the second week.

The contrast between the crushing work of the sub-commissions, and especially the drafters, and the broad, meandering oratory of the plenary sessions was striking.

The observers were freely invited and canvassed to take part in sub-commission work, and the plenary sessions were thrown open to them and the consultants for a period.

No topic of the conference was without interest, but those primarily concerned with Anglican–Roman Catholic relations naturally paid much attention not only to the section on Unity but also to the ecumenical attitude as it showed itself throughout.

This was first of all manifest in the courtesy and readiness to listen and ask for co-operation, already referred to. Father Herbert Ryan sj was even asked to collaborate with Dr Lesslie Newbiggin in making the first draft on Episcopacy submitted by sub-commissions 22 and 24 as well as that of the General Introduction to the whole of Section II on Ministry – this being revised by the Archbishop of York, Dr Coggan, and the Bishop of Warrington. L. A. Brown.

Roman Catholic observers were also co-opted in the later stages of drafting by the combined sub-commissions on Roman Catholic Relations and on Papacy and Episcopacy.

The sections of the Conference

I Renewal in Faith

The Catholic observers noted that the problems of this section were commonly attributed to three causes:

(a) The current turmoil in theology, philosophical theology and social thinking affecting a scholarly but undogmatic tradition.
(b) The presence in the section of a higher ratio of academics or former academics than in the other sections.
(c) The uneasy attempt to marry strictly theological questions with those which 'the world' (a term used far from homogeneously, like 'secular') feels the Church should be concerned with.

II Renewal in Unity

In the Renewal in Unity report, a re-wording of the famous Lambeth Quadrilateral of 1888 drew considerable fire. The 'historic episcopate' disappeared, to be replaced by 'a ministry through which the grace of God is given to his people'. Some fierce argument ended with a compromise: the 1888 version was printed as a footnote, which only emphasized the contrast. The report commented later that the Quadrilateral 'is not a static formulation of positions in which Anglicans are entrenched. Rather we see it in the context[3] of the vision of unity expressed at the WCC assembly at New Delhi' (which of course makes no mention of episcopate, historic or otherwise).

It was in this section that the eventually amalgamated sub-commissions no. 29, 'Relations with the Roman Catholic Church', and no. 23, 'Episcopacy, Collegiality and Papacy', reported. The tale needs telling in full.

No. 29 had been advised by Archbishop Ramsey to concentrate its attention on the Malta Report. It did so, and passed on its favourable reaction to the section. It was finally underwritten by the whole conference in resolution no. 52, while no. 53 recommended the setting up of a permanent joint commission and welcomed the work of the Joint Commission on the theology of marriage and its application to mixed marriages (see Chapter 24).

The work of sub-commission 23 had a rougher passage. The corresponding preparatory essay on 'Primacy and collegiality' by two Oxford scholars, D. W. Allen of St Stephen's House and A. M. Allchin, Librarian of Pusey House and editor of *Sobornost*, was excellent and fair, and was suggesting no more than that those separated from Rome 'look again at your objections and fears of a visible centre of unity'.

It traced particularly well how the eleventh-century reforms of the papacy had unwittingly altered the notion of primacy and of men's attitudes to it.

While they did not think that among Anglicans the notion of the Pope as anti-Christ had survived the early seventeenth century, they thought 'it might be argued that the idea of the Pope as anti-Christ involves a certain indirect recognition of the importance of the Petrine office'.

Humanae Vitae

By an unlucky coincidence the papal encyclical *Humanae Vitae* came out at the opening of the Conference. The press, hitherto rather lukewarm about Lambeth, made a meal of both the encyclical and the coincidence, but the Conference merely debated the matter for two days.

The Bishop of Newcastle, H. E. Ashdown, supported by Robert Mortimer of Exeter and Graham Leonard of Willesden, made a plea for recognition of 'the 90 per cent of value and truth in the document'. The point which aroused most opposition was the contention that birth control necessarily led to moral degradation. The Bishop of Kansas City, Edward Welles, insisted that it had not done so for him in X years of happy marriage. He was much headlined, which led to a decision to adopt the lesser of two evils and open the sessions to the press.

Eventually, resolution no. 22 took the unusual step of quoting three resolutions of the 1958 Lambeth Conference in full. The first two of these exalted marriage as a divine vocation to be controlled by discipline and self-restraint, the third laid the responsibility for number and frequency of children on the informed Christian conscience. This long quotation was preceded by the words:

Responsible Parenthood
This conference has taken note of the papal encyclical letter
Humanae Vitae recently issued by His Holiness Pope Paul VI. The
Conference records its appreciation of the Pope's deep concern for
the institution of marriage and the integrity of married life.

Nevertheless, the Conference finds itself unable to agree with the
Pope's conclusion that all methods of conception control other than
abstinence from sexual intercourse or its confinement to the periods
of infecundity are contrary to the 'order established by God'.

(*Reports and Resolutions*, p. 36)

The Roman Catholic observers wisely refrained from intervening in the discussion, but in the following January Cardinal Heenan, speaking in St Paul's Cathedral at the end of the Week of Prayer for Unity, had this to say:

The Anglican bishops made no attempt to criticize or condemn. Our
community, embarrassed by attacks on the Pope by some of its own
members, was grateful beyond measure for the forbearance and
compassion shown by Anglicans. I have deliberately awaited this
opportunity of speaking in St Paul's to express our thanks for that
great act of friendship.

What effect the encyclical had on sub-commission no. 23, charged with making a draft on 'Episcopacy, Collegiality and Papacy', can only be guessed. They had other aspects of the question to consider, notably a statement of Lambeth 1908, endorsed in 1920 and 1930.

> There can be no fulfilment of the Divine purpose in any scheme of
> reunion which does not ultimately include the great Latin Church
> of the West, with which our history has been so closely associated in
> the past and to which we are still bound by many ties of common
> faith and tradition.

The exact quotation appeared in the first draft and survived to appear in the plenary report. But the first draft went much further:

> Although as we understand them at present we are unable to accept
> the claims of the papacy to infallibility and immediate and universal
> jurisdiction, we believe that a considerable majority of Anglicans
> would be prepared to accept the Pope as having a primacy of service
> implying both honour and responsibility, in a renewed and reunited
> Church as would seem right on both historical and pragmatic
> grounds.

The passage just quoted was fallen upon less by bishops than by Protestant observers, with Lukas Vischer in the lead. As a result of these criticisms the words 'a primacy of service implying both honour and responsibility' were amended over the weekend to 'a primacy of love implying both honour and service' but in this form too it was rejected by the plenary fairly sharply, especially by the chairman who suggested a drastic reduction of the whole passage.

There followed an interesting episode on the Monday. The two sub-commissions concerned with the Roman Catholic Church, 23 and 29, met together, with Bishop Butler and myself as observers. The meeting began with solid opposition to the passage but ended with significant changes of heart reflected in the italicized passages:

> As a result of the emphasis placed on collegiality at the Second
> Vatican Council, the status of bishops in the Roman Catholic Church
> was in greater measure enhanced, though the teaching of the First
> Vatican Council on the infallibility and immediate and universal

jurisdiction of the papacy was unaffected. *We are unable to accept this teaching as it is commonly understood today. The relationships between the Pope and the episcopal college, of which he is a member, are, however, still being clarified and are subject to development.* We recall the statement made in the Lambeth Conference of 1908, and repeated in 1920 and 1930, 'that there can be no fulfilment of the Divine purpose in any scheme of reunion which does not ultimately include the great Latin Church of the West with which our history has been so closely associated in the past, and to which we are still bound by many ties of common faith and tradition'. *We recognise the papacy as a historic reality whose developing role requires deep reflection and joint study by all concerned for the unity of the whole Body of Christ.*[4]

III Renewal in Ministry

Sub-commission 21 in Section 2, 'Renewal in Ministry' treated a subject with a stormy future (it will be discussed in Chapter 25): the ordination of women to the priesthood. For the moment the reactions of the Roman Catholic observers at the time may be quoted.

There was deep division in the conference. The Archbishop of York and the Bishop of Chester were the two chief advocates and the Archbishop of Sydney the most passionate opponent, but the final version of the report and the accompanying resolutions are cautiously worded. They judged the theological arguments to be inconclusive and recommended study. (Resolution 34)

The Malta Report

A day or two after Lambeth '68 had ended, Bishop Willebrands wrote to Mgr Benelli requesting permission to send the Malta Report to the Catholic episcopal conferences. Any of them who had followed even casually the reports of Lambeth must have known that the conference had the report and must have felt aggrieved.

Five weeks later Willebrands wrote again, a long letter saying how valuable and approved the Malta Report had been at Lambeth and dilating on the reasons for publication, which was now inevitable. (Several newspapers were now believed to be in possession of it.) This letter was answered on 22 November. The answer was that the opinion of the Congregation for the Doctrine of the Faith had been sought and they had replied that the threat of publication by a newspaper did not appear to alter (*non sembra mutare*) the decision of the Congregation, sanctioned by the Holy Father, not to publish the document. This was because it contained some grave doctrinal errors, underlined by Fr Hamer in his *votum*, submitted also to the SPCU, and because it was not the practice of the Holy See to publish the text of a work produced by a preparatory commission.

It was further objected that the publication of the report after the Lambeth Conference had studied it would give it greater credit than it had last May, allowing it to be believed that the Holy See had accepted even the points incompatible with Catholic doctrine, while if a newspaper took the initiative in publishing it the Holy See would not be committed and would remain free to publish a correction if the text were to be interpreted tendentiously.

This letter was signed by Archbishop Benelli, one of the most intelligent men in the Vatican.[5] It was almost certainly drafted for him by somebody else, but it was incredible that he could have read it carefully before he signed it. He carried a formidable burden of work.

Of the twenty opinions given by the consultors of the CFD only one said that it was 'not acceptable to Catholics' – hardly the same as saying it contained 'grave doctrinal errors'. To say that this accusation was contained in Fr Hamer's *votum* was ludicrous and – I was told long afterwards – made him very angry.

The SPCU could not give their whole attention to the confusion over the Malta Report because, sadly, Cardinal Bea died. He had been ill for weeks.

The Report was published in *The Tablet*[6] on 31 November, with a reasonably thoughtful apologia.

Postscript

In 1968, the question 'Will there be another Lambeth?' came up for debate. What the bishops valued chiefly was what the modern idiom would call 'a boost to morale', but they themselves would have preferred to call spiritual reinforcement.[7] The Bishop of Durham, the philosopher Ian Ramsey, put it another way: 'We are still very provincial and one would not suspect, except for Lambeth, that we are an international communion.' The last word was significant – in its Greek form, *koinonia*, it was to become richer and more important with the progress of ecumenical dialogue.

NOTES

1. The two volumes of *Preparatory Information* and *Preparatory Essays* and that of the *Reports and Resolutions* were published by the SPCK.

   A short account compiled mainly from the Roman Catholic observers' reports is in the SPCU Information Service no. 6 (1968).

   J. P. Simpson and E. M. Story, *The Long Shadows of Lambeth X* (McGraw-Hill, 1969), is a lively American eye-witness record.
2. A professor from Uganda, John Monti, having read out to the plenary, amid nervous titters, a turgid passage, said 'Perhaps my trouble is that English is my third language'.
3. A word subject to slave labour in ecumenical discourse.
4. These short exchanges were an example of a good dialogue made possible by the Conference's generous involvement of observers. The Conference not only strongly encouraged Roman Catholic–Anglican dialogue – it provided many examples of it.
5. It should be said that afterwards, down to the time he left Rome for Florence, Benelli was a staunch friend and helper of the SPCU.
6. This was not of course the first publication. The US *National Catholic Reporter* had already assured the report's wide circulation.
7. The same question was discussed even more strongly and in the same terms at the meeting of the Anglican Consultative Council at Trinidad.

14

The Anglican–Roman Catholic International Commision

The Anglican Communion had for some time been under fire, mostly from across the Atlantic, for lack of organization of any compelling kind. Its only *regular* international expression (apart from the Lambeth Conference) was in the form of a group of 26 members called the Lambeth Consultative Body. The result of reflection on this was the decision to establish the Anglican Consultative Council, ACC as it quickly came to be called.

This was the subject of Resolution 69, which was to be submitted to member churches with a request for approval not later than 31 October 1969. Eight functions were proposed for it, and a draft constitution. Direct ecumenical interest centred on function 5:

> To encourage and guide Anglican participation in the ecumenical movement and the ecumenical organizations: to co-operate with the World Council of Churches and the world confessional bodies on behalf of the Anglican Communion, and to make arrangements for the conduct of pan-Anglican conversations with the Roman Catholic Church, the Orthodox Church and other Churches.

This was the only one of the eight in which the brief went beyond advice, encouragement or co-ordination.

The body which was to do this, however, was still only the object of a resolution not yet confirmed by the provinces. The conference report was still talking of The Lambeth Consultative Body or the Anglican Consultative

Council. Three weeks after the close of the Conference, Ramsey told Satterthwaite that the Lambeth Consultative Body had 'unfortunately' left the appointment of the new Anglican–Roman Catholic Commission in his hands. He proposed circulating names to the metropolitans, while sticking firmly to designating Bishop McAdoo as co-chairman.

On 10 December 1968 Ramsey summoned John Satterthwaite. He said the numbers could hardly be kept down to six as had been tentatively agreed during his visit to Rome; 'it would be a mistake' not to include one or two Anglicans from outside the United Kingdom (a revealing understatement).

The Archbishop began his overtures in the new Year, with the evangelical Michael Green, who had been a consultant at Lambeth. Green excused himself but strongly recommended a younger man, Julian Charley, who was just leaving London College of Divinity to become Director of Studies at Bristol. He also 'had the recommendation of being a bachelor'. (This presumably meant no more than that he would have more time for talking to Roman Catholics.)

Julian Charley, interviewed at Lambeth, was told that 'his Grace is eager to have someone who would be able to *represent in a very definite way* the conservative evangelical wing of the Church of England' (italics mine). He never failed this charge, but things happened to him as to all of us, as they should in dialogue, things that sometimes seemed to terrify.

The CFR were very worried about who was to be the Roman Catholic co-chairman of the joint commission. By some means it had become fixed in their minds that Bishop Langton Fox was the Roman Catholic choice and they did not want him. He had been a member of the JPC and was now a member of the separate joint commission on marriage and mixed marriages (see Chapter 24) which had already met twice, in April and December of 1968. As the note to the Archbishop put it:

> some of us feel [Fox] is merely a mouthpiece for the more conservative elements of the English Roman Catholic hierarchy.

So Bishop Butler's name was pressed upon the SPCU for Catholic co-chairman. Ramsey thought it 'essential to have two co-chairmen of high academic standing'. The SPCU was aware that it was desirable to have a chairman acceptable to both sides. It was difficult to find the Roman Catholic paragon who would be acceptable to Lambeth[1] at that moment. As Ramsey astonishingly put it later, he 'hoped that the Roman Catholic co-chairman would be someone of real standing who could have prestige in Anglican circles ... and not some ecclesiastical hack appointed to satisfy the English Roman Catholic hierarchy'.

The man eventually chosen, the recently consecrated auxiliary Bishop of Northampton, Alan Clark, was hardly the Olympian figure of the Lambeth specifications, but he fitted the bill. His appointment was, circuitously, one of the advantages that came of the pre-ARCIC work of the '1950s' group in which he had become known to some Anglicans of consequence.

The SPCU approach to the planning of ARCIC was rather different. It focused more on the Malta report and how it was to be implemented than on personalities. The staff met on 7 February to discuss in some detail the report and its prospects. They naturally welcomed the following assertion:

> we hope in humility that our work may so help to further
> reconciliation between Anglicans and Roman Catholics as also to
> promote the wider unity of all Christians in their common Lord.
> (Malta Report, FR, p. 109)

To welcome this was not of course to imply any preference for multi-lateral dialogue; it simply reflected the SPCU's wider mandate. Lambeth's Section II report spoke rather more bluntly of the 'divergences which required serious study'.

The great majority of both Anglicans and Roman Catholics were going to find that 'common inheritance' and 'living tradition', and the prospect of 'extensive sharing', were ambitious ideas which went against the feelings in their bones. Nowhere was this more evident that in the British Isles.

Under the general heading of 'Growing together' the Malta Report, Part II, proposed what amounted to a comprehensive programme of mutual education, stressing the need for all on either side to learn what was shared, and thus get differences in proportion and strip them of hostile emotion.

Lambeth resolution 1968 no. 446 (*Reports and Resolutions*, p. 41) had said

> We believe that prior attention in ecumenical life and action should
> be given to the local level and point to local ecumenical action as the
> most direct way of bringing together the whole Christian community
> in any area.

This 'priority' was fully accepted in the SPCU and applied as much to Anglican–Roman Catholic relations as to any other.

The practical proposals had been formulated already at Gazzada. They were slightly modified at Huntercombe and given general approval by the respective authorities and circulated to the Roman Catholic episcopal conferences with a request for views and information by the end of 1967. No less than fifty conferences replied during the succeeding months and by early November 1968 the SPCU had before it an analysis of the replies.[2]

In March 1969, a long letter was sent to the CFR summarizing these SPCU reactions and suggesting a meeting in London on 21 April 'for an informal discussion on how to organize the work of the Commission'. This received a reply which stated firmly that what was wanted were the names of the Catholic members and (even more firmly) the date of the next Mixed Marriage meeting. Whereas the Secretariat thought we should be clear about exactly what we wanted before selecting people to do it, this was seemingly interpreted as 'stalling'. Fortunately the letter from the SPCU was sent on to the Bishop of Ossory, who treated it rather more sympathetically.

On 13 April Willebrands was appointed president of the SPCU. Findlow announced this to the CFR, adding that Fr Hamer ('about the most conservative theologian in the SPCU', he said) was likely now to be the new secretary. He concluded by prophesying 'confidence and acceleration once Willebrands is firmly in the saddle'. He might have added that, contrary to what Lambeth tended to assume, the SPCU's difficulties were now almost always with the Curia and not with the English hierarchy.

Not all the difficulties about membership were on one side. Though the Anglican Communion was less authoritarian in spirit and practice there was not much doubt (least of all in American minds) about who did the choosing. On the other hand Anglicans if invited would find it psychologically easier to refuse than would Roman Catholics.

The man who became the most vital member of the Anglican team, Henry Chadwick, was reluctant to accept because of his many commitments but was, providentially, firmly persuaded by Ramsey to drop one or two of them. Even the co-chairman, the Bishop of Ossory, had to request to be allowed to give up his place in the Anglican–Orthodox dialogue.

From across the Atlantic difficulties of the opposite sort came. Peter Day, the PECUSA ecumenical officer, showed signs of discontent with American representation. There was only one American in the Anglican team and no American bishop, though the delightful Arthur Vogel of

Nashotah House became one soon afterwards.[3] The Bishop of West Missouri, Edward Welles, who had acquired some fame at Lambeth '68 as 'no. 309', took the initiative of writing to the Presiding Bishop, John Hines, offering his services, apparently without success.

But the Americans did not give up easily. Even after the first ARCIC meeting (see below) when Ramsey was in the United States he was tackled by four bishops – Hallock of Milwaukee, who was on the Mixed Marriage commission, John Allin of Mississippi, a future presiding Bishop, Higgins of Rhode Island and Welles himself – about the 'heavy weighting of ARCIC by Church of England men'.[4]

Ramsey's comment when he got home was that while he enjoyed meeting the American bishops, he was of the opinion that they were light-weight theologically, keen for better relations with the Roman Catholics but ignorant of the doctrinal complexities to be cleared up first.

During the first half of 1969 a great deal of thought and some wide consultation was given on the Roman Catholic side to the selection of members of the Anglican–Roman Catholic commission. Some of the problems, such as the need for geographical spread, and for diversity of scholarly specialization and pastoral experience, we shared with the Anglicans, whilst others were peculiar to ourselves, as will be obvious to those who have read so far.

Both sides saw the need to keep some continuity with the JPC. Five Anglicans were taken over from it, only two Roman Catholics. There was some divergence about numbers, but Archbishop Ramsey felt that adequate representation of various sorts could not be achieved with the originally canvassed number of six. This was almost certainly true and nine a side, excluding secretaries, was eventually agreed on.

On 8 May the present writer set out for London with the new General Secretary, Fr Jérome Hamer, for a series of consultations about prospective members. We had with us no fewer than 22 names, about which we intended to sound out Archbishop Heenan of Westminister, Bishop Butler, the Apostolic Delegate Igino Cardinale and Bishop Thomas Holland. All four were in favour of Bishop Clark as co-chairman. Another point that emerged was that there was good support for having a layman on the commission.

Next day Hamer and I had a long conversation with the Archbishop of Canterbury and John Satterthwaite. Ramsey's main points were:

(a) He thought poorly of the proposal with which Part II of the Malta Report began: 'an official and explicit affirmation of mutual recognition from the highest authorities of each communion' (acknowledging the elements of shared faith). It had already been represented in the SPCU that this might scare people off and the Archbishop now made the same objection, adding that the wording was premature and even rather naïve.

(b) He made the point about the minimum representative number.

(c) He was ready to join with the Pope in giving the new commission a new mandate, but it was quickly agreed that the Malta Report was mandate enough.[5]

(d) He had forgotten that he had limited the commission to three years until he was reminded by Satterthwaite, but said he had done so only because some members were unwilling to commit themselves for longer. He had no intention of limiting the work to three years.

(e) It was agreed that the first meeting might be at St George's House, Windsor, 6–13 January 1970.

Thus fortified, Hamer and I set off for Dublin, where we met up with Bishop Butler, Howard Root and John Satterthwaite Bishop McAdoo received us with spacious Irish hospitality.

The purpose was to plan the Windsor meeting and draw up a programme. Divergence in interpreting Section III of Malta soon surfaced. Fr Hamer was still stressing the function of *oversight* and *co-ordination* of future work undertaken together by our two communions – assigned in Malta, para. 21.

The concrete tasks of theological, or better, doctrinal investigation mentioned in Section III were to be assigned to sub-commissions, which, though responsible to the main commission, were to have some kind of continuous existence. In fact, the decisive work as embodied in the Final Report was done by the main commission itself, and the term sub-commission was used merely to describe the dividing up of drafting and similar work *within* the commission.

This bias already appeared in Dublin. For only one of the papers proposed for Windsor was outside help sought. The paper on 'Fundamentals' was assigned to Bishop Knapp-Fisher and to Edmund Hill OP, who lived relatively close to each other in South Africa.

Butler was loathe to take on his assignment to the Authority theme – probably because on this very theme he had recently caused offence to some of his fellow bishops. He recommended Robert Murray SJ,[6] who was more accessible to the other member of the duo, Henry Chadwick, but this was not accepted.

On the question of lay participants, the Anglicans claimed they had no objection in principle but had problems in finding someone: 'we are not as well off in this respect as you', they said, which was surprising since we were always hearing of the importance of the laity in Anglicanism (cf. Lambeth 1968, *Reports and Resolutions*, resolution 24–25, pp. 95ff.); but they were evidently thinking of lay *theologians*. In the event there was no Anglican layman, but one Catholic, Professor J. J. Scarisbrick, and he was a Professor of history.

Welcome was given to the idea of broadening the dialogue to embrace non-theological factors, and a joint paper on the subject was commissioned, but this was not destined for a great future in ARCIC I.

A number of practical details were discussed and in some cases led to 'resolution'. For instance, it was agreed that in future press releases should be much less restricted and more informative.

NOTES

1. On 29 April the Bishop of Ossory reported a conversation with Ramsey in which the latter said that the Roman Catholic co-chairman should be a scholar, otherwise the matter in his view would not be worth going on with – *nor should he be a convert*.
2. On 21 May 1969, a similar though more general enquiry about Anglican–Roman Catholic relations was sent by the CFR to Anglican metropolitans. The most ample replies came from the USA, Australia and New Zealand. In the USA a joint commission had existed since before the end of Vatican II.
3. Arthur Vogel is still serving on ARCIC II.
4. Four out of the nine were actually working in the Church of England at the time, but the two from Australia and South Africa were very much English. J. N. D. Kelly was originally appointed but was quickly replaced by Eugene Fairweather.
5. More than enough as it turned out, though not incapable of clarification.
6. See above, p. 94. Murray was a contributor to *Infallibility in the Church*, the symposium organized at Birmingham (Darton Longman and Todd, 1968).

ARCIC at Windsor I

At the meetings of the JPC Mgr Willebrands, by then titular bishop of Mauriana, had been present as secretary (or number two) of the Secretariat and had played a substantial part. He was now succeeded in office by Fr Hamer and the impression the latter formed on his visit to London and Dublin strengthened his conviction that he should follow precedent and take part in the commission himself.[1] He did suggest this in his written the Dublin meeting. With a very inexperienced co-chairman and a co-secretary who was still very much of a tyro, there was a lot to be said for the commission having a prestigious old hand involved. In the event, the need was supplied with immense success by Fr Pierre Duprey.[2] He had joined the Secretariat in 1963 and was under-secretary for the Oriental section.

The Roman summer recess followed hard on the return from Dublin, and it was not until 26–27 September that Willebrands wrote to Ramsey announcing the names adding that 'this does not exclude the possibility of Fr Hamer and myself taking part in some of the meetings if the turn of events should seem to call for it'.

Co-operation at Windsor . . .

On 9 January 1970 we converged on Windsor. This was the first of three meetings that were to be held there: it was there that we were to meet for the last time in 1981. But this, our first meeting, was still exploratory. We had agreed at Dublin that the ideal basis for work was joint papers, which meant that the first stage of dialogue was done for us in advance, but it proved to be an ideal hard to live up to.

We started with a true joint paper, that of Bishop Knapp-Fisher of Pretoria and Edmund Hill OP, and it has always struck me as a model of its kind. Their theme was predominantly positive – the agreement on Fundamentals of Faith referred to in the Malta Report, paras 3–5 and 7, which they enlarged on without glossing over differences. They took basic documents from either side as witness:

Anglican	*Roman Catholic*
The Thirty-Nine Articles	*De Fide Catholica* of Vatican I
The Revised Church Catechism	*De Revelatione* ⎫
The Book of Common Prayer	*De Ecclesia* ⎬ of Vatican II
The Report on Doctrine of 1938	⎭

The selected Fundamentals were:

1. *Revelation and faith*, where they found complete substantial agreement.
2. *Scripture and Tradition*. Here there was much agreement, strengthened at Vatican II, but some persisting difficulties. The unique authority of the Bible is not seen by either side as implying the Protestant *sola scriptura* position; Scripture needs interpreting. 'Tradition' is not by material accretion but by deeper penetration of the Gospel. The 'inerrancy' of the Bible must be carefully circumscribed (see *Doctrine in the Church of England*, no. 32).
3. *Church and authority*. Knapp-Fisher and Hill agreed on seeing the Church as 'the creation of Christ, the continuation among men of his incarnate and risen presence and his redemptive act'. This raises questions which are acute in a state of divided Christianity.

Dr Vogel and Fr Tillard gave papers named from the Malta Report, para. 22: 'To examine the question of intercommunion and the related matters of Church and Ministry'.

Bishop Butler and Professor Henry Chadwick were compelled by circumstances to write separate papers, but their very similar English classical academic backgrounds led them to approach 'Authority, its nature, exercise and implications' in much the same way. Chadwick's longer paper spent two-thirds of its length on securing the foundation.

Butler turned more quickly to the religious problem. Both said much about contrasting attitudes to authority both among those who exercise it and those who accept it. Neither questioned the fundamental hierarchy of Christian authority: God, Church, Scripture, Ministry; but this is a chain in which the human element enters. Chadwick wrote:

> In general the Anglican tradition has been both cheerfully optimistic about the irresistible gravitational pull of truth, talking as if mistaken opinion would never long survive examination by reasonable men, and simultaneously gravely pessimistic about the capacity of the human mind, *even with the help of grace*, to compass divine truth, talking as if some degree of inadequacy can never be wholly eliminated from any proposition or doctrinal definition.
> [Italics mine]

The writer was clearly not *boasting* about either of these Anglican attitudes. He was showing how they affected the movement of Anglican authority, its slownes, its caution, its holding off; by contrast Rome looks trigger-happy with definitions and sometimes proscriptions and sanctions – though no doubt he detected a change in these Roman attitudes in the decade since John XXIII: a change even in Roman curial attitudes, though much more marked outside Rome.

Windsor I was not attempting to provide more than an agenda, a *status questionis*, but these two papers were doing so with a clarity, a cooling effect, which if heeded would influence the principal debate on authority for the next decade. They are an example of trying to get away, by reflection, from the talismanic effect of words used as banners of loyalty.

Growing together

The last paper listed for Windsor I was in fact the first to be disposed of. The Common Declaration between Pope and Archbishop had made a somewhat unfortunate dichotomy between 'theological matters' and 'matters of practical difficulty felt on either side', by far the chief of which was mixed marriages (see Chapter 24). The Declaration added the hope that 'responsible contacts' between the Communions might induce them to 'strive *in common* to find solutions for all the great problems that face those who believe in Christ in the world of today' (FR, p. 118).

The phrase 'growing together' had come into use at Gazzada and was taken as the title of the Windsor Paper. The paper added the subtitle 'An assessment of the opportunities for collaboration between the two Churches beyond the theological field'. Plainly this did not mean 'unrelated to the theological field'. The current phrase 'non-theological factors' is normally taken negatively to mean things that divide us, whether we know any theology or not.[3] The paper chose to deal with those problems and opportunities for Christian *witness* in a world hugely different from that in which Anglicans and Roman Catholics had separated – a difference which was growing more startling every day. What had already been said from the beginning about our 'common inheritance' supported the paper's contention that 'the complex and difficult task of making the Christian commitment intellectually and imaginatively respectable' in a world which had largely lost its religious resonance cannot wait upon the solution of 'our historic differences'. Cannot and *need* not. The paper was applauded but it was becoming clear that the energies of the commission were to be confined to theology.

Sub-commissions

Quite early the Windsor I meeting broke up into three sub-commissions which prepared brief preliminary papers on the three doctrinal subjects of Eucharist, Ministry and Authority. The Eucharist paper was a joint statement, positive and even optimistic, though on some points it 'agreed' merely to differ. When presented to the full meeting it had to be enlarged by about 50 per cent with a section beginning boldly 'The doctrine expressed represents only one viewpoint among Anglicans'. This put rather a damper on the last words of the paper: 'we are agreed that there is not sufficient disagreement between us to constitute an obstacle to full communion.'

The paper on ministry was very much shorter, and devoted only a couple of paragraphs to delineating a shared doctrine of ministry. Its second section dealt rather confusedly with the question of Anglican Orders (a fuller and clearer paper had been supplied at Malta) and its last section showed some echoes of the 'Growing together' paper.

'Church and authority' was the most helpful of these papers. It was schematic, almost a syllabus. It defined its purpose in a way which would still govern the Final Report:

Not to describe positions which hold here and now, but to reflect on an *ecclesiology* which would shape the future *church*, built on the primary biblical concept of *koinonia*. This method enables us better to shed past accretions and to enrich authentic traditions, in order better to carry out the Church's mission to the world.

In fidelity to our resolve at Dublin our press release had more sting in its tail:

The measure of our agreement should be made known and the practical recommendations of the Commission should be promptly and hopefully adopted ... The pace of theological convergence is quickening, but not fast enough to dictate the tempo for our co-operation in joint projects for fulfilling the Church's mission to the world. Men cannot always, with whatever goodwill, set time limits to the resolution of theological differences, but can and should make no delay in growing together by facing together the mounting problems of mission to today's world.

The press was rather lukewarm. Its interest in religious affairs had cooled in the years since Vatican II and it hardly looked to Anglican–Roman meetings except for something like a dramatic 'deal' over Anglican Orders.

For most of 1970 sub-commission work went on with local assistance preparing for the next full meeting in September. There was some encouragement from Anglican-Roman Catholic events in other spheres.[4]

NOTES

1. He was already a member of the Methodist–Roman Catholic Commission.
2. He was prevented by illness from being at Windsor for the first meeting.
3. Some of these, but by no means all, have been touched on earlier in these pages.
4. At Windsor we had invited papers from outside experts on the subject of morals. No one pressed harder for this than the Anglican co-chairman, the Bishop of Ossory, and he found plenty of sympathy on both sides. Pairs of papers were to be asked for on two themes:
   1. *The making, commanding and enforcement of moral judgements within the Church.*
        Anglican – Professor G. W. Dunstan, King's College, London
      Roman Catholic – Philippe Delhaye, Dean of the Theological Faculty, Louvain
   2. *The relations of men and women*
        Anglican – Professor Gordon Dunstan
      Roman Catholic – Fr Maurice O'Leary, Director of the Roman Catholic Marriage Advisory Council.

16

Cardinal Willebrands
in England

Three days after the Windsor meeting finished, the Week of Prayer for Christian Unity began. On its first Sunday evening, 18 January, Cardinal Willebrands (he had been made a Cardinal in April 1969) preached to a packed church in Great St Mary's, Cambridge. The Cardinal began with a quotation from Langland's *Piers Plowman*:

> ... come with me you fools
> into Unity of Holy Church and hold we us there ...
>   And call we all to the commons
> that they come into Unity and there abide
> and do battle against Belial's children.

With a string of quotations from the New Testament, he illustrated the glory of unity. He summarized events from the beginning of the Vatican Council down to the 'first fruits' of Anglican–Roman Catholic resolve in the meeting just ended at Windsor.

He then moved on to his distinctive and striking theme. He quoted the Council's document *On the Bishop's Pastoral Office*, which asserts that the local or 'particular' Church is that in which the one holy, Catholic and apostolic Church is truly present and operates. He quoted the Decree on Ecumenism (para. 14):

> The heritage handed down by the apostles was received in different
> forms and ways, so that from the beginnings of the Church it has had

136

a varied development in various places, thanks to a similar variety of natural gifts and conditions of life.

The sermon was a long one – space allows only recalling a striking phrase or two:

If we are only going to fossilize, common sense would seem to suggest that it is not very important whether we do so together or separately. Unity is vital only if it is a vital unity.

The sermon ended with Philippians 2:1–2:

So, if there is any encouragement in Christ, any incentive of love, and participation in the Spirit, any affection and sympathy, complete my joy by being of the same mind, having the same love, being in full accord and of one mind.

It was a memorable visit, with a sermon which lifted ARCIC and became a landmark in ecumenical literature.

After preaching in Westminster Cathedral, the Cardinal moved north to Liverpool to preach in the Anglican Cathedral. For generations Liverpool had had a reputation which was the reverse of ecumenical. The Catholic population, with a high proportion of Irish immigrants, was well countered by a strong contingent generally described as 'Orange'. In recent years the principal church leaders had done much to cool animosity. By 1970 an excellent climate of friendliness had been achieved by three highly civilized men: the Catholic Archbishop Andrew Beck, the Dean of the Anglican Cathedral, Edward Patey, and the Methodist Superintendent, Reg Kissack.

The Forty Martyrs

In 1970 the religious thermometer had been raised above blood heat by the fact that the process of the honouring of forty Catholic martyrs was nearing completion. The process was in the hands of the curial Congregation for the Causes of Saints, separated only in May 1969 from the Congregation of Rites, which had dealt with canonizations since founded in 1588 by Sixtus V. Its prefect at the time was Cardinal Bertoli.

The 'postulator general' or man in charge of promoting the cause of the forty English martyrs (several of whom had been pupils of the English College in Rome where Ramsey had stayed in 1966) was the Jesuit Paolo Molinari. He was an Oxford graduate, completely bi-lingual, sharp of mind, but of the utmost courtesy. His English collaborator was a London Jesuit, Fr James Walsh.

Ramsey, who had been consulted at an early stage, now changed his mind and issued a statement printed in *The Tablet*, which began by asserting his belief in the rightness of honouring sanctity wherever found, but went on to say that he feared the canonization would encourage a 'siege mentality', 'polemical self-consciousness' a 'kind of martyrdom complex'. It is easy to be wise after the event, but hard to resist the thought that this statement was a miscalculation. With the canonization process so far advanced, anything that looked like an attempt to stop it was likely to do no more than aggravate the Roman Catholic emotions the Archbishop feared.[1]

The British Council of Churches, which had a joint working party with the (non-member) Roman Catholic Church, a group which included the Anglican Bishops of Bangor and Bristol, issued a cool and balanced statement.

On 21 December, the *Sunday Times* entered the lists with a leader:

If words have any meaning, [the martyrs] died for their faith.
Is it believed in Lambeth that obscurantist forces in Rome are
deliberately bringing the case forward now after so many years to
rebuff the ecumenical spirit? This supposes that there are some
Roman Catholics so Machiavellian as to anticipate the reaction
from Lambeth and if there are, Lambeth has risen to the bait.

On Christmas Eve, *The Times*, in a leader headed 'Martyrs Memorial', reminded its readers that the mills of the Vatican ground slow and that this particular mill had begun grinding in the 1880s. It suggested that the Archbishop was 'perhaps too apprehensive'. 'Polemical Christianity evokes so little response now when so many churchmen are rightly seeking ways towards closer unity, that any encouragement it receives is not likely to be lasting.'

On the same day Ramsey's press officer told the *Telegraph* that 'the Archbishop will not go on complaining about it'.

In Rome there was some slight rattling of nerves and it was suggested to the postulators that their communication with the SPCU might be stepped up, especially in anticipation of Willebrands' January visit, when 'it would be very difficult for him to avoid the subject'.[2] It was decided that the best occasion for him to meet it would be in his sermon at Liverpool. It turned out to be a happy choice, in one very strange way.

He was received everywhere with the greatest warmth, both ecclesiastical and civil – in the Town Hall by the Lord Mayor, in a busy parish church where the preacher was the Orthodox Archbishop Athenagoras of Thyateira and finally in the crowded cathedral.

The service began quietly enough, but as Archbishop Beck moved to read a gospel passage, well-orchestrated shouts came from groups of Protestant extremists dotted about the cathedral. The disturbance brought out the best in Willebrands. He stood motionless until the noise was quite finished, when he began his sermon[3] as if nothing had happened. Needless to say he had his audience pinioned from the first word.

> I find myself thinking here tonight in Lancashire of one special aspect of Christian witness, one which I am convinced you would not expect me honestly to remain silent about. The witness of martyrdom. [Lancashire has one of the highest numbers of Catholic martyrs in the country.] We think first and foremost of the martyr as one who witnesses to Christ in the face of Christ's declared enemies. But it is the ugliest and unhappiest mark on Christian history that men have been prepared to kill in the name of Christ. They have been prepared to brand as treason or as some other crime the faith of those who saw their loyalty to Christ in other terms, and no tradition can be alone assigned this melancholy distinction. So martyrdom has been possible even within Christian common-wealths.
>
> Those who have heroically taken up the Cross of Christ do not cease to live for us, or deserve our honour, because we have banished, we hope for ever, the wretchedness, the discord, the violence, the pride of the somewhat savage age in which they bore their witness. Still less does this blessed change mean that they, as privileged members of Christ's body, cease to intercede for us; it means only that, in the wisdom of eternal life, they will be praying with us for reconciliation, for a healing of the wounds of history, for a unity which will transform our ancestral pieties and our loyalty to our roots into an all-embracing charity.

The evening was a deeply satisfying one, though sadly I never came across any reference to the sermon in papers or correspondence south of the Trent – another example perhaps of the geographical lopsidedness of England.

There seemed however to be considerable echoes of it in the allocution with which Pope Paul VI announced the canonization to a consistory on 18 May. To the official allocution which he gave during the canonization liturgy Paul VI added a sentence of his own – in his own hand late on the night before the ceremony:

> There will be no seeking to lessen the legitimate prestige and the worthy patrimony of piety and usage proper to the Anglican Church when the Roman Church – this humble 'Servant of the servants of God' – is able to embrace her ever beloved Sister in the one authentic communion of the family of Christ.

There was no question of such an autograph addition being left out of the *Osservatore Romano* or the official *Acta Apostolicae Sedes* (AAS 62 (1970), p. 753), and though there were few Anglicans present in St Peter's (Dr Ramsey 'felt unable to be represented' other than by his resident representative in Rome, Dr Harry Smythe)[4] the sentence made a deep impression and found its way into ARCIC's report, 'Authority in the Church II' (FR, p. 91, note 2).

Regnans in Excelsis

By a not very happy coincidence, 1970 was also the fourth centenary of the papal bull *Regnans in Excelsis* by which Pius V had excommunicated Queen Elizabeth I. Even in the reign of the first Elizabeth this idea of papal power was denied by many canonists. By the time of the second Elizabeth it was merely quaint. In 1570 it helped to establish the idea that Catholics, even the recusant priests in spite of their steadfast denials, were hostile agents of a foreign power and hence political traitors and fifth-columnists. In fact all the bull did among the great majority of Catholics, who shared the sixteenth-century mystique of monarchy,[5] was to set up an intolerable conflict of conscience.

It was from Canada, strangely enough, that in June 1970 representations came to the SPCU through the British Ministry to the Holy See suggesting that the 1570 bull might be withdrawn or abolished. It was now so much of a museum piece that the idea was not pursued.

Small steps

In May 1970 there issued from the SPCU a further instalment of the *Directorium Ecumenicum*, which began three years earlier as a series of direction for putting into practice the Roman Catholic ecumenical policy, enshrined in the Second Vatican Council decree: the first part had been a slightly hurried attempt to guide a world-wide Catholic public still somewhat bewildered by the change of official attitude since the days when it was doubted whether they should say the Lord's Prayer with other Christians.

Even before this first part was issued many bishops and others saw that there was a long-term problem of education resulting from the rapid changes. The second instalment of the *Directorium* now addressed itself to one part of this problem under the heading *Ecumenism in Higher Education*, printed in the SPCU Information Service (no. 10, 1970/II).

The SPCU had full responsibility for the text, but it had not been arrived at except in various degrees of 'collaboration' which often involved strenuous argument with other departments of the Curia. This was reflected in the result. But it did, nonetheless, avoid the often criticized Vatican habit of seeming to tell every local church, of whatever location, tradition or culture, how to solve the innumerable problems of putting the ideal into practice.

Awareness of the limitations was more evident still in the next document, put out three months later. It was modestly styled 'a working instrument at the disposal of the ecclesiastical authorities', and given the title *Reflections and Suggestions Concerning Ecumenical Dialogue* (SPCU Information Service, no. 12, December 1970). It acknowledged its debt to a consultation of experts from many parts of the world actively engaged in ecumenical dialogue (held in February 1967) and to a similar paper put out by the Joint Working Group of the Roman Catholic Church and the World Council of Churches.

This last was about a third of the length of the SPCU paper, though both had sectional headings which were virtually identical: 'Nature', 'Bases', 'Forms and Participants', 'Themes', 'Conditions', and 'Method', or 'Practice'. It was crisper in style than the Roman Catholic document (the original of which was curial Latin) and not larded with quotations. Some of the reflections and suggestions may today sound platitudinous but that is hardly more than a tribute to the progress made in twenty years.

ARCIC in Venice

Going to Venice for its second meeting (21–22 September 1970) was a stroke of luck for ARCIC. Through the good offices of the late Don Germano Pataro, a Venetian priest, a theologian and a man of remarkable influence in the *Serenissima*, we were lodged at a convent near the Accademia and held our discussions in a fine renaissance room in the palace on the Isola Sangiorgio, looking across the lagoon to San Marco and the Doge's Palace.

It will be remembered that at Windsor subcommissions were assigned work on the three themes which ARCIC saw as central – Eucharist, Ministry and Authority. These subcommissions were based respectively in South Africa, USA/Canada and England (Oxford).

The Commission was conscious of the need to show that it was doing something and getting somewhere, but also of the danger of releasing partial statements which might be misunderstood.[6] It therefore hoped that by the end of Venice some preliminary published statement (claiming to be no more than a progress report) would be possible.

The Commission did achieve its purpose with the three Venice Papers as they came to be called.[7] The South African sub-commission did manage to work jointly, and its draft supplied much of the Eucharist paper.

At the other extreme, the Oxford sub-commission elicited a number of interesting essays on the problem of authority but there was simply no time to bring them to bear on the drafting of a joint statement. In themselves these three papers helped to set out the agenda rather than make progress with it. As the critic in *The Month*, Michael Walsh, put it, 'the decision to publish them at all is more important than the content of the documents'. Publication eventually took place in mid-February 1971, but in the three months before that a three-act comedy drama was played.

Act I. The Commission and their obliging publishers (*Theology*, *The Clergy Review* and *One in Christ*) had agreed on a January date. On 18 November the evangelical member of the Commission, Julian Charley, wrote to the co-chairmen and to the acting Anglican Secretary, Michael Moore, saying that it had been agreed at Venice that there should be no publication except with an extended joint comment by himself and the French Dominican Jean Tillard.[8] But since Tillard was in Canada, it would be impossible for him and Charley to concoct anything together in time for a February publication. He then put strongly his case for this comment. Charley's 'constituency' (that is, Evangelicals) was cool and suspicious about the Anglican–Roman Catholic dialogue, but was steadily growing in strength in the Church of England. Hence a joint comment by Tillard and himself was of more than personal importance – it could make reservations look less of a party matter.

Neither Michael Moore, the Anglican acting secretary, nor Gordon Dunstan, the editor of *Theology*, was sympathetic to his plea. The commission's co-chairmen, Bishops McAdoo and Clark, said they would accept a brief reference in an introductory note by the Anglican secretary, to be followed by the comment in a later number. This compromise was accepted and the curtain fell on Act I.

Act II was shorter, and the scene moved to Rome. The curtain rises on the present writer telephoning from his office to rural Norfolk informing the Catholic chairman that Cardinal Willebrands was fairly seriously ill in hospital, and could give no attention to the Venice Papers until it would be too late for a January publication. Meanwhile the proposed note by Michael Moore was sent to the SPCU, there amended, and publication was settled on for February. End of Act II.

Act III was almost pure comedy. Michael Moore circularized all concerned with the terrifying news that the Jesuit periodical *The Month* had got hold of the papers and was threatening to steal a march. In the end it turned out that all *The Month* had was a draft press release intended to go with the publication.

The reader must be indulgent if he feels that all this sounds faintly like MI5 and the CIA at their most whimsical. In 1970 both sides were treading on unsure ground. What now seems clear is that we were still looking for a firm language, a more unambiguous use of terms both traditional and newly fashioned. The venerable Lord Fisher, who could always be relied on for a tart comment, said that in the Eucharist paper I–II 'the only solid fact is that the Church is the *ecclesia*'. Not quite fair, but many others noted the lack of any coherent ecclesiology.

NOTES

1. The very gentle bishop of Lancaster, Brian Foley, reported that his clergy were 'climbing the wall: I have never seen them so incensed'.
2. Letter from Heenan to Willebrands, 22 December. When this reached London it had become 'disturbing reports that the SPCU sent a protest to the postulation and requires no decision to be made until you (Willebrands) reach London'.
3. The full text is in the SPCU archives. The section on martyrs is printed in SPCU Information Service.

4. Harold Wilson's government was represented by Robert Mellish, the Chief Whip – who was a Catholic.
5. Vividly present in Shakespeare, though consistent with quiet criticism of government and institutions.
6. An article in the *Washington Post* just after Windsor (12 January) under the headline 'Anglican/Roman Catholic talks produce little results' showed how, in spite of the clear statement on the Malta Report, it was assumed that a frontal attack on the problem of Anglican Orders should be a priority.
7. They were quite distinct of course from the Venice Statement (1976–77) better known as 'Authority I' and forming part of the *Final Report*.
8. These two had become close friends and their mutual sympathy was to be a very positive factor in the Commission's work.

17

Windsor Meeting II:
the Eucharist

After the Venice meeting it was clear that the Commission needed to concentrate on one subject at a time. This subject for Windsor was the Eucharist, and the immediate point of departure was the Venice 'trial' paper.

ARCIC was not alone or even first in the field. In France the Groupe des Dombes had been studying the subject since 1964, though it did not publish its Agreement until 1972. In USA a 'Statement' had been issued by a Lutheran–Roman Catholic group in 1967. In August of that year the Faith and Order Commission of the WCC, meeting at Bristol, had resolved on a 'Resumé of the emerging ecumenical consensus on the Eucharist' which drew on work going back as far as the Lund Conference of 1952. This was published in 1971.[1] Already the two subjects of the 'real presence' and the sacrificial character of the Eucharist had been seen as central. ARCIC stood out in its belief that 'substantial agreement' could be achieved on these central themes.

The Venice paper was content to lean quite heavily on the working paper supplied by the South African Anglican–Roman Catholic Commission. The first three Venice paragraphs are taken almost word for word from the South African paper. In turn echoes of both are found in the Windsor statement, that is, the completed Agreed Statement which forms the first part of the *Final Report* (FR, pp. 12–16).

The Windsor statement should never be read apart from the Elucidation which was printed in 1979 to meet the criticisms which followed Windsor's publication.

The Windsor statement begins with a paragraph taken straight from the South African paper, where it appears under the heading 'Eucharistic language'.

> In the course of the Church's history several traditions have
> developed in expressing Christian understanding of the Eucharist.

Windsor goes on:

> Our intention has been to seek a deeper understanding of the reality
> of the eucharist which is consonant with biblical teaching and with
> the tradition of our common inheritance.

The last phrase caused difficulty for some readers. Where did this 'common inheritance' end? In 1971 the average Roman Catholic, neither a historian nor a theologian, if asked what Anglicans believed about the Eucharist would probably have answered 'I doubt if they believe in the real presence' or 'they put the martyrs to death for celebrating the sacrifice of the Mass' or 'they don't all believe the same thing'. He would have felt more confident in denying that an Anglican minister, whatever he believed the Eucharist to be, had any power to celebrate it – he had heard of Leo XIII and Anglican Orders. Hence when the programme for Anglican–Roman Catholic dialogue was first made known, the assumption at all but the highest levels was that the question of Anglican Orders would be among the first to be broached.

It was common enough to hear Catholics who had occasion to attend an Anglican Eucharist (a rare thing) in some types of church remarking 'Why, it is very like Mass'. (The reverse was also true.) An instructed Anglican might answer that it had never been the intention of his forebears to found a new Church, but only to return to the purer forms of the historic Church which involved getting rid of a good deal that could be lumped together as Romish corruptions. Thus the famous Thirty-Nine Articles which the Anglican found bound at the back of his Prayer Book were a curious mixture of things he was expected to believe and things he was told to disapprove of.

The Articles

By the time Anglican–Roman Catholic dialogue began officially in the 1960s many Anglicans felt the need to clarify the position of the Articles. They were a sixteenth-century production which had evolved over the very disturbed early years of the English Reformation, reflecting much of the intermittent continental Protestant influence of those times and little of 'classical' Anglicanism, generally reckoned to have been inaugurated by Hooker. Yet Anglican ordinands were at that time still expected to subscribe to them.

In 1968 a very distinguished commission produced the report *Subscription and Assent to the Thirty-Nine Articles* (SPCK, 1968),[2] which came out in time for the Lambeth Conference of that year. Looking at the origin of the Articles, the report says 'the wish for a solid front against Rome was undoubtedly the dominant motive'. Para. 59 attempts a definition or short description: 'The Articles are agreed propositions showing what attitude the Church of England took on certain controverted points of divinity in the sixteenth century.' Para. 65 adds 'much of the treatment from No. 9 onwards is controversial, polemical and negative, reflecting either the assumptions of or a reaction against late medieval theology'.

To the question, 'What function have they today?' the commission discerned at least four possible answers:

1. To define orthodoxy and heresy.
2. To be an 'identity card' for the Church of England.
3. To serve as title deeds for an Evangelical standpoint with the Church of England.
4. As a minimum doctrinal standard or agreed syllabus.

None of these four was generally felt to be satisfactory. The preface noted with approval that in the Roman Catholic Church the anti-Modernist oath and the Tridentine *professio* had been replaced by a much briefer *professio* which was 'generally being interpreted in the more liberal spirit of the theology of Vatican II'.

We may seem to have dwelt rather long on the Articles in view of the fact that they played very little explicit part in the ARCIC discussions, but critics of ARCIC were often ready to appeal to them.

Doctrine in the Church of England

Whatever the range of its thinking, ARCIC was always conscious that its ultimate agreed statements would be addressed to others than its scholarly peers. Hence its difficult task of keeping the statements short and as simple as possible. The twentieth century has been one of great activity in eucharistic theology. Professor Fairweather in an introductory paper noted that much of this found no expression in official texts.

In 1938 there had been published the report *Doctrine in the Church of England*. The commission which compiled it had been set up as early as 1922, and four conditions were laid down for its make-up:

1. There should be a wider representation of all parties.
2. They should be men of wide and tolerant temper.
3. They should be constructive, imaginative minds able to create a synthesis.
4. They should be young enough to leave hope of finishing the job (under 45, it was suggested).[3]

Thus *Doctrine in the Church of England*, though so different in tone from the Thirty-Nine Articles, was like it in being not a full statement of Anglican doctrine but a reaction to a situation.

This characteristic was not least evident in the central section on 'Sacraments' (more than a third of the book). More than half of this was devoted to the Eucharist. William Temple, in his introduction, admitted 'wide divergences within our Church, but to a great extent they are divergences rather of emphasis than of substance'.

In the body of the report, treatment of the Eucharist follows much the same order as ARCIC's except that it includes a section on 'Priesthood' (p. 156), which for ARCIC comes in the agreed statement on Ministry, known as the 'Canterbury'. In reading the ARCIC statement it is necessary to remember this: some of our earliest critics did not.

Sacrifice and agreement

The Windsor statement attracted much comment by confining its mention of the Catholic doctrine of transubstantiation to a footnote (para. 6) and using the word 'sacrifice' very sparingly, again adding a highly compressed historical footnote. Considering the vast bulk of literature on both subjects during the late Middle Ages, the Reformation and the Counter-Reformation and in the first half of the twentieth century, this could hardly fail to strike many readers as rather too much of a *tour de force*.

To this several answers could be given:

1. A high proportion of this enormous literature is polemical. This is true even of some of the twentieth-century writing, for example, that which has been prompted by the revived discussion of Anglican Orders.
2. Much of the literature was not concerned with what ARCIC was looking for: 'agreement on essential matters where it considers that doctrine admits of no divergence'.
3. Dr Mascall, in the foreword to his *Corpus Christi*, commands some sympathy when he writes:

    the great tragedy of the reformation lay in the fact that, while the great majority of the Reformers were desperately anxious to return, for both their ecclesiastical order and their liturgical reforms, to the practice of primitive Christianity, neither they nor anyone else at that time had any adequate knowledge of what primitive Christianity was.

4. Many of the 'reforms' introduced in the sixteenth century concerned not so much doctrine as discipline (vernacular liturgy being the most obvious example); they were considered by Trent though not adopted and have been recently taken over in the Roman Catholic Church.

In dealing with doctrine Dr Fairweather had pointed out the lack of parallel between Roman and Anglican eucharistic literature. It is clear that Rome offers more documents with what Fairweather called 'a high degree of formal authority', which of course does not exempt them from interpretation.

Eucharist sacrifice: subcommission work at Oxford

A subcommission met at Oxford in England months before the Windsor meeting to provide material for the latter's discussion of 'Sacrifice'. It had no simple task of confronting a Roman Catholic and an Anglican position, since Anglican statements on doctrine seldom give only one point of view.

John Halliburton, who had taken over the mothering of this English (Oxford) sub-commission, reported that the need to provide more than an Anglican position and a Roman Catholic position was quickly recognized. Halliburton had in fact provided an introduction and bibliographical (historical) guide which owed much to Mascall's work already cited. It ended by stressing that concern for the subject was just as great among

Evangelicals as among Anglo-Catholics. The two concerns had recently shown less contrast and more convergence. Following the collapse of the English Anglican–Methodist unity scheme, members of the two parties had collaborated in yet another 'response to a situation', a book called *Growing into Union* (SPCK, 1970). This was a kind of alternative scheme, but also contained as an appendix a joint essay by Dr Mascall and the evangelical scholar Michael Green called 'Eucharistic sacrifice – some interim agreement'.

Evangelicals would normally be thought of as still taking no. 31 of the Articles of Religion seriously – more seriously anyway than Anglo-Catholics:

> The offering of Christ once made is that perfect redemption,
> propitiation and satisfaction for all the sins of the whole world, both
> original and actual; and there is none other satisfaction for sin but that
> alone. Wherefore the sacrifice of Masses, in which it was commonly
> said that the Priest did offer Christ for the quick and the dead, to have
> remission of pain or guilt, were blasphemous fables and dangerous
> deceits.

It was the second half of this that caused trouble: the first half was fully accepted by Roman Catholics and had been since Trent, though many Evangelicals still doubted the fact.

The second part has of course attracted the attention and the dislike especially of Roman Catholic readers. Modern commentators on the Articles have denied that it is intended to reject the sacrificial character of the Eucharist. Indeed, Bicknell begins his commentary categorically:

> The New Testament says very little in detail about the Eucharist as a
> sacrifice, but it leaves no doubt, wherever it is mentioned, that the
> Church regarded it as such.

Preparatory papers

Edward Yarnold's first paper for the Oxford preparatory group (he contributed three) offered comment on the classical Tridentine passage from Session XXII (DS 1743). Beginning 'It is quite clear that the Council is far from teaching that the Mass adds anything to Calvary', he asks 'what does it teach?' He answers: (a) the Mass applies the sacrifice of Christ to our daily need for forgiveness and in *this* sense is 'propitiatory' (a word abhorred by Protestants), and (b) the Mass is a commemoration of Christ's sacrifice. He suggested that some expressions of Trent led post-Tridentine theologians to assume that Christ is sacrificed afresh in some sense in each Mass. This kind of thought had been generally abandoned by Roman Catholic theologians. He discerned in recent authoritative documents 'an attempt to make less use of the word sacrifice in explanation of the Mass'.

Bishop Christopher Butler developed much further Yarnold's intimation of the *sacramental* nature of the eucharistic sacrifice, expounding its link with the Pauline use of *mysterion*: he was suspicious of relying too much on Old Testament models (St Thomas would have agreed strongly).

Fr Yarnold described his second paper as 'an attempt to produce a statement avoiding the term sacrifice' and indicating what seem to be points of disagreement as well as agreement.

Julian Charley's paper (no. 10) offers simply some comments on the other sub-commission papers.

Another sub-commission met under Bishop Clark's roof at Poringland from 12 to 16 April. It produced two draft paragraphs: 'The Mystery of the Eucharist' and 'The Eucharist and the sacrifice of Christ'. These became, after much discussion, sections I and II of the Windsor statement (FR, pp. 12–14; no part of the *Report* better illustrates the value of small group discussion and conversation). Seven pregnant lines were added:

> In the eucharistic prayer the Church continues to make a perpetual memorial of Christ's death, and his members, united with God and one another, give thanks for all his mercies, entreat the benefit of his passion on behalf of the whole Church, participate in these benefits and enter into the movement of self-offering. (FR, p. 14)

The word 'sacrifice' has a very long history. The two dozen lines devoted by ARCIC to 'The Eucharist and the sacrifice of Christ' are carefully chosen and the statement very compact. The Commission's aim was not to provide a comprehensive theology of the Eucharist, still less a history of the theories and disputes which had befallen it, but to provide (if it could) a statement of substantial agreement. This involved examining much of this history – not only the history of Anglican–Roman Catholic controversy but also that of pre-Reformation teaching about the Eucharist.

Bishop Harry McAdoo, Anglican co-chairman, described the Agreed Statement on Sacrifice thus:

It is moving out of past ideas such as 're-sacrificing Christ', past ideas such as that there can be no legitimate place in eucharistic theology for sacrificial language.

It should be said that many Anglicans had attempted this sort of examination before.[4]

Under its second sub-heading, 'The Eucharist and the sacrifice of Christ', ARCIC states:

Christ's redeeming death and resurrection took place once and for all in history. Christ's death on the cross, the culmination of his whole life of obedience was the one, perfect and sufficient sacrifice for the sins of the world. There can be no repetition of or addition to what was then accomplished once for all by Christ. Any attempt to express a nexus between the sacrifice of Christ and the eucharist must not obscure this fundamental fact of the Christian Faith. (FR, p. 13)

It would be difficult to argue that the Church had ever questioned this fundamental fact, less difficult to point to practices and to language which have obscured it.

The introduction of '*memorial*', in italics, which catches the eye (p. 14), as a seeming substitute for 'sacrifice' would summon up in most minds those things put up in so many market places after the 1914–18 war. Yet St Thomas Aquinas, for example, apostrophizes the Eucharist as

> memoriale mortis domini
> panis vivus vitam praestans homini

> O thou memorial of our Lord's own *dying*
> O *bread* that living art and *vivifying*

ARCIC uses a Greek word, *anamnesis*. When Christ spoke at the Last Supper he was clearly not just recommending to the apostles an anniversary party after his death. ARCIC called this *memorial* 'the Church's effectual proclamation of God's mighty acts . . . of the *totality* of God's reconciling action in (Christ)'.

Again Aquinas, that master of the succinct, rare among theologians, had anticipated this:

Se nascens dedit socium
Convescens in edulium
Se moriens in pretium
Se regnans dat in praemium

Being born, he gave himself
    as comrade, as friend;
eating with them he gave himself
    as their food;
dying he gave himself as the price
    of their redemption;
reigning (in heaven) he gave himself
    as their prize.

The last line brings in an element which Aquinas' philosophical contemporaries loved to wrestle with but whose reality they took for granted – the relation between time and eternity. It is an element indispensable from the mystery of the Eucharist.

The Eucharist is not merely a memorial, however effectual. It looks forward – it shows forth the death of the Lord *until he comes*. It cannot be considered apart from eschatology, or the last things. It is a pledge of future glory which is eternal glory. But in the meantime it clearly involves a traffic between heaven and earth. To remember that time and eternity are incommensurable is to avoid pitfalls in the understanding of the Eucharistic sacrifice and anamnesis.

Reception

ARCIC was received with some appreciation, but also, on the Roman Catholic side at least, with reservations and hostility. The then Bishop of Portsmouth, Derek Warlock, spotted that some of the comments published in the press were made with such speed that they must have been prepared without reference to the statement.

We must see how the commission classified the reactions on 'Sacrifice' and how it handled them.

The policy of 'Elucidation' was not arrived at without discussion. Other courses were open:

— to launch into debate, which hardly anybody thought likely to advance our aim, least of all before our Final Report was submitted;
— to tinker with the statement, which would diminish our credibility;
— to elucidate what we had said, which would absolve us from the charge of pontificating and perhaps widen the range of sympathy and understanding.

The whole of the full meeting at Chichester Theological College (20 August–8 September 1977; FR, p. 104, para. 9) was devoted to deciding on this and allotting the work to subcommissions.

Elucidation on the Eucharist statement was published on 7 June 1979 (FR, p. 104, para. 10). It was much longer than the original statement. It began by reiterating what it meant by substantial agreement[5] as explained in both the Eucharist and Ministry statements. It went on to list the more representative and important criticisms.

> *In spite of the firm assertion* ... of the once for all nature of Christ's sacrifice, some have still been anxious that the term *anamnesis* may conceal the reintroduction of the theory of a repeated immolation. Others have suspected that the word refers not only to the historical events of salvation but also to an eternal sacrifice in heaven. Others again have doubted whether *anamnesis* sufficiently implies the reality indicated by traditional sacrificial language and the adequacy of the Commission's exegesis of *anamnesis* has been questioned.
> (FR, p. 17, para. 3)

A common feature of the language of the 'representative' criticisms may be noted. Words like 'anxious', 'conceal', 'suspected' too easily reflect what the late R. P. C. Hanson in a witty essay[6] called the 'conspiracy' theory of ecumenism. Only a few extremists (see below) openly charged the Commission with *consciously* having such unworthy aims, but even Cardinal Heenan went so far as to write that 'ecumenists are *tempted* to find formulas like *politicians*' (italics mine).

The Commission had little trouble finding sources, ranging from the New Testament to recent liturgical revisions and instructions, to support its use of *anamnesis* (FR, pp. 18–19). It was satisfied that the word expressed 'the traditional understanding of *sacramental* reality'. I have italicized the word. The common feature of the criticisms cited was to fail to appreciate the unique nature of this reality.

The Real Presence

The Venice paper had treated the Presence of Christ in the Eucharist very briefly, noting how controversy had caused attention to be focused too narrowly on the *way* in which Christ is present in the consecrated bread and wine. J. M. Tillard, in a key ARCIC paper (no. 29) entitled 'The presence of the Body and Blood of the Lord', says

> This question [of the Presence] harks back to the question of the Sacrifice, and unless we have first clarified this latter question we cannot say we are in complete agreement on the former.

From the time that eucharistic theology assumed such prominence in the early Middle Ages, discussion was dominated by the Presence. This imbalance was reflected in much of the abusive practice of which the Reformers complained – the concentration on the elevation, the infrequency of communion and so on – though Protestants often went far beyond mere reactions to abuses. Here again, both abuse and reaction stemmed from a failure to understand the nature of sacramental reality.

Proper sacramental language, though it cannot escape the use of terms like 'in', 'under', and even 'veiled', does not involve 'localized' presence. Nevertheless to the question 'What is this?' the believer who receives the Eucharistic bread has to reply, according to *his faith*, 'It is the body of Christ, who gives himself as food, as the Bread of life' (op. cit., para. 12).

The term *transubstantiation* is introduced in a footnote (FR, p. 14, para. 6f.) Tillard turns to its content:

> Communion with Christ in the Eucharist presupposes his *true* presence *effectually* signified by the bread wine which in this *mystery* *become* his body and blood. [Italics mine]

Some thought that the footnote was taking away what the sentence had just conceded. These were the people who talked of the 'dogma of transubstantiation'. There is only a dogma of the true, real and substantial presence of Christ in the sacrament, which we perceive by faith, and which comes about through a *mirabilis conversio*, what the footnote calls a 'mysterious and radical change'. Those who coined and put into circulation the term 'transubstantiation' and the Fathers of Trent who thought it an 'apt and convenient' way of describing the *mirabilis conversio* did not think they were *explaining* the *mystery*. Tillard and others have argued that they were more concerned to *guard against* explanations of an improper kind – not only to safeguard the reality of the presence but also to avoid heavily materialistic or physical ideas of this presence (op. cit., para. 13; cf. *Doctrine in the Church of England*, p. 173).

The rest of the opening paragraph (FR, p. 14, para. 6) warns against treating the real presence in isolation from the whole of Christ's redemptive action.

Paragraph 7 stresses the various ways in which Christ is present to the faithful. It echoes the even stronger paragraph 9 of 'Eucharisticum Mysterium' (the Instruction of 1967) especially its last sentence: 'the presence of Christ under the species is called "real" not in an exclusive sense as if the other kinds of presence were not real, but *par excellence.*' Paragraphs 8, 9 and 10 of 'Windsor' taken together with the lengthy paragraphs 6 and 7 of the Elucidation deal with the complex question of the role of faith in the Eucharist and, by implication, with the elusive doctrine named (apparently no earlier than 1867) as Receptionism, though found at the Reformation. The famous footnote on Transubstantiation (FR, p. 14) twice uses the word 'change' with regard to the elements, and paragraph 10 (pp. 15–16) says 'the bread and wine *become* the body and blood of Christ'. In its Elucidation on this point (one of the strongest passages in the *Final Report*) the Commission noted that some had been 'unhappy' and suspicious of this 'realistic language' as seeming to involve a physical change in the elements. The first sentence of paragraph 8 of the statement:

The sacramental body and blood of the Saviour are present as an offering to the believer *awaiting his welcome*. [Italics mine]

is logically incompatible with making the offering dependent on the welcome or making it the product of the welcome. The next two sentences put the matter beyond doubt.

When this offering is met by faith a life-giving encounter results. Through faith Christ's presence which does not depend on the individual's faith in order to be the Lord's real gift of himself to his Church – becomes no longer just a presence *for* the believer, but a presence *with* him. It is a life-giving encounter, the presence *with*, that comes from faith.

(Tillard develops this in his paragraph 10.)

The Agreed Statement says quite enough to exclude the doctrine of Receptionism in its strict sense but the Elucidation under the heading 'Gift and reception' (no. 7) ventures an 'opinion' that the acute difficulties of the past have really been a matter of different complementary movements within an indissoluble unity: Christ giving his body and blood, and the communicants 'feeding upon them in their hearts by faith'.

The last Elucidation was on 'Reservation'. No one questioned that the practice of reserving the sacrament for communicating the sick was ancient. It was agreed that historically this purpose had become obscured by the practice of veneration in some of its forms. This was a practical problem on which there was no simple division between Roman Catholics and Anglicans. Briefly, Anglo-Catholics liked Eucharistic devotions and Evangelicals heartily disliked and distrusted them.

In the Roman Catholic Church recent liturgical reforms, some of them amply pre-dating Vatican II, had implicitly acknowledged some undeniable trends in extra-liturgical devotion. The Instruction of 1967 had devoted its entire chapter III to the matter and began by affirming the 'primary and original purpose of reservation' (para. 49, quoted by ARCIC). Its next paragraph, 50 (already obviously alluded to in ARCIC), began:

When the faithful adore Christ present in the sacrament they should remember that this presence derives from the sacrifice and is directed towards both sacramental and spiritual communion.

The Elucidation candidly admitted (para. 9; FR, p. 24) that Evangelicals would not be reconciled to the idea of any adoration at all. This paragraph contains the only allusion in all the Final Report to the Thirty-Nine Articles – and it is of course to Article 28.

The Sacrament of the Lord's Supper was not by Christ's ordinance reserved, carried about, lifted up or worshipped.

As it moved to its goal the Commission philosophically repeated 'Difference of theology and practice may well co-exist with a real consensus on the essentials of Eucharistic faith – as in fact they do *within* each of our communions'.

Introducing the Elucidation in response to selected criticisms (FR, p. 18, para. 4) the Commission wrote:

Behind these criticisms there lies a profound but often unarticulated
anxiety that the Commission has been using new theological language
which evades unresolved differences. Related to this anxiety is the
further question as to the nature of the agreement claimed by the
Commission. Does the language of the Commission conceal an
ambiguity (either intentional or unintentional) in language which
enables members of the two churches to see their own faith in
the Agreed Statement without having in fact reached a genuine
consensus?

The preface to the Agreed Statement, signed by the co-chairmen, did
its best to state exactly what the document was: 'agreement on essential
points of Eucharistic doctrine', not a 'comprehensive treatment of the
subject'; but 'nothing essential' had been ommitted; it was an expression
of 'consensus at the level of faith'.

The co-chairmen added a description of the Commission as officially
appointed, drawn from many countries and theological backgrounds, and
charged to submit their findings to their respective authorities.

Publication

Anglicans, and particularly Evangelicals, were keen to publish the Report.
Julian Charley put it very well in a letter to Bishop Clark:

> There is nothing more odd than to have made public the fact that we
> have reached a consensus and then to withhold any publication of
> what it contains. I am already meeting with considerable voices of
> alarm in our constituency about what has been agreed and I believe
> it to be absolutely imperative to being everything out into the open
> as soon as possible.

Bishop Clark's approach was rather different. He had written first to the
Archbishop of Canterbury, saying that the statement needed some
'external authority'. Charley predictably replied to this:

> I do not see how it can possibly be given any more 'external'
> authority until it has been made fully public and been open to
> careful consideration.

The two were plainly thinking of two quite different sorts of 'external authority'.

The Tablet invited Bishop Butler to write about ARCIC. He gave a skilful and impartial summary of it with some pointers to further reading and ended:

> I have said that the statement has no ecclesiastical authority. I hope it will be approved by the authorities both at Rome and Canterbury as 'true so far as it goes' and as really disclosing substantial agreement. But it is important that it shall also seem acceptable to 'ordinary believers' and to 'the people of God' in the full richness and complexity of that term. The people of God cannot judge it till they have seen it. So I hope it will be published before long.

This somewhat fruitless insular discussion was happily settled by a letter from Paul VI to Archbishop Ramsey, positive in tone though indicating the limits of the statement and concluding:

> Questions about the continuation of the dialogue, including the publication of the statement, will be dealt with on our side by our Secretariat for Promoting Christian Unity.

The Agreed Statement was published on 31 December 1971, three and a half months after its existence was announced in various newpapers.[7] Unfortunately this allowed time for extremists on either side to work themselves up into a state of hysteria at the very idea. The *Church of England Newspaper* advertised an ultra-Protestant meeting to pray against it in a London church.

On the Catholic side this delay allowed the onset of some cold feet. Fr Flanagan had written to the *Church Times* and *The Tablet* in the name of a group which, with some nerve, had arrogated to itself the title of Catholic Priests Association,[8] attacking the statement at most of its nerve points and calling on the Catholic bishops to repudiate it clearly and emphatically.

But by February 1972, Fr Richard Stewart, summarizing comment to date, was able to show that general press reporting had been welcoming, citing 'warm endorsement' by the Archbishop of Canterbury in the Canterbury *Diocesan Gazette*, and instancing already serious attempts to study the Agreed Statement among clergy and laity in various kinds of groups.[9] Cardinal Heenan got the bishops to supply each his own critique.

Most of them were in some degree sympathetic; a few described the language as 'unfamiliar but sound', and Michael Bowen said outright:

> One must not hastily qualify as ambiguous or falsely irenic language which is merely unfamiliar, not traditional in our own usage.

He was then Bishop of Arundel and Brighton (from whose diocese Fr Flanagan and others had fought the good fight) and had recently taught theology in Rome. It was a nice irony that the second most sympathetic comment came from an Irish bishop, William Philbin, whose diocese, Down and Connor, was effectively Belfast.

It was hard for Englishmen and Irishmen, especially Catholics with their past four centuries, to assimilate, still more identify, 'a common tradition'.

Some, in spite of assurances that there was still 'work in progress' and that there was more to be done, could not shake off the idea that the question of Orders was somehow being shirked.

It was a happy thing that the episcopal conference of England and Wales had an official Theological Commission which co-opted the two episcopal members of ARCIC, Butler and Clark, for its examination of the ARCIC statement. Its report was brief, restrained, cool and judicious.

Cardinal Journet of Fribourg, a theologian much trusted by Paul VI (cf. Chapters 1 and 2 above on the 1950s conversations), contributed the most helpful judgement that the sacrificial character of the Eucharist was adequately asserted in the statement.

In Rome things got off to an unfortunate start. The London *Times* had given quotations some time before the agreed deadline. This was spotted in the Secretariat of State and sharply commented on to the SPCU. A press handout was hastily produced, playing the statement down, describing it as a *simple document d'étude*, 'not yet complete', leaving *essential* points to be clarified. This last phrase was of course a contradiction of the Commission's claim to 'substantial agreement'. This gave aid and comfort to the self-appointed inquisitors in England, but the ultimate effect of the hiccup was small.

NOTES

1. These documents were later collected in the booklet *Modern Eucharistic Agreement*, with an excellent Introduction by Bishop Harry McAdoo, co-chairman of ARCIC (SPCK, 1973).

2. Six members of the commission had taken part in the pre-ARCIC conversations described above.

In *Subscription and Assent* (para. 75) one way of dealing with the Articles which was canvassed but not adopted was called 'light revision', which chiefly would 'remove out-of-date language and delete phrases which have created difficulty'. A model of such revision was given in an appendix, and while Article 31, part 1, was left intact, part 2 was replaced by a bit of good up-to-date ecumenical theology:

The offering of Christ once made upon the Cross is that perfect redemption, propitiation and satisfaction for all the sins of the whole world, both original and actual: and there is no other satisfaction for sin, but that alone.

In the Sacrament of the Holy Communion a perpetual memory is made of the oblation of Christ. No addition to his self-offering on the Cross is intended or conveyed. Therein we offer ourselves and our gifts, and receiving the spiritual food of the Body and Blood of Christ, are made one with him and are incorporated into his mystical Body, which is the blessed company of the faithful both living and departed.

The second version uses just the first sentence finishing at 'Christ'.

Therein too we receive through the operation of the Holy Spirit by faith the saving benefits of Christ's death and resurrection.

Cf. O. O'Donovan, *On the Thirty Nine Articles: A Conversation with Tudor Christianity* (Paternoster Press, 1986).

3. The commission in fact lost seven members, six by death, before it finished its work. Burge, the chairman, died in 1925 and was replaced by William Temple, the future Primate.

4. *Doctrine in the Church of England* (pp. 141–83) was a worthy example by a team of distinguished people. Other familiar twentieth-century examples are: Charles Gore, *The Body of Christ* (1901); Darwell Stone, *History of the Doctrine of the Holy Eucharist* (1904); A. J. MacDonald, *The Evangelical Doctrine of the Holy Communion* (1930); E. L. Mascall, *Corpus Christi* (1965); Gregory Dix, *The Shape of the Liturgy* (1943).

5. Inevitably some regarded as substantial matters which they thought had been left out, but surprisingly the majority of Catholic commentators were reasonably content. One bishop from a remote province thought that substantial agreement meant agreement on transubstantiation.

6. Part of *A Critique of Eucharistic Agreement* (SPCK, 1975), which deals with several attempts at eucharistic agreement.

7. *The Church of England Newspaper* and *Church Times* (10 September); *The Tablet* (18 September).

8. It was an interesting sociological fact that this movement was also centred in the southern counties, not in the north of England where Catholics were supposed (in London at least) to be arch-conservative, narrow-minded, etc.

9. One participant in this was Raymond George, who had been one of the non-Catholic observer–consultants at the Consilium Liturgicum in Rome for implementing the Council's Constitution on the Liturgy. He was also a moving spirit in international dialogue between the Roman Catholic Church and the World Methodist Council.

18

Ministry

In responding to the ARCIC Agreement on Eucharist, the Scottish Episcopal Church had asked for 'clearer demarcation' between Faith and Theology.

This need became more urgent when the Commission turned to Ministry. The link between the two themes is evident. Difficulties about the sacrificial nature of the Eucharists are intimately connected with difficulties about the priestly or sacerdotal character of the ordained ministry. These difficulties are compounded by uncertainties about the early history of ministry. Two things follow: (1) Scholars, historical or theological, have to interpret the limited evidence and fill gaps – sometimes by educated guesses or speculation. The Reformation intensified this challenge and increased the number of theories or views, some of them decidedly *ex parte.* (2) Certain key words came to be used in ambiguous or mistaken ways.

In an ecumenical context the two areas of Sacrifice and Presence could soon be identified as areas where doctrinal differences had arisen concerning the Eucharist. By contrast, Ministry involves a great variety of human relations about which humans can differ, not merely theologically but because of the very different and changing patterns of societies and cultures. To *isolate* what are in ARCIC's words 'essential matters where [it considers that] doctrine admits no divergence' was no easy matter; to achieve consensus on them was a formidable task.

The opening sentence of the ARCIC statement on Ministry and Ordination says:

162

Our intention has been to seek a deeper understanding of ministry which is consonant with biblical teaching and with the traditions of our common inheritance, and to express in this document the consensus we have reached, (FR, p. 30, para. 1)

The very title of the statement implies setting the ordained ministry within the framework of all Christian ministry.[1] Baptism incorporates us into Christ, which means into a life of service. 'The ordained ministry', says the statement, 'can only rightly be understood within the broader context of various ministries, all of which are the work of one and the same Spirit' (FR, p. 30, para. 2).

The subject of ministry had arisen periodically in the dialogue ever since the first papers were presented to the JPC, particularly in relation to the Eucharist, where conception of the minister's role cannot be separated from conception of what the sacrament is. This last question lay at the heart of the greatest of all Anglican–Roman Catholic differences – that of the 'validity' of Anglican Orders. When the ARCIC statement on Ministry came out, the first question all journalists asked was (in the words of the Elucidation, FR, p. 40, para. 1) 'about the bearing of the statement upon the problem of recognizing the validity of Anglican orders'.

In fact, para. 19 of the Malta Report had already said:

It is only when sufficient agreement has been reached as to the nature of the priesthood and the meaning attached in this context to the word 'validity' that we can proceed, working always jointly, to the application of this doctrine to the Anglican ministry today.

None of this prevented the Venice 'trial' paper (1971) on Ministry devoting three long final paragraphs, under the heading 'The problem of Orders' to Anglican Orders.[2]

Gazzada II, 1972

ARCIC began its discussion of Ministry and Ordination at Gazzada II, from 30 August to 7 September 1972. It naturally did so having very much in mind the reactions to its first offering, the statement on Eucharist. Apart from the intrinsic connection of the two themes, the Commission could not fail to be interested in the plentiful reactions to its style and method, summarized in a report to the sub-commission which met two days in advance and discussed by the full Commission. The latter then proposed a 'text for publication'[3] outlining what it felt they had learned from the criticisms.

When ARCIC came in 1979 to select those points of its Ministry and Ordination statement which criticism showed required Elucidation, it chose this one first:

> insufficient attention was given to the priesthood of the whole people of God, so that the document seemed to have too clerical an emphasis.[4]

It is unlikely that any member of ARCIC wished to lend support to this 'too clerical' emphasis. The first section of its statement, headed 'Ministry in the life of the Church', was concerned entirely with Ministry as belonging to the Church as a whole – to the People of God, to the baptized, to all Christians who are a 'community of reconciliation within the whole history of mankind'. The document *Baptism, Eucharist and Ministry* (Faith and Order Paper no. 111, WCC) puts it thus: 'The word ministry in its broadest sense denotes service to which the whole people of God is called.'

The key word in the criticism cited in the Elucidation above is 'priesthood'. Both in its origin and in its subsequent use, it had been an ambiguous word. ARCIC, which had a slight weakness for handing out important learning in small sips in a footnote, put it thus:

> In the English language the word 'priest' is used to translate two distinct Greek words, *hiereus* which belongs to the cultic order and *presbyteros* which designates an elder in the community.

The trouble is that the word 'priest' derives etymologically from the second (and secondary) meaning. English has also the adjective 'sacerdotal' deriving from *sacerdos* but has no noun to express distinctively this personage. The personage and office were much older than Christianity, and were found in both Jewish and pagan cults. They were associated with ritual sacrifice.

In Christianity there was only one 'priest' in the literal sense. But he is the fulfilment of what in the Old Testament had been 'types and shadows'.[5] He is the one mediator 'both priest and victim', the one reconciler. How then is it possible to speak of the priesthood, *hierateuma*, of all the baptized?

The first answer is that St Peter does so, explicitly in his first epistle (2:9–10). He was certainly not harking back to the Old Testament priesthood. He was seaking of something which belonged to the people of the New Covenant, of something linked with the unique and unrepeatable sacrifice of Christ. It belonged to the baptized because they were baptized *into* Christ. Plenty of modern texts could be cited to show that Roman Catholics and Anglicans fully understood and shared this conviction. Lambeth '68 had said 'All Christians share in the priesthood of their Lord'. The Roman Catholic International Theological Commission, meeting in October 1970, had used almost the same words:

> In the New Testament there is no other priesthood but that of Christ. This priesthood is the fulfilment of all the ancient priesthoods and supersedes them. *All the faithful in the Church are called to share in it.*
>
> (see Appendix, ARCIC 76, 3)

It is surprising that ARCIC at Canterbury had approached this matter somewhat obliquely, in para. 7 in a descriptive passage which ends 'The goal of the *ordained* ministry is to serve this priesthood of all the faithful'. The Elucidation seemed perhaps conscious of this obliquity in its para. 2, 'Priesthood', which runs:

> In common Christian usage the term priesthood is employed in three distinct ways: the priesthood of Christ; the priesthood of the people of God; the priesthood of the ordained ministry. The priesthood of Christ is unique. He is our High Priest who has reconciled mankind with the Father. All other priesthood derives from it and is wholly dependent upon it.
>
> The priesthood of the whole people of God (1 Peter 2.5) is the consequence of incorporation by baptism into Christ. This priesthood of all the faithful (para. 2) is not a matter of disagreement between us. In a document primarily concerned with the ordained ministry, the Commission did not consider it necessary to develop the subject further than it has already done in the statement. Here the ordained ministry is firmly placed in the context of the ministry of the whole Church and exists for the service of the faithful.
>
> (FR, pp. 40–1, para. 2)

This clarification was admirable and necessary but more was needed on the same point. If the priesthood of the faithful was 'not a matter of disagreement' the term 'priest' when applied to the *ordained* ministry clearly was. Roman Catholics used nothing else: some Anglicans used it; other Anglicans and all Free Churchmen avoided it altogether.[6] Those who avoided it could find support in the New Testement. It is never used there to designate an ordained minister or ministry.

On the other hand ARCIC, in one of its key paragraphs (FR, p. 35, para. 13), says 'Christians came to see the priestly role of Christ *reflected* in these (ordained) ministers and used priestly terms in describing them'. The rather weak word 'reflected' was dealt within the Elucidation of 'Ministry'. Very succinctly, it repeated 'The statement (para. 13) explains that the ordained ministry is called priestly principally because it has a particular *sacramental* relationship with Christ as High Priest'. The content of sacramental relationship is hardly conveyed by 'reflected'.

The Commission starts from the Christian community: 'The goal of the ordained ministry is to serve this priesthood of all the faithful', which itself is a ministry and mission of service, aimed at building up the community. The metaphor of building is important. The process of building calls for cohesion, assignment of different functions to parts, fitting together, order. The result of building is an edifice, which has various attributes and functions. It is a focus of unity, but not of uniformity; of stability but not of rigidity. If a cathedral was *completely* rigid it would fall down in a storm.

The metaphor or image of a 'body' brings out these requirements even more forcefully (Eph 4:16). Neither metaphor must be pressed too far. The spread of the gospel called at once for the foundation of local churches, but these were not 'a loose aggregation of autonomous communities' (FR, p. 32, para. 6). How were the attributes of a building and a body main-tained not only within them but *among* them?

ARCIC turns first to the New Testament, from which it draws certain inferences:

1. In the early Church the apostles exercised a ministry which remains of fundamental significance for the Church of all ages (para. 4 *sub initio*).
2. Within the New Testament ministerial actions are varied and functions *not precisely defined.*
3. More precision develops and some form of *recognition* and *authorization* is already required in the New Testament period for those who exercise ministerial functions in the name of Christ.

4. Here we can see elements which will remain at the heart of what today we call *ordination* (para. 6).
5. The New Testament shows that ministerial *office* played an *essential* part in the life of the Church in the first century and *we believe* that the provision of a ministry of this kind is part of *God's design* (para. 6).
6. Normative principles governing the purpose and function of the ministry are already present in the New Testament (Matt 10:5): service (Acts 20:28), guardianship, example, teaching, preaching (1 Tim 4:12–16), and shepherding, not domineering (1 Peter 5:1–4) (para. 6).
7. In the New Testament a variety of images is used to describe the functions of the minister (servant, herald, ambassador, authoritative representative, teacher, shepherd, steward, example; cf. Congregation for the Doctrine of the Faith observations).

Six of these seven points are made in Part I of the statement, 'Ministry in the life of the Church': only the last in Part II, 'The ordained Ministry'.

From para. 6 (point 5 above) there emerges, from much that is non-committal, a clear agreed doctrinal statement:

> The New Testament shows that ministerial *office* played an essential part in the life of the Church in its first century and we believe that a ministry of this kind is part of God's design for his people.

This seems to match what the International Theological Commission says in the first of its six propositions (cf. also *Doctrine in the Church of England*, p. 115).

Cautious as this was, it went too far for some of the critics. The Elucidation of 1979, para. 4, addressed itself to these critics, circumscribing the Commission's position yet more closely:

> It is enough for our purpose to recall that, from the beginning of the Christian Church, there existed *episcope* in the community, however its various responsibility were distributed and described and whatever the names given to those who exercised it. (Cf. paras 8, 9 and especially 6; FR, p. 43)

Para. 9 is the first place in the statement in which the Greek noun *episcope* appears. It is usually translated in English as 'oversight'. The cognate word *episcopos* (in English, bishop) means one having responsibility for oversight, but the statement is clear that the term *episcope* applied to other ordained ministers besides *episcopoi*. The fundamental *episcope* is that of Christ, but *episcope* is also an essential element in the functions of those who are authoritative representatives of Christ (para. 9).

Of the many images used in the New Testament to describe the functions of the ordained minister perhaps the most inclusive is that of 'shepherd'. It joins the idea of service, of care, to that of leadership, of discipline and the maintainance of order. It was dilated on in a familiar Old Testament Psalm (23, or 22); it was used of himself by Christ (John 10:11–18), it was the most venerable of the artistic images of Christ. The word 'pastor' (simply Latin for 'shepherd') and more commonly the adjective 'pastoral' are hence familiarly used as synonyms for ordained ministry and ministers.

One of the reasons the Second Vatican Council had spoken of the Anglican Church as 'holding a special place' among the Reformation Churches was that it had retained the 'threefold ministry' of bishop, presbyter and deacon. The statement introduces this theme very gently, in the historical context. *Presbyter*, a word translated into English as 'priest', simply means an elder person; a deacon, one who performs services. In the last sentence of its section on ministry in general, the Commission simply says

the full emergence of the threefold ministry of bishop, priest and deacon required a longer period than the apostolic age. Thereafter this threefold structure became universal in the Church. (FR, p. 134)

The relevant Elucidation in response to criticism enlarged on this. The Commission was concerned not with the problem of primitive nomenclature, but with the primitive existence of ordination and oversight and with the emergence 'early in the second century' of the threefold ministry *centred upon* episcopacy, and in continuity not only with the apostolic faith but also with the commission given to the apostles (cf. *First Epistle of Clement* 42): 'We both maintain that *episcope* must be exercised by ministers ordained in the apostolic succession' (FR, p. 43).

In this second section the statement, without losing sight of history, shifts its attention much more to theology, to Church order, and to what Catholics and Anglicans still see as the apostolic function and character of the ordained ministry (FR, paras 7 and 9, p. 32).

A familiar, marked contrast between Catholic and Protestant worship

– a contrast reflected in the arrangements and furnishings of churches – was the different accent on Word and Sacrament; in more familiar terms, between services dominated by preaching, Bible reading and hymn singing and those dominated by Mass and Benediction. This was not a straightforward contrast where Roman Catholics and Anglicans were concerned. It could be noted easily between say, Westminster Cathedral and All Souls, Langham Place, but no less easily between All Souls, Langham Place and All Saints, Margaret Street, both Anglican. These examples of Anglican comprehensiveness did not however obscure the fact that Anglicans typically paid more attention to what we all now call the ministry of the Word and Catholics to what Belloc called 'the blessed mutter of the Mass'.

Yet the distinction was fundamentally misconceived. 'In both word and sacrament', said the statement crisply, 'Christians meet the living Word of God' (para. 11), and paras 9 and 11 amply reinforce this.

The next paragraph of the statement begins with a reminder that ministry in the Church is one of reconciliation – the reconciliation which Christ accomplished and of which his Church is the instrument.

The central act of worship, the Eucharist, is the memorial[7] of that reconciliation and nourishes the Church's life for the fulfilment of its mission. Hence *it is right* that he who has oversight in the Church and is the focus of its unity should preside at the celebration of the Eucharist. [Italics mine]

Julian Charley, our Evangelical member, in a commentary which he published hard on the heels of the statement, hastened to add

The statement says nothing about a 'priestly character' necessary for such a responsibility by which an ordained man is *empowered* to do something which *no layman can do*.[8] [Italics mine]

The statement does not use the word 'character', nor had the International Theological Commission's six propositions (June 1974), but, having explained in no. 2 why and how the episcopal and presbyteral ministry is 'sacerdotal', the ITC goes on:

The Christian who is called to the sacerdotal ministry therefore received by ordination not merely an external function but a special share in the priesthood of Christ, by virtue of which he represents

Christ before the community and at its head. Hence ministry is a specific form of the life of Christian service in the Church.

Several distinguished Roman Catholic critics, including Congar, Schnackenburg and Lanne, were satisfied that para. 15 dealt with the matter of priestly character, even without the word.

Paras 14 and 15 dealt with the question of the *sacramental* status of ordination. The Council of Trent had laid down that Orders were 'a true and proper sacrament instituted by Christ' (DS 1774, 1766). The Twenty-fifth Article of Religion placed it among

the five commonly called sacraments . . . not to be counted for Sacraments of the Gospel, being such as have grown partly of the corrupt following of the apostles, partly are states of life allowed in the Scriptures; but yet have not the nature of Sacraments with Baptism and the Lord's Supper for that they have not any visible sign or ceremony ordained by God.

To the Tridentine canon the statement makes no allusion. Positively, the ARCIC text calls orders a 'sacramental act' and attributes to it not only the elements of a sacrament but also those of a 'character': 'the Spirit seals . . . the gifts and calling of God are irrevocable. For this reason ordination is unrepeatable.'

Nevertheless in the Elucidation of 1979 (FR, p. 42, para. 8) the Commission acknowledged that the phrase 'in this sacramental act' had caused anxiety on two different counts: that this phrase seems to give the sacrament of ordination the same status as the two sacraments of the Gospel, and that it does not adequately express the full sacramentality of ordination. The Elucidation (ibid.) sensibly reiterated what it had said and added:

Both traditions affirm the pre-eminence of baptism and the Eucharist as sacraments necessary to salvation. This does not diminish their understanding of the sacramental nature of ordination, as to which there is no significant disagreement between them.

Para. 13 of the statement (FR, pp. 35–6), still grappling with the use of the word 'priest', dilates further on the relation between the ordained ministry and the eucharist:

1. Because the Eucharist is the memorial of the sacrifice of Christ, the action of its presiding minister in reciting again the words of Christ at the last supper and distributing to the assembly His Holy gifts is seen to stand in a *sacramental relation* to what Christ himself did in offering his own sacrifice.
2. It is because the Eucharist is central in the Church's life that the essential nature of the Christian ministry, however this may be expressed, is most clearly seen in its celebration.
3. Ordained ministers, particularly in presiding at the Eucharist, are representative of the whole Church in its priestly vocation of self offering to God.

These three sentences, especially the last two, show signs of having been hammered out with sweat and blood. They are followed by another which in interested circles has achieved some fame: 'Nevertheless the ordained ministry is not an extension of the common Christian priesthood, but belongs to another realm of the gifts of the spirit.' This sentence was clearly devised to avoid the customary Roman Catholic expression, still found in *Lumen Gentium* and *Mysterium Ecclesiae*, that the two differ *essentia et non gradu*. This seemed to non-Catholics too strong a dissociation. The substitute phrase was of French origin and 'realm' was used as a replacement rather than a translation for *registre* – a favourite word of Fr Tillard's. In its musical usage – register or compass – it seems a better term.

In the Elucidation of 1979 the Commission explained the change at some length.

> The word *priesthood* is used by way of analogy when it is applied to the people of God and to the ordained ministry. These are two distinct realities which relate, each in its own way, to the high priesthood of Christ, the unique priesthood of the new covenant, which is their source and model. These considerations should be born in mind throughout para. 13, and in particular they indicate the significance of the statement that the ordained ministry 'is not an extension of the common Christian priesthood but belongs to another realm of the gifts of the Spirit'.

In para. 16 the statement touches rather laconically on the significance of ordination rites for 'apostolic succession' – two words which appear only as the last two of the paragraph. Para. 4 had said why the *Church* was apostolic 'not only because (1) its faith and life must reflect the witness of Jesus Christ given in the early Church by the apostles, but (2) because it is charged to continue in the apostolic commission'. This second point carried the dialogue into its thorniest field, that of 'Authority in the Church'.

NOTES

1. The BEM (WCC) document emphasizes the ecumenical significance of this:
   'As they engage in the effort to overcome these differences [about the place and forms of ordained ministry] the Churches need to work from the perspective of the calling of the whole people of God.' See also *Doctrine in the Church of England*, p. 114.
2. The section of this trial paper headed 'Apostolic ministry' was laconic. Eight lines sufficed to state points of agreement: that ordained ministry derived not from the community, but from Christ by way of His Commission to the apostles, though the historical relation of the traditional threefold ministry to the apostles had not yet been traced in any detailed way. The rest of the section – five paragraphs making up 55 lines – dealt with papal primacy, already treated under 'Church and authority', where it really belongs.
3. Whether it was ever published I cannot discover.
4. The subject of the priesthood of the faithful is treated at some length in Pius XII's encyclical on liturgy of 1947, *Mediator Dei*.
5. The words derive from the familiar Latin hymn *Tantum ergo*, one of the many places in which Aquinas insists on this idea: *antiquum documentum novo cedat ritui*.
6. Mistrust of the word and hints of the reason are reflected in such derivatives as 'priest-craft' and 'priest-ridden'.
7. The special sense already established: *anamnesis*.
8. In fact para. 9 does say that presbyters and bishops are given authority to preside at the eucharist and pronounce absolution. 'Deacons are not so *empowered*.' If deacons are not, *a fortiori* laymen are not. The Elucidation is clearer (FR, p. 41).

19

Authority I: Venice

Jean Tillard wrote in 1976 that the Venice agreement ('Authority I') was a 'normal and necessary sequel to the Canterbury agreement' ('Ministry'). He dismissed the idea that its aim was simply an agreement on the papacy – a conclusion jumped to by many. There were several aspects of authority to be examined before this question-in-chief. The origin of the Anglican–Roman Catholic separation had been a repudiation of papal authority, and such discussion as there had been since was largely of a polemical sort centred on this repudiation. The Thirty-Nine Articles confined comment on it to this crisp sentence: 'The Bishop of Rome hath no jurisdiction in this realm of England.'

Nobody of any consequence was any longer concerned to dispute or hinder the spiritual or ecclesiastical jurisdiction which the Pope exercised over Catholics in English-speaking lands. But there were plenty of people who heartily disliked and repudiated most of the 'papal claims' which had been embodied in the first Vatican Council and in particular its dogmatic constitution *Pastor Aeternus*. Chief and most notorious among these claims was that of Infallibility. Thus there was every good reason of strategy as well as of logic for starting with a search for agreed principles of a general kind about authority and moving on to Authority in the Church.

Questions of authority had of course been raised from the very beginning in the Joint Preparatory Commission. After preliminary papers at Gazzada the scheme for the Huntercombe paper had as its full title. 'The authority of the Word of God and its relation to the Church'.

The Malta Report used the word 'authority' very sparingly, but the many-sided concept runs through the text as a leitmotiv, and para. 20 (FR, p. 115) records agreement that

> a serious theological examination should be jointly undertaken on the nature of authority with particular reference to its bearing on the interpretation of the historic faith to which both our communions are committed.

When ARCIC first met at Windsor, the joint paper by Bishop Knapp Fisher and Fr Edmund Hill OP, and two papers (originally intended to be one joint paper) by Professor Chadwick and Bishop Butler treated of authority (see above, pp. 132–3). Chadwick and Butler dwelt on the contrasting attitudes of Anglicanism and Roman Catholicism both among those who exercise authority and those who accept it. These attitudes reflected differences about how far truth could be attained – though the Roman Catholic attitude had been changing.

Chadwick reflected on two questions: (1) What today are the fundamental differences on Authority which Anglicans and Roman Catholics have inherited and which still have influence on conversations between them? (2) What prospects are there for a re-statement of religious authority in this modern world? Here were two questions, one looking backward, one forward, which needed to be asked; but the answer to one would be unattainable or sterile without the answer to the other.

Prompted by these papers, a sub-commission drew up a short scheme which embodied the ideal for the Authority debate of 1974–76:

> Not to describe positions which hold here and now but to reflect on an ecclesiology which would shape the future Church, built on the biblical concept of *koinonia*.

When ARCIC met for the second time (Venice, 21–28 September 1970) it had firmly in mind to produce a *ballon d'essai* on each of its three subjects. Not too much was claimed for these progress reports, but when they were completed it was evident where the chief burden of difference lay. 'Church and Authority' was not only the longest of the three; it devoted only one-third to matters of agreement, two-thirds to doing what the Windsor scheme vowed not to do: 'describing positions held here and now'. After some very tense discussion (which used to show on the faces of the sub-commission as it emerged for meals) this had appeared unavoidable. The 'Ministry' sub-commission too devoted a fair slice of its contribution to the papacy.

After the usual shufflings about publication the 'Venice papers' appeared in *Theology* and *The Clergy Review* in February 1971.[1] Perhaps, as Michael Walsh said in *The Month*, 'the decision to publish them at all is more important than the content'. They gave readers something to bite on rather than guess about.

The fruits of Grottaferrata, 1974

ARCIC finally turned its full attention to Authority at Grottaferrata, near Rome, 17 August–5 September 1974, and completed its first agreed statement on the subject just two years later.[2]

A certain progression in the type of problem faced by ARCIC in its three statements, on the Eucharist, on Ministry and on Authority, is discernible. The Common Declaration of 1966, basing dialogue on 'the Bible and the ancient common traditions', could be relatively easily kept in view. Anglicanism at its most 'Protestant' moments did not repudiate the Eucharist. There were points of doctrine to be cleared up, but no one could say that Roman Catholics and Anglicans stood ranged in total contradiction on the subject.

When it came to ministry the matter was complicated by the fact that periodically, and most gravely in 1896, the papacy had judged that the Anglican Church had so defective an idea and intention about ordained ministry that its orders could not be considered valid. ARCIC claimed that its own work on the doctrine of ministry 'put the question of orders in a new context'; in plain English, called for its joint re-examination in a spirit and with an equipment quite different from that of 1896.

The problem of Church and Authority was of a different order. In 1870 Vatican I had made fateful pronouncements about Authority in the church, especially the authority of the Bishop of Rome. The history of the development of that bishop's authority is long and complex. The ARCIC statements had to confront doctrines about the papacy which Vatican I *appeared* to place on the same level as the constituents of the Chicago–Lambeth Quadrilateral. To a Church which first assumed its separate existence by repudiating all papal authority, this might (and to many did) seem to raise an insurmountable obstacle even after Vatican II. Fortunately there was plenty to talk about before the subject of the papacy was approached.

In one sense the transition from 'Canterbury' to 'Venice' was easy and inevitable, as Tillard had said: ministerial function implies, calls for, some authority. The life and ministry of Christ knew no dichotomy, no opposition between service and authority. The community of reconciliation requires shepherding. The New Testament imagery for ministerial function implies authority; the minister is a 'steward who may only provide for the household of God what belongs to Christ' (FR p. 33). This is a responsibility which is inseparable from authority.

But from what authority? Certainly not just his own. Venice says:

> The Spirits of the Risen Lord, who indwells the Christian community,
> continues to maintain the people of God in obedience to the
> Father's will. He safeguards their faithfulness to the revelation of
> Jesus Christ and equips them for their mission in the world. By this
> action of the Holy Spirit the authority of the Lord is active in the
> Church. (FR, p. 53, para. 3)

If anybody, from Pope to curate, exercises his 'authority' with any other idea of its source or purpose than this, he is merely hindering its effectiveness. But if the Holy Spirit is to use human beings as his instruments they must exercise guardianship, which at times will require firmness and discipline, for example 'when fierce wolves will come in among you, not sparing the flock; and from among your own selves will arise men speaking perverse things' (Acts 20:29–30).

There is a delicate balance in *episcope*, oversight; the task of the shepherd, 'Command and teach' (1 Tim 4:11), is in counterpoint with 'not by constraint but willingly' (1 Peter 5:2).

The authority of the Risen Christ is unique and comprehensive, but as Julian Charley says,[3] 'the difficulties begin when we try to define how this authority is mediated to and through the Church'. A very famous text touches on this. 'All authority in heaven and on earth is given to me' (Matt 28:1). The Venice statement begins with and proceeds from those to whom Christ spoke these words, the apostolic community, which had not only heard and seen the salvific words and deeds of Christ, but had been promised that he would continue to be with them through the Holy Spirit. His presence would ensure that the community would remain, to be brought to perfection not only by spreading abroad but by growth in understanding of the Truth, which would be passed on inviolate to every local Church which the apostolic zeal caused to be founded.

Assisted by the Holy Spirit they transmitted what they had heard and seen of the life and words of Jesus and their interpretation of his redemptive work. Consequently the inspired documents in which this is related came to be accepted by the Church as a normative record of the authentic foundation of the faith. To these the Church has recourse for the inspiration of its life and mission, to these the Church refers its teaching and practice. Through these written words the authority of the Word of God is conveyed. Entrusted with these documents, the Christian community is enabled by the Holy Spirit to live out the Gospel and so to be led into all truth. (FR, p. 52)

This is an attempt to find the true way through a minefield of problems which has been with us since the sixteenth century but which some modern developments have added to.

The passage quoted begins as an historical account of how the Scriptures came about, then modulates into an 'ideal account' of how they function in the Church. Sometimes it may seem that ARCIC fails to be perfectly clear in maintaining the line between the ideal and the actual; but when it is seeking consensus or doctrinal agreement it is right to be concerned chiefly with the ideal.

The uniqueness of Church authority is that it claims to transmit the Word of Him who is the Way, the Truth and the Life. It does so because the Church believes that it shares in the life of the Spirit of God. Much in history seems to tell against this claim.

The Christian Church is spoken of as a 'community of faith' and the Venice statement makes much of this. First let us be clear what it does not mean. It does not mean a collection of persons individually guaranteed against error or ignorance, or behaviour inconsistent with faith and obedience. It does not even mean that local Churches are immune from error – otherwise there would never have been schisms. Yet Vatican II said that 'by the power of the Holy Spirit . . . the Church . . . has never ceased to be a sign of salvation on earth' (*Gaudium et Spes*, no. 43).

In its chapter II on *Authority in the Church* the Venice statement recognizes other kinds of authority besides the hierarchical: first the diversities of graces recalled by St Paul (Eph 4:11; 1 Cor 4:11) and above all the 'eminent holiness' (to borrow a catechism phrase), the inner quality of life, of those who respond more fully to Christ's call. This pattern of different kinds of authority illuminates the quality and importance of *koinonia* which reaches out into human activity as a saving and sanctifying force.

Section II (FR, pp. 53–5) tries to show how the Holy Spirit sustains this *koinonia* and works through it: A 'continuing process of discernment and response . . . the faithful may live freely under the *discipline* of the Gospel . . . taking full account of human weakness . . . a *continual* summons to reform' (italics mine).

That the search for unity is a prompting of the Spirit only very obstinate Christians now deny, but problems arise in putting this into action. These problems are most immediately known in the parish. Parish priests, the immediate representatives of the ordained ministry, 'exercise their authority in fulfilling *ministerial* functions' (see FR, p. 54, para. 6, citing Acts 2:42). Their authority is respected to the extent that they are seen to serve. Yet if discords and other signs of human frailty arise, they must appear as a contradiction, a reproach when the community gathers at the Eucharist.

This picture repeats itself at ascending levels of Church authority. The bishop of a diocese in modern conditions cannot visit a parish community very regularly or frequently, but celebrating mass, administering the sacraments, preaching and exhorting, he exemplifies authority as a form of care and service. Chapter II of the Venice statement dilates on the living process, an ordered fellowship 'in which faith is expressed and the Gospel is pastorally applied' (FR, p. 54, para. 6).

Chapter III broadens the picture. Each local Church (the term is generally used to mean the diocese) *is* the Church insofar as it 'is rooted in the witness of the apostles and entrusted with the apostolic mission'. But it is associated with the other local Churches in these essential features and in its responsibility for world-wide mission. The *koinonia* is not merely local but also universal – that of the *one* Church of Christ.

Again we have here the statement of an ideal (cf. Acts 15) but one which the Church very early 'realized the need to express and strengthen' by meeting in *council* from time to time 'to discuss matters of mutual concern and to meet contemporary challenges'.

Through such meetings the Church, determined to be obedient to Christ and faithful to its vocation, formulates its rule of faith and orders its life . . . Its decisions are authoritative when they express the common faith and mind of the Church.

If the decisions are those of an *ecumenical* nature they bind the whole Church.

Para. 10 shows how a closely related means of maintaining unity among local Churches was that of primacy – assigned to the bishops of principal sees and exercised over other bishops of their region. Again, the purpose is to promote unity, right teaching, mission and (though the word is not used) to admonish.

> When the primate perceives a serious deficiency in the life or mission of one of the Churches he is *bound*, if necessary, to call the local bishop's attention to it and to offer assistance. There will also be occasions when he has to *assist* other bishops to reach a common mind with regard to their shared needs and difficulties. (Para. 11.)

In the next paragraph (12), 'within this context' the subject of the Bishop of Rome is slid in. A lot of summary assurances are hastily given that even Vatican I had not defined the authority of a dictator, and that Vatican II had gone much further in repudiating this. In the second half of the paragraph we return briefly to history and are reminded that the talk is of the 'ideal' and 'the primacy rightly understood', not of the history of the papacy. 'Neither theory nor practice has *ever* fully reflected these ideals' (p. 58).

Para. 13 speaks of those responsibilities of the local Church which take it beyond its internal life; it is not truly itself unless it looks outwards and sees itself as a constituent part of the one Church of Christ, and its mission. The mandate of ARCIC was an ecumenical one and the Commission could not have come to exist if the Spirit had not renewed this realisation and the scandal of its neglect, in our time.

The formulation of the Scriptural canon, of creeds, of conciliar definitions, were all in their different ways designed to maintain the apostolic *memory*.

'The Church', says para. 18, 'has the obligation and the competence to make declarations in matters of faith.' Later it says:

> When conflict endangers unity or threatens to distort the Gospel, the Church must have effective means for resolving it.

Authority is a form of service and the principal service is to maintain the Church in the truth.

What are the *effective* means of doing so? The Church cannot add anything to the deposit of faith; it can only make it clear. The task of making the Gospel clear to people of cultures different from that from which it emerged was formidable.

The responsibility of 'oversight' was hence heavy. For a time the immediate apostolic tradition could be appealed to directly, especially in those churches of apostolic foundation. The Scriptures, the creeds, the Fathers of the Church, the definitions of early councils were decisive because they maintained and embodied the apostolic tradition, but though documents and statements could be appealed to as fundamental, they could be variously interpreted and often were. There remained always the need for judging such varieties and making sure they did not compromise 'the rule of faith'. Para. 18 proclaims the special responsibility of bishops for promoting truth and discerning error in interaction with the Christian community, the *sensus fidelium*.[4]

ARCIC was not writing apologetics. All Christians accept that 'the Spirit abides in the Church', but differ about how this is seen to operate. In the decisions of General Councils? These are agreed by ARCIC to be in some cases 'protected from error' but only in 'fundamental matters of faith' which formulate the 'central truths of salvation' (FR, p. 62, para. 19). This was not clearly grasped at first, and was taken as contradicting no. 21 of the Thirty-Nine Articles and had to be reaffirmed in the Elucidations of 1981 (FR, pp. 71–2).

The last sentence of Section IV describes as *Christian hope*:

we believe that Christ will not desert his Church and that the Holy Spirit will lead it into all truth. That is why the Church in spite of its failures, can be described as indefectible.

This is the first appearance in the ARCIC report of the word *indefectible*. It appears again in a footnote to that section of the second statement on Authority which deals with Infallibility:

This is the meaning of *indefectibility*, a term which does not speak of the Church's lack of defects but confesses that, despite all its many weaknesses and failures, Christ is faithful to his promise that the gates of hell shall not prevail against it. (FR, p. 91).

The last words are of course part of the famous 'Petrine text' (Matt 16:18). They stress again that the heart of the matter is *salvation* – the goal.[5] Doctrine is *saving truth*.

There is really no Anglican–Roman Catholic problem about indefectibility except that the *word* has been associated with Anglican opposition to papal infallibility. Neither word is of ancient use. Chillingworth (1602–40) said 'that there shall always be a Church infallible in fundamentals we easily grant, for it comes to no more than this, that there shall always be a Church'. But after 1870 Anglicans were convinced that Rome was saying more than that. As Julian Charley put it in his commentary on 'Authority I',

> Protestants are not generally aware of how extensive were the rigorous conditions laid down by the First Vatican Council for hedging round the doctrine of infallibility.

Section V of the Venice statement makes a comparison between the authority of councils and that of primates which is complementary. Councils have an authority which is binding when it treats of 'central truths of salvation'. Paras 20–23 speak of primates. It seeks, and para. 24 claims that it achieves, 'a consensus on the basic principles of primacy'. What are these?

1. Primacy is an expression of the collective responsibility of the bishops over whom it is exercised, though
2. the primate may on occasion be expected to take the initiative in speaking for the Church.
3. Primacy is a service to the *koinonia* (i.e. to unity and love, to the future of Christian life).
4. It respects and promotes Christian freedom and spontaneity.
5. It does not seek uniformity where diversity is legitimate.
6. It does not centralize administration to the detriment of local Churches.

Para. 23 adds that this balance between primacy and conciliarity in *episcope* needs to be realized at the universal level. This brings the Commission to the see of Rome.

> It seems appropriate that in any future union a universal primacy such as has been described should be held by that see. (FR, p. 64.)

The Venice statement had introduced the matter first in para. 12 (FR, p. 59):

The see of Rome, whose prominence was associated with the death there of Peter and Paul, eventually became the principal centre in matters concerning the Church universal. The importance of the Bishop of Rome among his brother bishops, as explained by analogy with the position of Peter among the apostles, was interpreted as Christ's will for his Church.

Para. 17 adds:

In addition the Bishop of Rome was also led to intervene in controversies relating to matters of faith – in most cases in response to appeals made to him, but sometimes on his own initiative.

Para. 24 (FR, Section VI; p. 64) begins by claiming that

what we have written here amounts to a consensus on authority in the Church, in particular on the basic principles of primacy.

If this claim extends to para. 23, then it is a consensus on the need for a primate at the universal level. But para. 24 at once adds:

It is when we move from these basic principles to particular claims of papal primacy and its exercise that problems arise.

Papacy and criticisms

The setting out of these matters in para. 24 constituted the programme for the last phase of ARCIC I's work. The problems were:

1. The Petrine texts
2. The 'divine right' of the papacy (DS 3058)
3. The infallibility of the Pope
4. His universal immediate jurisdiction.

The 'Conclusion' of Venice (FR, pp. 66–7, para. 26) consisted of a prod to the authorities. Recalling Malta's idea of unity by stages, it went on:

We have reached agreements on the doctrines of the eucharist, ministry, and, apart from the qualifications of para. 24, authority.

Doctrinal agreements reached by theological commissions cannot, however, by themselves achieve the goal of Christian unity. Accordingly we submit our Statements to our respective authorities to consider whether or not they are judged to express on these central subjects a unity at the level of faith which not only justifies but requires action to bring about a closer sharing between our two communions in life, worship, and mission.

ARCIC sat down (at Chichester, 30 August–8 September 1977) to examine the criticisms of its Venice statement.

Many people suggested that ARCIC had somehow managed to discuss authority without any reference to the much-canvassed 'crisis of authority' in the contemporary world: the decline in church-going, in Church influence and educational opportunity – these were only symptoms of doubts and disturbances which had been at work for much longer. There was little doubt that Anglicans and Roman Catholics began with different presuppositions, which often led to each viewing the other's crisis as more important and soft-pedalling its own. The proper approach to an ecumenical discussion of authority was not indeed to ignore contrasts, but to get to the root of them and see what common principles of authority lay there.

When ARCIC spoke of the 'ideal' it was referring to the ideal as willed by Christ – the authority of Christ as maintained in the apostolic tradition through the action of the Spirit. In its Section I on Christian Authority, speaking of the transmission of the apostolic tradition, it said 'the inspired documents in which this is related came to be accepted by the Church as a normative record of the authentic foundation of the faith' (FR, p. 52, para. 2).

Yet when they came to write the Elucidation in 1981, they found underlying the many criticisms a persisting suspicion that Scripture was being undervalued. They devoted two pages to refuting the charge.

Though the Venice statement had professedly limited itself to general principles of authority and primacy (para. 24), and even set out in some detail problems still to be faced, this did not deter some critics from already dilating on these problems. The Commission contented itself with referring these critics to 'Authority II' (FR, p. 68, para. 11).

In Section V of 'Venice' what was said of General Councils came under fire from two sides. It was accused of contradicting no. 21 of the Thirty-Nine Articles, by saying that General Councils are

protected from error in fundamental matters of faith which formulate
the central truths of salvation and which are faithful to Scripture and
consistent with Tradition. (FR, p. 62, para. 19.)

The CDF, on the other hand, seemed to think that this *restricted* the
authority of General Councils, and was inconsistent with para. 10 of
Canterbury (FR, p. 34) (which, however, was not talking about General
Councils or their inerrancy).

To claim *total* inerrancy for General Councils would be unrealistic and
unhistorical. Not even Vatican I claimed *total* infallibility for the Pope; it
restricted it very precisely and in any case equated it with the 'Infallibility
with which Christ wished to endow his Church'. See 'Authority II' (FR,
pp. 91–8).

In Elucidation 3 (FR, p. 72) the Venice statement considers the
questions asked by critics 'whether reception by the whole people of God
is part of the process which gives authority to the decisions of ecumenical
councils',[6] a tricky question undoubtedly connected with Elucidation 4,
'The place of the laity'. ARCIC did well to say at once what it meant by
the term 'reception'.

> By 'reception' we mean the fact that the people of God acknowledge
> such a decision or statement because they *recognize* in it the
> apostolic faith. They accept it because they *discern* a harmony
> between what is proposed to them and the *sensus fidelium* of the
> whole Church. [First two italics mine]

It is necessary to understand exactly what is this *sensus fidelium* before
judging what part it plays as 'a vital element in the comprehension of
God's truth'. The Latin phrase occurs only twice in the statement, but
reflections of its meaning are scattered throughout the Final Report.

Baptism enrols the Christian in a community of faith. There are diversities of gifts, as St Paul insisted, and some of these are given to persons as
persons, others to those ordained for specific functions. But the gifts are not
confined to ordained ministries – not even the gift of discerning God's will
for his Church (FR, p. 54, para. 6); the passage goes on:

> All who live faithfully within the *koinonia* may become sensitive to
> the leading of the Spirit and be brought to a deeper understanding of
> the Gospel and of its implications in diverse cultures and changing
> situations.

But it would be a gross mistake to think of the *sensus fidelium* as some prerogative of the educated. It is not a *consensus doctorum*, an agreement among the learned. It is something belonging to *all* the faithful. Newman thought of it as a 'sort of instinct', a corporate apprehension, the Church's apprehension of what is Christian, to do with the Spirit's maintaining the sacramental life of the community of faith.[7]

The ordained ministry is an integral part of this life and this community, not something standing over and apart from it. 'The *interaction* of bishop and people (in promoting truth and discerning error) is a safeguard of Christian life and fidelity.' The section concludes (FR, p. 72):

> The Commission therefore avoids two extreme positions. On the one hand it rejects the view that a definition has no authority until it is accepted by the whole Church or even derives its authority solely from that acceptance. Equally, the Commission denies that a council is so evidently self-sufficient that its definitions owe nothing to reception.

Elucidation 5 (p. 74) faces the objection to the phrase 'requires compliance' to episcopal authority (p. 54, para. 5):

> Both our communions have always recognized this need for disciplinary action on exceptional occasions as part of the authority given by Christ to his ministers, however difficult it may be in practice to take such action.

Elucidations 6 and 7 on jurisdiction and regional primacy were to be taken up in the appropriate section of 'Authority II' (FR, pp. 88–91), but in the last Elucidation on primacy and history (no. 8; FR, pp. 76–8) paragraphs were devoted to the question whether 'the Commission . . . suggests that a universal primacy is a theological necessity simply because one has existed or been claimed'. The allusion is to the Venice statement, paras 10–23. If the Elucidation is re-read carefully in conjunction with these paragraphs, and bearing in mind the work that had to be done on Anglican objections to papal primacy, it is hard to see how this assertion could be maintained.

The editor of the *Clergy Review*, Michael Richards, who had been a member of the JPC, wrote of the Venice statement:

> in the first two statements one felt that one was reading the work of theologians who, working together, had produced new insights – a

fresh synthesis from which all could profit. In this one the strong impression is given of a Catholic team working hard (too hard) to answer the questions of an Anglican one.

The first Anglicans did not argue away papal primacy. For complex reasons they repudiated it. The Articles of Religion, as we have seen, simply said 'the Bishop of Rome hath no jurisdiction in this realm of England'. Now, four centuries later, Anglicans were at least prepared to consider putting an end to an old break, but before they could accept the papacy they would have questions needing answers.

It was necessary for agreement about *principles* of authority to be reached before the questions could be focused. Paras 22 and 23 of Venice summed up these required principles. 'It is when we move from these basic principles to the *particular* claims of papal primacy and to its *exercise* that problems arise', said Venice, para. 24, and proceeded to list the chief ones (see above, p. 182). They became the subject of dialogue which was to culminate in the statement called 'Authority II', completed at Windsor, August–September 1981, and published in 1982. Seen against the background of four centuries of history as well as fifteen years of dialogue, the last paragraph of this statement (para. 33; FR, pp. 97–8) deserves contemplation:

> We have already been able to agree that conciliarity and primacy are complementary ('Authority I', 22–23). We can now together affirm that the Church needs both a multiple, dispersed authority, with which all God's people are actively involved, and also a universal primate as servant and focus of visible unity in truth and love. This does not mean that all differences have been eliminated; but if any Petrine function and office are exercised in the living Church of which a universal primate is called to serve as a visible focus, then it inheres in his office that he should have both a defined teaching responsibility and appropriate gifts of the Spirit to enable him to discharge it.
>
> Contemporary discussions of conciliarity and primacy in both communions indicate that we are not dealing with positions destined to remain static. We suggest that some difficulties will not be wholly resolved until a practical initiative has been taken and our two Churches have lived together more visibly in the one *koinonia*.

During the time in which ARCIC I's reflections on Authority in the Church were maturing the practical force of the topic was brought home to the Catholic Church in England. In November 1975 John Cardinal Heenan died after a long illness and in March 1976 he was succeeded by Basil Hume. The previous four cardinals had been English College, Rome men.

Apart from personal factors it took little knowledge of history to foresee that Authority, which is much a matter of exercise and human relations, was likely to present a new face in a man who had spent 35 years as a Benedictine, thirteen of them as Abbot. Ever since Anglican–Roman Catholic discussion of authority formally began in 1970, it had become clear to those involved that style in the practice of authority was what concerned Anglicans more than theory. It was this that had opened up visions in the short pontificate of John XXIII. By 1976 the visions were ready for refocusing and not only in Rome.

NOTES

1. One might ask how many of those who settle a matter by saying 'I read it in the *Guardian*' could tell you the name of the editor at any one time.
2. The considerable work put in in the interval is briefly described in FR, pp. 103–4, paras 6–9.
3. *Agreement on Authority* (Grove Books, no. 48), p. 17.
4. The distinguished theologian Stephen Sykes (now Bishop of Ely), in a searching paper on 'Authority in the ARCIC document', is highly critical of what is said first in para. 15 about Tradition and Restatement and about the *sensus fidelium*. Perhaps the paragraph itself is capable of fruitful restatement.
5. The whole final section (FR, pp. 91–8) should be read in conjunction with section IV of 'Authority I', of which it is a thorough expansion.
6. We should remember that at this stage ARCIC is strictly talking only of those councils acknowledged in the Lambeth Quadrilateral. Differences about the subsequent history of councils are alluded to in a footnote (FR, p. 63).
7. Cf. Cardinal Willebrands' address to the plenary meeting of the SPCU (nos 13–18, 1978): 'I freely acknowledge that "the faithful as a whole" who have received the anointing of the Holy Spirit (cf. 1 John 2:20–27) is incapable of being at fault in belief.' Cf. *Lumen Gentium*, 207. (Information Service no. 39, p. 2.)

CHAPTER

20

Archbishop Coggan in Rome

The year following the completion of 'Venice' offered several occasions for testing the waters beyond the limits of ARCIC. Before the statement was published the SPCU had judged it prudent to get Fr Christophe Dumont OP, a venerable ecumenist who also enjoyed the confidence of the CDF, to attach to the publication a long and reasonably sympathetic comment. They had also solicited comment from Yves Congar OP, whose international reputation was such that inquisitorial reactions to him were no longer very likely.

During 10–18 November 1976 the Plenary session of the SPCU took place in Rome, bringing together all the bishops from the Catholic world who were members of the Secretariat. This was much too early an occasion for a serious discussion of the Venice Statement, which was still in the bureaucratic limbo between completion and publication, but reactions among the members to a summary account of it were encouraging. More significantly Paul VI exhorted the members to 'intensify their efforts' towards unity – a phrase which the *Osservatore Romano* splashed across its front page.

The Secretary General of the Anglican Consultative Council, Bishop John Howe, had suggested to Cardinal Willebrands as early as 1974 an annual series of *informal talks* between small groups chosen by the SPCU and himself. The agenda for these was to be topical. The second of these 'conversations' took place in Rome the week before the Secretariat plenary just mentioned – 3 November 1976. It discussed mainly the report

188

of the third meeting of the Anglican Consultative Council held in Trinidad the previous spring, and especially those sections of it which dealt with 'Church and Society' and 'Mission and Evangelism'.[1]

Here was a handy and flexible instrument which has continued annually down to the time of writing. It was also a regular reminder that dialogue was between the Roman Catholic Church and the Anglican Communion.

Paul VI spoke to a general audience at the beginning of the Week of Prayer for Unity, 19 January 1977. Hope was based on theological foundations such as those encountered in *Lumen Gentium* and *Unitatis Redintegratio*, but 'also based on, and sustained by, the positive results which the search for unity among Christians *is* obtaining'. He added:

> We do not look on Peter's see in any other way than as a particular form of service to the unity of the Church.

The visit

During the early months of 1977 preparations were going on for yet another visit to Rome and its bishop by the Archbishop of Canterbury. This took place slightly more than eleven years after that of Michael Ramsey and nearly seventeen years after that of Geoffrey Fisher. (It will be remembered that the one before that was in 1397.)

When Donald Coggan reached Rome, 27 April 1977, the noble enterprise launched by his predecessor had more than a decade of experience behind it. Of this experience the central element was the ARCIC dialogue. When Pope and Archbishop met, a common declaration was expected, even inevitable, in addition to courtesy speeches. The latter presented no difficulty, the former rather more. What could be said briefly that was more than vaguely encouraging? Between November 1976 and April 1977, drafts and visits between Rome and Lambeth were exchanged at several levels and revision discussed and made.

The visit followed broadly the pattern of 1966. The Archbishop was lodged at the English College. He was accompanied by five bishops, all closely connected with Anglican–Roman Catholic relations:

JOHN HOWE, Secretary General of the Anglican Consultative
    Council[2]

EDWARD KNAPP-FISHER, a member of ARCIC

JOHN SATTERTHWAITE, Bishop of Fulham and Gibraltar, formerly
     secretary of the CFR and first co-secretary of ARCIC
JOHN TRILLO, Bishop of Chelmsford and President of the Church of
     England Committee for Roman Catholic relations
ERVINE SWIFT, Bishop of the 'convocation' of the American Anglican
     church in Europe

Also with him were;

THE REVD CHRISTOPHER HILL, co-secretary of ARCIC and a
     counsellor on CFR
CANON HARRY SMYTHE, Director of the Anglican Centre in Rome.

The party arrived on Wednesday afternoon and were welcomed at
the airport by, among others, Cardinal Willebrands of the SPCU and
Archbishop Giovanni Benelli of the Secretariat of State. The party
had been forced at a late hour to take an earlier plane from London and
this proved useful for two reasons. It gave time for the Archbishop
and Cardinal Willebrands to talk over the text of the declaration along
with the ARCIC co-secretaries. This proved invaluable and might have
been even more so if one or two of the less agreeable and co-operative
Vatican officials had not been present.

The Archbishop was immediately a relaxed and easy guest, friendly
and appreciative. There was still time to spare after the conversation and
he readily agreed to take a drive and a stroll on the Janiculum hill – the
best place from which to appreciate the topography and historical growth
of the city. Just below the hill is the venerable church of Santa Maria
in Trastevere with its nave arcade of ancient Roman columns and its
superb mosaics. One felt here, and later in the Catacomb of St Priscilla
and in the excavations under St Peter's, that he was conscious of the
primitive gospel – or that in a more than conventional sense he was at
home.

He was at home too, as his predecessor had been, with students. After
supper he was taken to the English College common room – a place long
famed for grilling visitors, without excessive regard for rank and still less
for the requirements of diplomacy. He disarmed them in the best way – by
being in no wit disconcerted and saying exactly what he thought without
patronage. Such delicate issues as women priests and 'establishment' were
raised for the only time during his visit.

On the next day, Thursday 28 April, Dr Coggan was received in the Pope's library. Cardinal Willebrands and Bishop Torella from the SPCU were also present, and Bishops Howe and Knapp Fisher from the Archbishop's party. Afterwards the whole party came in, and Pope and Archbishop exchanged short formal speeches.

The visitors were entertained to lunch at the residence of the British Ambassador to Italy. A list of guests was fortunately given in advance to the SPCU by the Minister to the Holy See, Mr Dugald Malcolm. It was found to contain not a single Roman Catholic name. I telephoned hastily. Invitations were rushed to Cardinal Willebrands, and Archbishops Casaroli and Benelli, of the Secretariat of State.

In the afternoon the Archbishop was at the crowded American Episcopalian Church in the Via Nazionale, and in the evening it was the turn of the Church of England to be hosts at a very large gathering arranged through the Anglican Centre.

On Friday morning, 29 April, a service of prayer took place in the Sistine Chapel. The planning of this was something of a tug-of-war. A week or two in advance I was invited to collaborate with Peter Coughlan, who was then attached to the Congregation of Rites in producing a draft service. The Congregation of Rites already had a number of ideas of their own about the service. They showed no idea at all of what Englishmen and particularly Anglicans were accustomed to. Such music as there was was almost entirely in the hands of the Sistine choir, which was at that time probably at the lowest point in its long and distinguished history.

Coughlan and I co-opted a good musician, Bruce Har, a former Oxford junior don studying at the English College, and got to work putting a strong accent on congregational singing and on English works to be sung by the English College choir. We submitted our draft to Monsignor Noè, the secretary of the Congregation, who promised to give it full consideration. After several days' delay, I was summoned to Noè's office and presented with an 'amended' draft. To my consternation it showed only ghostly traces of what we had proposed. I decided the situation was too desperate for meekness or even diplomacy, and listened, faintly surprised, to myself telling this considerably higher-ranking official what was and was not tolerable for this historic occasion, and even adding my opinion (a widely shared one) that the current state of the Sistine choir must have Palestrina and Victoria turning in their graves. To Noè's great credit, he took this well. Having assured me superfluously that the choir-master, if he heard me, would go up in the air (*saltarebbe in aria*), he proceeded to hint very broadly that he rather agreed with me. 'The Sistine choir', he said quite correctly, 'has historic rights.' Then, with a well-timed pause, 'but we try to restrict those rights'.

It was all very Italian and good-tempered. We hammered out a compromise which in the end was successful. It was Eastertide. The Pope and the Archbishop processed into the Sistine Chapel to a translation of the paschal hymn *Ad regias Agni dapes* ('At the Lamb's high feast we sing') sung to the chorale 'Salzburg'.

The Pope's failing health was evident (it was a little more than a year before his death), his voice was hoarse and faltered a little over the English, but in the substance of what he said there was deep and thankful appreciation of the visit and of its significance – a symbol of hope, of perseverance, of increased desire for common witness to the Gospel. These themes found echo in the Archbishop's words at many points, and the Pope's words on study and meditation of the Scriptures must have warmed Donald Coggan's heart.

Everybody who had taken an active part in the service now followed the Pope and the Archbishop into the Pauline chapel for the reading of the Common Declaration (see text in FR, p. 119).

After the strenuous morning, the ecumenical party moved to the Benedictine headquarters of Sant'Anselmo in its cloisteral calm on the Aventine. The principal guest was doubtless reminded of the sixth-century Roman and monastic origin of his see. He was carried further back in history after luncheon, to the Catacomb of St Priscilla, meticulously cared for by the Benedictine nuns and containing perhaps the earliest painting of the Madonna and Child, astonishingly mature.

The rest of the time was taken up with social events, sightseeing and farewells. On the last morning of his visit, the Archbishop prayed at the tomb of John XXIII. Archbishop Benelli then joined the party, bringing last greetings and prayers from Paul VI, and accompanied the guest to the airport.

Responses to ARCIC

In the following October the Synod of Bishops gathered in Rome. Their principal theme, decided by the Synod committee, was 'Catechesis'. A draft agenda had been circulated in advance and comments invited. The subject of ecumenism was hardly touched, as the SPCU noted.[3] Speaking on the secretariat's behalf at an early session, Cardinal Willebrands strongly criticized this glaring lacuna.

> Sometimes in the past catechesis actually was a source of prejudice, false interpretation, hatred for others.

Listing some of the necessary ecumenical elements of catechesis he was able to draw plentifully on conciliar texts and also on the papal document *Evangelii Nuntiandi* which itself was based on the findings of the Third Episcopal Synod.

In a later speech the Cardinal took the chance of telling the Synod about the activity of the SPCU – a matter about which it could be safely surmised that its members were very unequally informed. He spoke of the various dialogues and said particularly:

> On the subject of what is to be done with the results of the Anglican–Catholic dialogue there are some interesting elements in the Common Declaration of the Holy Father and Archbishop Dr Coggan, published on the occasion of the Archbishop's recent visit to Rome. After referring to the three documents mentioned above it says 'We now recommend that work ... begun be pursued, through procedures appropriate to our respective Communions, so that both of them may be led along the path towards unity.'

What follows is significant: 'The moment will shortly come when the respective Authorities must evaluate the conclusions' (SPCU Information Service no. 34, p. 4). With regards to the fruits dialogue will bear for the two communions, the statement continues:

> The response of both communions to the work and fruits of theological dialogue will be measured by the practical response of the faithful to the task of restoring unity, which, as the Second Vatican Council says, 'involves the whole Church, faithful and clergy alike, and extends to everyone, according to the talents of each. (*Unitatis Redintegratio,* no. 5; SPCU Information Service no. 34, p. 4).

It goes on to say that such practical response has been encouraging.

Throughout 1977 and 1978 it became increasingly obvious that Venice ('Authority I') was attracting more attention than its predecessors. The nearest thing to an immediate official Anglican judgement (reaction is a better word) was in the meeting of the General Synod in February 1977.

The report had a mixed reception, not merely in the sense that some liked it and some did not. One or two speakers welcomed the statement while questioning its claim to provide any basis for *immediate* action – a very arguable position. While ARCIC had always envisaged (if rather vaguely) the idea of communion by stages, it could hardly suppose that full sacramental sharing could be justified at the present stage of agreement about papal authority. What the synod debate revealed was not so much the persisting differences isolated in Venice, para. 24, but the profound psychological differences between liberal academic Anglicanism and the Catholic conception of Church Authority. An editorial in *Theology* (no. 30, 1977) exalted such diverse independent spirits as Kierkegaard, Péguy and Simone Weil at the expense of the 'cloying institutional solipsism' of ARCIC, and concluded:

> if we forget such people, we may arrive at our *Italian ecumenical destination* sooner, but only to discover that something absolutely indispensable has been left behind. [Italics mine]

Commenting on some of Bishop Montefiore's not unrelated difficulties, Professor Henry Chadwick observed. 'If one is setting out to reformulate an objective basis for unity, the requirement of unity of *faith* is not a sign of obtuseness' (italics mine).

From the collation of these responses and those of the Lambeth Conference, the ACC hoped to elicit: (a) an affirmation of the congruence of the three ARCIC statements with Anglican teaching; and (b) an affirmation that the three statements provided a sufficient basis for further official dialogue between the Roman Catholic Church and the Churches of the Anglican Communion, with 'united not absorbed' as its goal. The Church of England handed over this task to its Faith and Order Advisory Group (FOAG), which however did not produce its answer until some weeks after the Lambeth Conference – December 1978.

In the months preceding the Conference, the ACC had received answers to its enquiry from many provinces of the Communion, the USA, New Zealand, Australia, Canada, South Africa, Scotland and Wales. None of them went quite so far as the eventual Lambeth resolution except the Episcopal Church of the USA. Its long response said:

Despite historically conditioned differences [United States] ARC finds, after nineteen joint consultations, that they have such profound agreement on the level of faith as to be sister churches.

In other provinces the typical response to the ACC's first question was that the ARCIC documents provided a good basis for further dialogue.

NOTES

1. The topic of the ordination of women priests began to surface. It should have done so earlier, as Archbishop Ramsey said.
2. Bishop Howe retired in 1982 and was succeeded by Canon Samuel Van Culin of ECUSA.
3. For some time there had been pressure for a synod on Ecumenism and this would have been a good time for it, but there was no enthusiasm in the Curia for the idea.

Lambeth Conference 1978: Authority II

Lambeth

The mood of the Lambeth Conference of 1978 was certainly one of concern about unity and authority, but this mood arose only very indirectly from the deliberations of ARCIC. It was as much an internal Anglican problem arising from the divisions about the ordination of women to the priesthood. One division *was* about the ecumenical aspect of this matter. Some thought it of decisive importance, other were rather touchy and impatient of its being overstressed. The organizers were clearly anxious that the issue of women priests should not devour the conference's attention.

Of the 197 pages of preparatory essays, only two short papers were directly concerned with Ecumenism. One by Ian Fraser (the Dean of Mission at Selly Oak Colleges) was largely concerned with cutting commissions of professional theologians down to size; the other, by the veteran ecumenist and former Bishop of Bristol, Oliver Tomkins, concentrated on the general pattern and development of Anglican participation in the Ecumenical Movement, though stressing the decisive effect of Roman Catholic entry into the movement.

More directly important to ARCIC was the section on Episcopal Ministry, which opened with a characteristically brilliant essay by Henry Chadwick on 'Episcopacy in the New Testament'.

Even more concise and riveting was the speech on 'Roman Catholic relationships' which he delivered to the full conference. When he had done, there was not much excuse for anyone remaining fluffy in his mind about what ARCIC was doing or what its statements meant.

Turning to Authority, on which Anglicans and Roman Catholics are accustomed to widely differing styles, he dwelt on the bases of authority: 'on all this Rome and Canterbury agree'; 'dispersed authority' as treasured in Anglicanism does not mean 'so dispersed that you cannot find it', but it does mean that 'We fear concentration of authority in one person alone whose judgement can be swayed by his background, experience and national culture'.

Venice had set out to see whether these two different concepts of authority could be reconciled. It has 'a central basis – that primacy and conciliarity are complementary, but about primacy it sets out difficulties still in process of resolution'.

The Archbishop of Canterbury also dwelt on the nature and practice of Anglican authority. To have a single head is 'not of the genius of Anglicanism'. The Lambeth Conference? No. The Anglican Consultative Council? No. A Doctrinal Commission? I believe the Communion needs one, he said, but added that it could only function for doctrine. He inclined to the idea of regular, well-briefed meetings of primates, in the very closest and most intimate contact with the ACC.

There is a difference between a 'dispersed' authority in the sense of multiple sources (like the Lambeth Quadrilateral) from which decisions are drawn and by which they must be tested, and an authority dispersed among living persons. The first kind is as much Roman as Anglican in the sense that both need it, inescapably. The second is where the rub comes. Both sides admit that there has existed group authority in the form of ecumenical councils. Only one side has a Pope. Is he in fact the very negation of group or conciliar authority, or must his *primatial* authority be in balance or harmony with it? Venice agreed that it must, but Anglicans were not at all convinced that habitually it was. At the same time they were showing signs of wanting somebody who, in the words of Venice, para. 12, 'exercised his oversight in order to guard and promote the faithfulness of all the Churches to Christ and to one another'.

The Lambeth Conference of 1978 welcomed the work of ARCIC, and recognized it as a 'solid achievement in which we can recognize the faith of our Church'. The Conference invited the Commission to consider responses and provide further explanation. It also invited the respective authorities to consider the Agreed Statements in the light of the Malta Report, 'with a view to bringing about a closer sharing between our two communions in life, worship and mission'.

No. 4 was of course giving a Conference answer to the question asked in the last sentences of Venice (para. 26; FR, p. 67).

ARCIC was due to hold its annual full meeting shortly after the Lambeth Conference but plans were disrupted by the death of Paul VI. The Conference reacted to this with most generous sympathy, inviting the three Roman Catholic observers to celebrate a requiem Mass for the Pope which nearly all attended.

Some days later a successor, John Paul I, was elected. Grief followed too quickly with his sudden death and in October his successor, the present Pope, was installed.

Back to ARCIC

ARCIC was unable to arrange its full meeting before 12–20 January 1979, but sub-commissions met twice to examine the reactions to the three statements and prepared the Elucidations which were published in the following June, dealing with the statements on Eucharist and Ministry.

By the time the full Commission assembled again at Venice, 28 August–6 September 1979, it had accumulated a mass of material for its two remaining tasks – its assault on the four serious problems of Venice para. 24, but also material which called for elucidation of 'Authority I'.

This latter included the relevant parts of the 'Responses' of the Church of England prepared by the Faith and Order Advisory Group, which should have been presented to the Lambeth Conference (see above, p. 194) but did not appear until December 1978. Some account of this should now be given before turning to criticism from the Roman Catholic side.

The Faith and Order Advisory Group (FOAG) began by asking ACC what it meant by 'congruent' with Anglican teaching. Did it mean (a) permissible within the Church, given goodwill; (b) representative of mainstream Anglican thought; or (c) what might be considered authoritative teaching with mandatory force? ACC opted for (b) but FOAG eventually chose its own formula: 'acceptable to all the mainstreams of thought within our Church'.

On turning specifically to the Venice statement, the FOAG response emphasized several points. How far is freedom to dissent compatible with the preservation of true *koinonia* (40)? Behind the Venice sentence 'Restatement builds upon and does not contradict the truth intended by the original definition', does there lurk a Roman Catholic tendency to what might be called a merely cumulative view of truth (43)? ARCIC it felt to be still too inclined towards an automatic ratification of the past (44).

FOAG recognizes that 'any process of attempting to discover the *sensus fidelium* cannot but be a long and complex matter' but welcomes agreement on the importance of co-operation between clergy and laity.

FOAG (agreeing with Yves Congar, for example) puzzles over the Venice sentence 'Local Councils from the second century determined the limits of the New Testament'.

FOAG followed many Anglican critics in seeing Venice contradicting Article 21 by saying 'ecumenical councils' decisions on fundamental matters of faith exclude what is erroneous'. It questioned whether Venice's description of an (ideal?) universal primacy does justice to the full position held by the Roman Catholic Church.

Finally FOAG said (very reasonably at that stage, it seems to me):

> What we have to ask is whether any of these questions is so fundamental and important that it must be resolved before further action can be taken to bring about a closer sharing between our two communions in life, worship and mission.

This multiple and precise question is hardly susceptible of a plain 'yes' or 'no'. FOA6 ended with this brief verdict:

> We report that in our view the three Statements are sufficiently congruent with Anglican teaching to provide a theological basis for further official dialogue between the Roman Catholic Church and the Churches of the Anglican Communion.

CDF observations

Among Roman Catholic reactions to 'Venice', that of the Congregation for the Doctrine of the Faith was of practical importance.

The CDF's first complaint was that Venice had 'failed to utilise the significant gains of the statement on ministry'. It seemed to think that Venice had to *repeat* the ministry statement – though they were both intended to be part of a single Final Report.

They detected a covert attack on clerical status in the paragraphs on reception, which they took as saying that doctrinal decisions on the part of the episcopal authority are conditioned by acceptance on the part of the faithful. This they took as attributing to the faithful an authority co-equal with that of an ecumenical council. Fr Tillard, replying to the CDF's

Observations, detected here, not surprisingly, a confusion between *sensus fidelium* (a subtle concept) and *consent* of the faithful as some kind of counting of heads. The matter was later clarified in Elucidation 3 (FR p. 72) though in fact it was clear enough in para. 12.[1]

Venice was also said to 'limit the *authority* of ecumenical councils to doctrinal decisions on fundamental matters of faith' and 'the central truths of salvation'. This was an evident misreading of para. 14, which did not limit the authority of ecumenical councils but their *inerrancy*.[2] This too is dealt with in the first part of Elucidation 3. On these grounds the CDF proceeds to conclude that the document seems to '*omit* the basic principle of episcopal authority for which the Commission had already prepared the way in the document on Ministry'. What about the basic principles of primacy?

The CDF's 'Observations' take exception to the first part of Venice, para. 12, which speaks of the primacy of Rome as 'emerging in an historical context by a providential process'. The 'Observations' object that according to the faith of the Church, 'the Roman primacy was not merely a providential happening but was an actualization of the constitutive intention of Christ himself'. If that last phrase means 'what Christ intended', how great is the difference implied by 'not merely'? (But see also Elucidation 8, 'Primacy and history', FR, p. 76; and the excellent 'Co-Chairmen's Preface'. FR, p. 49.)

The 'Observations' did not finally regard Venice as more than 'The first step in a dialogue which calls for more research and reflection'.

In an article in *The Month* in March 1977, Edward Yarnold pointed out that the Venice argument for papal primacy was 'hardly compelling enough to counter the Anglican feeling that it would be an unjustifiable risk to put themselves at the mercy of Roman government'. As Yarnold put it, 'the onus is on Rome to make Roman primacy practically as well as theologically credible to Anglicans'. ARCIC still had work to do on the theological credibility, it could do little or nothing about the practical. The onus was one which Paul VI had been aware of: it rested lightly on the shoulders of most of the Curia.

Return to Venice

The *Final Report* tell us (p. 104): 'The Commission resumed its discussion of authority at the Casa Cardinale Piazza, Venice, 28 August 1979', to consider the paper listed as ARCIC 204, which was the work of Jean Tillard OP and the Evangelical Anglican Julian Charley, a 'Draft Continuation of Venice 24'. In nearly ten years of ARCIC dialogue these two had become very close friends.[3]

There was of course other material at the Commission's disposal, but in fact the meeting at once set about discussing the Tillard/Charley draft, plunging without preliminary into Section I on the 'Petrine texts'. This problem had been stated in Venice 24 in this laconic fashion:

> Claims on behalf of the Roman see as commonly presented in the past have put a great weight on the Petrine texts (Matt 16:18–19; Luke 22:31–32; John 21:15–17) than they are generally thought to be able to bear. However, many Roman Catholic scholars do not now feel it necessary to stand by former exegesis of these texts in every respect.

It would be hard to think of a more gossamer-like way of dissociating oneself from the heavy tread of Vatican I's *Pastor Aeternus*, composed of course in a very different age and circumstances, but leaning heavily on the texts. Robustly, Professor Lampe at the Synod of 1977, discussing the Venice statement, expressed his satisfaction that 'the Petrine texts, which never had anything to do with the papacy anyway, seem at last to have been jettisoned'.

In a paper supplied to ARCIC no. 107, not dated), 'The New Testament basis for a Petrine Office peculiar to Peter himself within the Apostolic Community', Bishop R. P. C. Hanson, having examined the evidence, proclaimed himself an unrepentant Western Latin Christian and, acknowledging the part that the papacy had played in history, admitted he could in certain circumstances 'be induced to acknowledge the primacy and authority of the Pope *ex animo* and *ex conscientia*'.

> What I could not imagine myself ever agreeing to is the acceptance of the views that Papal office and Papal power are based upon an institution by our Lord in the days of his flesh or that they are in any serious sense witnessed to in the New Testment.

ARCIC refused to be shaken out of its pacific stand. It rehearsed (FR, pp. 81–2, para. 3) the many Petrine texts, saying that they witness to an early tradition and special place which Peter clearly held during Christ's ministry. It distinguished those texts which applied equally to all the apostles (para. 4), emphasizing that responsibility for pastoral leadership was not restricted to Peter. It pointed to those distinctive features of Peter's ministry – service, not domination, strengthening the brethren, overcoming threats to unity – 'which help clarify the analogy that has been drawn between the role of Peter among the apostles and that of the Bishop of Rome among his fellow bishops' (para. 5).

Only an analogy? Para. 6 goes on:

> The New Testament contains no explicit record of a transmission of Peter's leadership nor of apostolic authority. Furthermore, the Petrine texts were differently interpreted as early as the patristic age. Yet the Church at Rome 'the city in which Peter and Paul taught and were martyred, came to be recognized as having a special responsibility for unity and fidelity to the apostolic inheritance'.

Its last paragraph, no. 9, gave first a description of the Church which echoes Article 19 of the Thirty-Nine Articles, and concluded:

> In a re-united Church a ministry modelled on the role of Peter will be a sign and a safeguard for such unity.

Divine right

Venice 24b (FR, p. 64) said that the language of divine right used in Vatican I of the successors of Peter 'has no clear interpretation in modern Roman Catholic theology', but that 'if it is understood as affirming that the primacy of the Bishop of Rome is part of God's design for the universal *koinonia* then it need not be a matter of disagreement'. This was certainly true if you subscribed to the argument of 'Authority I'. 'Authority II' put it more bluntly: 'What does the language actually mean?' The key words in chapter 2 of *Pastor Aeternus* are *ex ipsius Christi Domini institutione seu jure divino*. We have no means of knowing (or showing) that Christ *instituted* the Roman primacy in the ordinary sense of the term, except from the New Testament, and in 24a it was agreed that the New Testament does not provide this direct evidence. What then does *jure divino* signify?[4] 'Authority II', still following the Tillard/Charley draft, spoke of what it did and did not mean. Para. 11, giving the first innings to the Catholics, recognized that (a) it means at least that universal primacy expresses God's will for the Church; (b) it does not mean that it was founded as an institution by Christ during his life on earth; (c) it does not mean that the universal primacy was a source of the Church, as if Christ's salvation had to be channelled through it; (d) rather, the universal primate is the sign of the visible *koinonia* of the whole Church.

'Authority II' (FR, p. 87, para. 13) went beyond discussion about the meaning of *jus divinum*.

Given the above interpretation of the language of divine right in the First Vatican Council, it is reasonable to ask whether a gap really exists between the assertion of a primacy by divine right (*jure divino*) and the acknowledgement of its emergence by divine providence (*divina providentia*).

Jurisdiction

'Authority II', para. 16, addresses itself to 'Authority I', para. 24d.

Jurisdiction in the Church may be defined as the authority or power (*potestas*) necessary for the exercise of an office. In both our communions it is given for the effective fulfilment of office and this fact determines its exercise and limits. It varies according to the specific functions of the *episcope* concerned. The jurisdictions associated with different levels of episcope (e.g. of primates, metropolitans and diocesan bishops) are not in all respects identical.

Critics had asked what was meant by jurisdiction. The Vatican I decree *Pastor Aeternus*, chapter 1, had declared that the Lord had given to Peter a primacy which was not merely of honour but of 'true and proper jurisdiction' (DS 3055): full, supreme, truly episcopal, ordinary, immediate, which therefore now belonged to the Bishop of Rome.

In a paper supplied to ARCIC, 'The concept of jurisdiction in the Catholic Church', Professor Alberigo of the University of Bologna had pointed out that *jurisdiction* was a word used in the Church only since the Middle Ages, and had been subject to wide fluctuations of meaning and loose use. Vatican I had given it as wide a meaning as possible.

There were some among both the minority and the majority at Vatican

I who sought for a principle on which the limits of papal juridiction could be indicated. It was a principle long afterwards adopted by ARCIC.

The discussion of authority continued over three meetings and seven or eight re-drafts of the Tillard/Charley paper. The final draft took the sensible course of beginning with its own brief definition of jurisdiction: the authority or power (*potestas*) necessary for the *exercise of an office*. As such of course it existed for both Anglicans and Roman Catholics. The words I have underlined are key. They send us back to the statement on Ministry (FR, p. 33, para. 9). An essential element in the ordained ministry is the responsibility for oversight (*episcope*). It was already clear and agreed that the ministry of *episcope* is exercised at various levels, that is in the various offices or *munera*. But what all these have in common is not that they exercise identical or universal jurisdiction but that they serve the *koinonia* – that which *unites* all 'local' churches. The chief *munus* (function) of the *episcope* of the universal primate is 'to serve the faith and unity of the whole Church' and 'to exercise the jurisdiction necessary for the fulfilment of his functions' (ibid.)

Jean Tillard in his book *The Bishop of Rome* shows clearly that the idea of determining papal jurisdiction by focusing on the *episcope* of unity was aired and welcomed in the debates of Vatican I. As *Pastor Aeternus* put it, however:

> But that the episcopate should be one and individual and the whole multitude of the faithful preserved in unity of faith and communion through a united priesthood, he placed Peter at the head of the apostles as the perpetual principle and visible foundation of this twofold unity. (DS 3050)

Vatican II in *Lumen Gentium* set out, as everybody knows, to redress the balance by refashioning the theology of Church and episcopate.[5] It did not do this by repudiating what Vatican I had said about jurisdiction (*potestas*). It simply put it in its proper place. In the third chapter we get to the 'Hierarchical structure with special reference to the episcopate?' Already if we have read the first two chapters we can never again read the canons of *Pastor Aeternus* in the same way. We are now talking about a *communion*, of people and of churches, which all authority serves. The words *supreme*, *ordinary*, *immediate* and so on have lost their 'political' resonance.

This is the line of thought that runs through 'Authority II' on Jurisdiction; certain points stand out:

1. The authority of the bishop, i.e. jurisdiction, is not the arbitary power of one man over the freedom of others but a necessity if the bishop is to serve his flock as its shepherd.
2. This applies equally to the universal primate. Several thoughts occur about this. (a) Till the crack of doom there will be parish priests, bishops, metropolitans and Popes who are by nature inclined to authoritarianism, just as there are prime ministers who are bossy or nonentities. What matters is the force of the checks and balances built into the system. This brings us to: (b) In a world organization it is utter nonsense to talk simply of the arbitary power of one man.
3. Para. 18 of 'Authority II' (FR, p. 89) tries defusing Anglican anxieties by explaining that 'ordinary' and 'immediate' are technical, canonical terms which mean that jurisdiction belongs to the office, to the episcopal order, and is not something stuck on afterwards, and that it is only called universal because the unity it administers is universal.

Paras 19 and 21 (FR, pp. 89 and 90) come back to the generalized assurances based on the newly stressed collegial character of primacy and the 'moral' limits to universal jurisdiction.

Infallibility

ARCIC had already agreed on the *sources* of authoritative teaching, in Venice, para. 18 (FR, p. 61): Scriptures, Creeds, Fathers, Early Councils. It went on to recognize the possibility of human error among those responsible for teaching, but added what was in fact a proper description of the Anglican doctrine of indefectibility. Mistakes and abuses cannot destroy the Church's teaching ability. Christ will not desert his Church and the Holy Spirit will lead it into all truth. What does 'papal infallibility' add to this?

Indefectibility is not an exclusively Anglican word. The original comprehensive schema *De Ecclesia Christi* of fifteen chapters, called *Supremi Pastoris*, distributed to Vatican I in January 1870 but never used, had a chapter (VIII) on the Indefectibility of the Church and another (IX) on its Infallibility.[6]

Chapter XI of the same schema was *De Romani Pontificis Primatu*. This was eventually enlarged and brought forward in the agenda to form *Pastor Aeternus*, where the infallibility of the *Pope* was now included. A considerable part of the council opposed the definition, and when Pius IX refused a last-minute request to modify the text, many departed before the last session rather than sign the decree (DS, p. 595).

In ecumenical discussions of it the Catholic side has tended to appear in the dock and the other on the bench. This tendency was not wholly absent from ARCIC's discussion of the topic, but a brave effort was made to rise above it in approaching 'Authority II' – in, for example, a paper entitled '1870: in search of a definition of the problem' (on internal evidence ascribable to Henry Chadwick).

The Christian faith – according to this paper – has two aspects. It is a *deposit*, which implies protection, looking after in proportion as you value it. But the deposit of faith is a living treasure, given by the Lord and redeemer and sustained by the Spirit; but it needs to be commended to 'all sorts and conditions of men' in every age, and at the same time to be protected. This is not done by adding to it.

Faith belongs to the Church, and the Church is a living organism, keeping alive a living organism. Living things need foods: spiritual food first – what old-fashioned Christians call charity and grace, and sacraments. But next, food for the understanding, which grows strong and repels disease. Anglicans and Roman Catholics could agree on all this, but not necessarily on where to turn to for medicine in case of illness.

ARCIC's 'Authority II' begins with Christ, the way, the truth and the life. It goes on to the Spirit-guided witness of the Church with its prophets, saints and martyrs of every generation.[7] It then considers the *magisterium*, the teaching authority; first in general. Teaching, has already been agreed on as an integral part of the *episcope* of the ordained ministry – though not confined to that ministry ('Ministry and Ordination', paras 8–10).

Then comes the crucial question of

> whether there is a special ministerial gift of discerning the truth and of teaching bestowed at crucial times on one person to enable him to speak authoritatively in the name of the Church in order to preserve the people of God in the truth. (FR, p. 92, para. 23)

To answer this, the statement (FR, pp. 91–2, paras 24–26) rehearses what has in general terms been agreed, that 'at certain moments, the Church can in a matter of essential doctrine make a *decisive judgement* which becomes part of the permanent witness'. In one of its best passages 'Authority II' then describes the character and conditions of such judgements and argues that, if you recognize the need for a universal primate, you must recognize that he can make such judgement 'in matters of faith and so exclude error'.

Paras 27–30 (FR, pp. 93–6) continue to enlarge on the character, conditions and limitations of these judgements: they are judgements of recall and emphasis, elucidating truth, exposing error, showing how faith applies to contemporary issues. The Church can only serve the needs of successive generations if it is faithful to the Gospel through all modes and changes of expression.[8] It maintains this faithful service by the co-operation of the teaching authority and the theologians: their mutual suspicion can only weaken it, shadow the light of the Spirit.

Attributing the power of decisive judgement on matters of faith to the universal primate, the statement, admitting that Popes have often preserved the Church from error, recalls the stringent qualifications of *Pastor Aeternus* (DS 3065–3074), chapter 4, but concludes:

> If the definition proposed for assent were not manifestly a legitimate interpretation of biblical faith and in line with orthodox tradition Anglicans would think it a duty to reserve the reception of the definition for study and discussion

This brings us to para. 30 and to the dogmas of the Immaculate Conception and the Assumption of Our Lady. It had been restated neatly enough in the original Tillard/Charley draft:

> Anglicans for their part have no difficulty in recognising that the universal primate, who has to speak in the name of his fellow bishops for the sake of the *koinonia*, especially when the issue is a crucial one, is assisted by the Holy Spirit to express the mind of the Church. *But* they do not consider that the two infallible definitions given by the Bishop of Rome fulfil the necessary conditions. They call in question the legitimacy and possibility of making infallible statements on subjects such as these.

What ARCIC says in FR, pp. 95–6, para. 30 shows some advance in agreement on what these dogmas *mean*. What Anglicans cannot understand is why they had to be defined as dogmas.

Having entitled its treatment of Venice 24 'Infallibility' (FR, p. 65), ARCIC in 'Authority II' went on to discuss its pros and cons for nine long paragraphs (FR, pp. 91–9) before using the word.

Roman Catholics must bear much of the blame for the historical fact that Anglicans (and others) have grown up with distorted ideas of papal primacy. It is fairly easy to set out and explain the history, but much less easy to dispel the present facts. The distorted ideas existed on both sides. Secondary things like paraliturgical growths – the tiara, silver trumpets, St Peter's, and so on – helped to build up a cult which had little to do with doctrine.

Popes since John XXIII have done much to dispel exaggerations of cult and to stress and justify what always lay behind them, the affectionate conception of the primate as a Father, which is deeply theological. People see John Paul II and his conception of his office in different ways, but it is laughable to think of him as remote.

But para. 33 (FR, p. 98) admits the changes that are occurring:

> Contemporary discussions of conciliarity and primacy in both communions indicate that we are not dealing with positions destined to remain static. We suggest that some difficulties will not be wholly resolved until a practical initiative has been taken and our two Churches have lived together more visibly in one *koinonia*.

NOTES

1. Cf. Yarnold/Chadwick, p. 20: 'The Faith which all Christians share is primarily a personal faith in Jesus Christ and only secondarily the ability to make orthodox statements of belief about him. Belief in the *sensus fidelium* does not imply a belief that every Christian is a reliable exponent of theology.'
2. This is very much as Vatican I limits papal infallibility.
3. Tillard's substantial work *Eglise d'Eglises* (Cerf, 1989) is dedicated to Julian Charley.
4. Cardinal Ratzinger, in the interview given to the German news agency KNA shortly after the publication of the 'Observations', remarked 'there is quite a varying content in the interpretation of the divine right, which must remain a subject for reflection before one can simply say that the difference has been eliminated'. He felt that the claim conceded in the *Final Report* was 'more pragmatic and less fundamental'.
5. For fuller comment on this and the perceptive reactions of Prof. Fairweather, see pp. 69–70 above. Fairweather was a member of ARCIC and an observer at Vatican II.
6. Cf. *Papal Primacy and the Universal Church*, p. 144.
7. But not leaving out Pascal's applewoman or retired colonels in a General Synod. They all share the *sensus fidelium*, properly understood.
8. The poet, whose tools are words, is more sensitive to their qualities and dangers:

> words strain
> Crack and sometimes break, under the burden
> Under the tension slip, slide, perish

Decay with imprecision, will not stay in place
Will not stay still. Shrieking voices
Scolding, mocking, or merely chattering,
Always assail them. The Word in the desert
Is most attacked by voices of temptation,
The crying shadow in the funeral dance
The loud lament of the disconsolate chimera.

T. S. Eliot, *Four Quartets: Burnt Norton*

The Pope in Great Britain

Before ARCIC broke up for the last time, 8 September 1981, its co-chairmen wrote to John Paul II and to the Archbishop of Canterbury putting two questions:

— whether the Agreed Statements on Eucharistic Doctrine, on Ministry and on Authority in the Church (I and II), together with the Elucidations, are consonant in substance with the faith of the Roman Catholic Church and the Anglican Communion;
— whether the Final Report offers a sufficient basis for taking the next concrete step towards the reconciliation of the Churches grounded in agreement in faith.

The next sentence of their letter showed that they were expecting no prompt answer:

Even while these questions are being deliberated we recommend the setting up of a new commission.

This would be to 'work out the implications of such reconciliation in the event of a favourable answer' and 'suggest the stages through which the two Churches would eventually move towards organic unity' ...

There was an important background to this. From 26 April to 2 May there had been a meeting of the Anglican Primates in Washington DC to which Archbishop McAdoo, the co-chairman of ARCIC, had supplied a memorandum. Instancing a general sense of urgency about what would happen following the Final Report and referring to Anglican 'dispersed authority', the Archbishop went on:

> we are left in certain cases with a need to express ourselves as a total communion. Should this be done and can it be done? How can it be done in a way consistent with our Anglican ethos?

The solution he proposed was precisely the co-chairmen's letter just quoted, which would then come before the attention of the fifth meeting of the Anglican Consultative Council, which was to be held at Newcastle in September 1981.

The ACC proposed that the next ARCIC should devote itself to promoting 'reception', which is not merely the acceptance of statements by the authorities but a new spirit of reception created throughout the respective communions.

The Roman response to the ARCIC co-chairmen's letter was totally different. Their problem was to involve those members of the College of Bishops who had to deal regularly with Anglicans and with the ecumenical attitudes of their own flocks. It was not an insuperable *practical* problem. The SPCU was perfectly accustomed to circulating ecumenical texts to episcopal conferences. But the attitude of the Congregation for the Doctrine of the Faith was very different. They pointed out that, in accordance with a decision taken on 18 May 1977, the report should not even be sent to the episcopal conferences before being examined by the CDF, and suggested that a commission formed of some members of the SPCU and some of the International Theological Commission chosen by the Secretariat might help the Congregation for Doctrine, and even that a few ARCIC theologians might present the report to the CDF *consulta* before the Congregation began to form its judgement.

There was another complication which made for urgency. The Pope was to visit Britain in a few months, and the Catholic authorities in England made little secret of the fact that, if the report were still in bond when the papal visit took place, the impact of the visit and the atmosphere surrounding it would be seriously impaired.

On 27 November, the undersecretary of the SPCU, Fr Pierre Duprey, visited Mgr Bovone of the CDF to explain this urgency and to request for the ARCIC report not a *definitive* judgement, but a *declaration* (interim judgement) to the effect that the Report is a serious theological work, that may be published on the sole responsibilities of the members of the Commission. This would seem perfectly natural to the Anglican authorities and create a better impression in England. The SPCU was prepared also to follow the procedure adopted with 'Authority I' (see above, Chapter 19) and invite a theologian esteemed by both the Congregation for the Doctrine of the Faith and the Secretariat to write an accompanying critique. (This time it was Père Lecuyer CSSP.)

Mgr Bovone replied that he was familiar with these arguments but unimpressed by them. He saw no reason why the full procedure of the Congregation for a definitive judgement – one or more consultations, a cardinals' meeting and a papal audience – should not be possible before the end of January 1982, provided the material was ready in the next few days and *nothing equally urgent required study in the meantime* (italics mine).

Two days after this meeting the new Prefect of the Sacred Congregation for the Doctrine of the faith, the Cardinal Archbishop of Munich, Joseph Ratzinger, took up his place in the Palazzo Sant'Uffizio.

It was 14 January 1982 before any more news was forthcoming, and it was hardly glad tidings. The Secretariat of State informed the SPCU that the Congregation for Doctrine would finish its examination of the Final Report on 24 February and report its findings to the Pope on 26 February. There was one comfort. The idea of a *definitive* verdict had been given up. The CDF was to confine itself to 'Observations', which were eventually dated and published on 29 March.

In the meantime, Cardinal Willebrands had the draft and seemed not very pleased with it. Although the contents of the report had been widely leaked, the CDF intended to distribute the text of the report *with* its own observations and covering letter to the episcopal conferences. This had always previously been done by the SPCU but now they were only even notified of it by letter on 16 April.

In the meantime the Congregation learned that there was to be a press conference presenting the Final Report in London on publication date, 29 March. The Congregation then took the extraordinary step of sending its official, Mgr Bovone, to London with a letter signed by Cardinal Ratzinger and addressed to Bishop Clark, the Catholic co-chairman of ARCIC. The latter was summoned to the papal nunciature on the late evening of 28 March (all the way from rural Norfolk) and told that he must read the letter to the press conference on the following day. This he refused to do, but said that he would give the substance of it in indirect speech. The retort was that in that case the letter would be published in next day's *Osservatore Romano* (afternoon of 30 March with date of 31 March). All of this was done without reference to the SPCU.

At Castelgandolfo on 4 September 1980 the Pope had congratulated ARCIC thus:

> . . . you have gone behind the habits of thought and expression born and nourished in enmity and controversy to scrutinize together the great common treasure, to clothe it in a language at once traditional and expressive of the insights of an age which no longer glories in strife but seeks to come together in listening to the quiet voice of the Spirit.

Plainly the CDF did not share this view of ARCIC's approach. In a dozen places it complained of ambiguity, and of phrases which 'could be read in more than one way'.[1]

The present writer reached the age of retirement from the Vatican service in May 1981. It was a few weeks before the last meeting of ARCIC I, and a very few more before the fifth meeting of the ACC at Newcastle. Apart from any personal considerations, if this had been rigidly enforced it would have borne hard on any successor however well-equipped. This was represented by the SPCU to the relevant authorities, who after much consideration reprieved me until the end of the calendar year. I left my office on New Year's Eve, with feelings it would be complicated and of no consequence to describe, though with many grateful memories.

What therefore follows here is of a different character, still reliant on the sources described but no longer to the same extent on personal memories. It owes much to conversations with my accomplished and lamented friend and successor, Richard Stewart, whose sadly sudden death deprived Anglican–Roman Catholic relations of an outstanding servant.

Roman arrangements

It was naturally to be expected that the coming of Joseph Ratzinger from Munich to the Roman CDF would have a considerable impact, not least at this critical moment in Anglican–Roman Catholic relations. He came of a strong Bavarian Catholic background, but had academic experience in Bonn (1959), Münster (1963), Tübingen (1966) and Regensburg.

It is not easy to distinguish the part played by the new prefect in the 'Observations'. They were already well matured when he took his place. The letter which was sent to Bishop Clark in advance of the publication was decided on at an ordinary meeting of the CDF (24 March) and received papal approval two days later. But the style of the letter suggests that before signing it Cardinal Ratzinger did something to soften its tone and make it more positive and hopeful.[2]

Peter Hebblethwaite, writing in *The Tablet* a month before the 'Observations' were published, quoted the Cardinal's letter that some points in the *Final Report* 'do not seem to be easily reconciled with Catholic doctrine'. Hebblethwaite commented benignly 'Cardinal Ratzinger does not imply that it cannot be done but he would like to be shown how. That is a perfectly legitimate request.'

The next immediate and practical question was how the Pope's coming visit to England could be turned to the best ecumenical advantage. On the eve of the Epiphany, Professor Henry Chadwick was in Rome and met those staff members of the SPCU concerned with Anglicans, together with the Director of the Anglican Centre, Canon Root (an ARCIC member) and the Revd Christopher Hill, Anglican co-secretary of ARCIC. Professor Chadwick was clearly acting as envoy for the Archbishop of Canterbury.

John Paul II was aware of this meeting and most anxious for it to take place. Professor Chadwick began by stressing the historic and very present importance of the papal visit. It was a unique opportunity for ecumenical common witness – for joint manifestation of allegiance to Christ. Anglican primates from overseas, and Orthodox and Free Church leaders would be invited.

The next day but one, Professor Chadwick had an audience with the Pope – which lasted through lunch. The question of an Anglican eucharist at Canterbury was raised. The Pope had clearly been thinking in other terms, but was far from rejecting the idea out of hand – he wanted more time to think and pray. Other proposals for Canterbury were discussed and raised no real problem: a common declaration, which would include the announcing of a new dialogue commission 'whose first task would be to examine the reconciliation of ministries'.

Finally the question of leaders from 'free' Protestant Churches was broached. The Pope seemed to hope to meet them on a 'human' level, outside the formalities of a liturgy, and the Archbishop had already anticipated this.

English arrangements

In England Cardinal Hume and his fellow bishops had many things to occupy their minds concerning the visit, but were far from ignoring its ecumenical aspect. They were aware that this was the aspect which in previous papal journeys had been widely regarded as least satisfactory. With the Pope's visit to England almost coinciding with the ARCIC report, the delicacy of the situation was doubled. The English Cardinal was resolved on three things: (1) that the report should be available in advance of the Pope's arrival; (2) that he, the Cardinal, should not concern himself directly with the strictly interchurch encounter, especially that at Canterbury; and (3) that he should forestall the chance that the Pope, through bad advice, should do or say anything which might be adversely interpreted in a country with which he was unfamiliar.

For Catholics, to insist on the 'pastoral' character of the visit was right, provided it was remembered that the pastoral concern of the Church now included (since Vatican II) the search for unity. It was not so very long since a tiny but loud minority of Catholics had been calling for sanctions on members of ARCIC. A badly managed papal visit could have stirred up stagnant waters again.

The Tablet had the bright idea of running a series of short articles under the general title 'Five minutes with the Pope'. There was a wide variety of contributors, including Professor Henry Chadwick himself. He pointed out that the convergence achieved in the ARCIC report was the work not of the Church of England but of the Anglican Communion in which the Church of England played a very important but not wholly characteristic role. He also stressed that if the Canterbury ceremony were to appear as an isolated exercise in ecumenical window-dressing it would be no good for inter-church relations.

The visit

The visit of a Pope, without historical precedent, was a journey over difficult and uneven ground. It could have done without the complication of the Falklands war. Repeatedly as the Pope moved about the country, beginning at Westminster Cathedral, he made brief allusions to the far-off hostilities in the Falklands. The theme never seemed obtrusive; he thought only of reconciliation, which is the binding force of the sacramental system

– the leitmotiv of his journey. Yet whenever the war was briefly mentioned it seemed to be underlined as a contrast to what the journey of faith meant.

At Westminster the Pope's discourse moved neatly from the cathedral – its architecture recalling Christian universality but also symbolizing the faith and energy of modern English Catholicism – to Canterbury where he would be next day.

> There everything speaks of ancient common tradition[3] which in this modern age we are ready to stress together. I too want to speak in this way – to mourn the long estrangement between Christians.
> My deep desire, my ardent hope and prayer is that my visit may serve the cause of Christian unity.

The Canterbury ceremony stood out in several respects. It was quieter, more circumscribed, yet reaching out to involve the heads of Anglican Churches from every part of the Communion, heads of the British Free Churches and through television, to many millions of all sorts. It combined dignity and warmth because eye and ear were drawn back to common origins. Though no Bishop of Rome had ever set foot here, one of the greatest of them, Gregory I, had sent a monk from Rome to found this Church.

The Pope spoke of the modern martyrs, Catholic and Anglican, the Pole Maximilian Kolbe and the Ugandan Anglican Archbishop Janani Luwum, who are commemorated in Canterbury Cathedral, also of all who had suffered in our time. He concluded:

> If we remember that beginning in Jesus Christ our Lord, if we can face the suffering involved in travelling his way, if we can lift our eyes beyond the historic quarrels which have tragically disfigured Christ's Church and wasted so much Christian energy, then we shall indeed enter into a faith worthy of celebration because it is able to remake the world.

John Paul II's sermon was longer but no less charged with feeling – with hope, with Christian love, with resolve, with petitions. Dwelling this Whitsuntide on the power of the Spirit of truth and unity which is poured out on us,

> let us open ourselves to his powerful love as we pray that, speaking the truth in love, we may all grow up in every way into him who is the head, into our Lord Jesus Christ.

Perhaps the most solemn moment of this historic gathering was the ceremonial renewal of baptismal vows in which every Christian there joined.

In the fashion first established in 1966 (see p. 95) the Pope and Archbishop signed a Common Declaration. It looked back thankfully on the work of ARCIC and forward to the next stage, announcing a new commission:

> Its task will be to continue the work already begun; to examine,
> especially in the light of our respective judgements on the Final
> Report, the outstanding doctrinal differences which still separate us,
> with a view towards their eventual resolution; to study all that
> hinders the mutual recognition of the ministries of our communions,
> and to recommend what practical steps will be necessary when,
> on the basis of our unity in faith, we are able to proceed to the
> restoration of full communion.

The Declaration ended with a new element, not explicit in earlier declarations but referred to in the Preface to the *Final Report*:

> Our aim is not limited to the union of two communions alone, to the
> exclusion of other Christians, but rather extends to the fulfilment
> of God's will for the visible unity of all his people. Every dialogue
> represents a renewed challenge to abandon ourselves completely to
> the truth of the Gospels.

This graceful acknowledgement of the presence, sympathy and participation of so many Christian leaders was followed later by a conversation between them and the Pope. This was necessarily too short[4] and John Paul II invited them to come to Rome to continue it. (This they did in a stay of several days in the autumn of the same year. All who observed those days were moved by the prodigious expenditure of time and labour given by the visitors, sometimes far into the night.)

On the evening of the Canterbury ceremony, the present writer moved from Canterbury to Liverpool, committed to help with a broadcast from the Anglican cathedral there. As the Pope walked down the nave to warm applause a good woman at the nave end of a bench was so excited that she dropped her rosary at his feet. Almost without pausing he stooped down, picked it up and handed it back to her.

For Anglicans, there was little or nothing the Pope said which could not be echoed as an act of common witness. More even than all this, the 'language of signs and events' – especially in Canterbury and Liverpool, but also in Scotland – spoke eloquently of new possibilities in places where the cynical commonplace had long held that 'No Popery was the residual religion'.

It was a high moment, needing to be followed up hard lest it should be subject to the law of diminishing returns.

NOTES

1. Interesting to compare this with Michael Ramsey's comment in *Theology* (May 1982): 'The reader is likely to be impressed that while there are within the process some recastings of statement, some questions unanswered and some areas of uncertainty, there is throughout the discussions an intellectual coherence and *a refusal to accept the superficial or the ambiguous*. There is a moving impression of integrity and perseverance which makes the authors resemble Jacob wrestling until the break of day' (Italics mine).
2. It was widely felt at the time that the interview given by the new president to the German news agency KNA reflected much more faithfully his own approach to the Final Report than did anything in the 'Observations'. It was a momentous departure from precedent – but not the last – for the head of the SCDF to descend into the public arena to discuss the subject of a document recently issued officially by the Congregation. (Interview printed in large part in *The Tablet* (1 May 1982), pp. 434–5; cf. also Chapter 21 above.)
3. The phrase was lifted from the Rome *Common Declaration* of 1966.
4. It was not, however, so short but that Cardinal Willebrands could tell the SPCU plenary early in 1983 'I have been told by some of these leaders that the ecumenical situation in Great Britain following the Pope's visit was quite different from what it had been some weeks earlier. Clearly we should be open to this visitation of grace ... ' (Information Service, no. 51.)
   Cardinal Ratzinger concluded his article of March 1983 (see below, pp. 220–1):

   The problems belong to the realm of thought, the hopeful signs to the realm of life. The Pope's visit was a clear indication of this because it was a lived event, it was also a gesture of hope.

Reactions to the ARCIC Final Report

CDF reactions

Something should now be said of the fortunes of the ARCIC Final Report and something of Anglican–Roman Catholic relations at large beyond the confines of theological commissions.

In a lecture given at Fribourg University, Fr Jean Tillard said

At the moment when we disbanded, the most senior member of our group, Bishop Butler, confided to Julian Charley and myself, who were the youngest, what he called his 'envy': *we* were going to see Unity and sing the *Magnificat* while he would only be able to join in 'with the angelic choirs'. Alas, everything suggests that on this point dear Bishop Butler was wrong.

What kind of response did the Final Report evoke on both sides in the early 1980s?[1]

One of the earliest comments on the Final Report is found in an article in *La Croix* of 12 May 1982 by Fr Congar. He asked 'If each side judges attempts at agreement according to confessional criteria, must not union be regarded as chimerical, hopeless?' He told the story of St Nicholas of Flüe, a retired judge living as a hermit who was approached for arbitration by delegates of two quarrelling Swiss cantons. He took his girdle off, tied a simple knot in it, and handed it to them. 'Untie that knot', he said. 'That's not difficult', they said, and did so. 'But you wouldn't have been able to do

it if you'd each pulled on your own end', he said. 'What', goes on Fr
Congar, 'does it mean for us to stop pulling on our own end of the cord?
It means continuing to apply the ARCIC method, tackling with healthy
realism the questions which come up.'

The occasion of the article was the recent appearance of the SCDF
'Observations'. It was not in Congar's nature to indulge in Curia-bashing,
but he did allow himself to say that the *tone* of the remarks

> recalls that of the schoolmaster making red-pencil marks on the
> margin of an exercise, and would strike the public as little suited to
> welcoming dialogue after four and a half centuries of estrangement.

On 6 May the Anglican chairman of ARCIC, Archbishop McAdoo,
made a public comment on the 'Observations'. He acknowledged the
sympathetic generalities with which they began, but was disappointed to
find that in substance 'the "document" appears to be on a quite different
wave length from that of the Final Report'.

In March 1983 Cardinal Ratzinger again descended into the public
arena with an article in the recently inaugurated review *Insight*. The title
was 'Anglican–Catholic dialogue – its problems and hopes: the position
of the Roman Congregation for the Doctrine of the Faith'. The Cardinal
was an academic theologian of European reputation, and proposed to
write his article in a detached way. He pointed out (what ARCIC had
repeatedly admitted) that its findings were a service to be submitted to
the respective authorities.

> Since [ARCIC's] purpose was not merely academic but focused on
> ecclesiastical reality, the statement had to go through an official
> ecclesiastical process of examination and judgement.

This indisputable sentence was followed by a much less happy one. '*This
took place when the sessions came to an end in September 1981*' (italics mine).

In 'Observations', what the Cardinal himself had described in March
1982 as 'a contribution to dialogue' had now become 'an ecclesiastical
process of examination and judgement'. Had fifteen years' work been
dealt with in about as many days?

The Cardinal went on to say that, if this authoritative answer had caused
surprise and even 'resulted in misunderstanding and bad feeling', this was
simply because the Congregation commissioned by the Pope as the central

organ of ecclesiastical authority had set to work examining the texts as soon as they were completed. 'On the other hand the text left one completely in the dark as to the concrete structure of authority in the Anglican community.'[2] Further on, the article says 'This [the procedure just described] was an example of the functioning of precisely that structure of authority sketched out by Vatican II'.

> One can clearly recognise three characteristic elements of that structure – the office of Peter's successor, the worldwide college of bishops, and relation in dialogue to other Christian Churches and denominations. In this case we see ecumenical dialogue raised from the sphere of particular groups – which are not yet authoritative however well authorised and important they may be – and transferred to the level of matters concerning the whole Church in a universal and obligatory way. *Then the see of Peter speaks through one of its central organs,* not indeed in a definitive manner, yet with an authority which carries more weight in the Church than a merely academic publication about the question would. *Based on the teaching of the Church*, the document *provides guidelines for further development of the dialogue.* And *finally the whole college of bishops*, as successors of the apostles, *are drawn into dialogue* in their capacity of responsibility for the whole Church. [Italics mine]

We have seen that in writing to Bishop Clark in May 1982 (see above) Cardinal Ratzinger had presented the 'Observations' as 'a contribution to dialogue', a description which both surprised and impressed those familiar with the history of the Holy Office. The oscillation between this and the language of the *Insight* article must have puzzled and disillusioned them.

On the other hand, Ratzinger's actions in writing publicly showed courage and modesty. Fr Tillard, who had more than once challenged the SCDF's comments on ARCIC, wrote two long articles [3] under the general title (perhaps editorial) 'Dialogue with Cardinal Ratzinger'. He noted the problem of the dual *persona*:

> It is difficult to understand how a person who is at the head of an official body can distance himself from a document which was prepared and published by that body. But this matters little. What is of vital importance is that the opportunity has been presented for dialogue in an atmosphere of openness and tranquility.

Anglican reactions

In June 1982, the Church of England Evangelical Council published an 'Assessment and critique' of the ARCIC Final Report. The Foreword began:

> We write in the warm afterglow of the Pope's visit to Britain. He seems to irradiate the love, joy and peace of Christ. We have been challenged by his evident godliness and goodness . . . the ecumenical euphoria surrounding the Pope's visit needs to be balanced by and has set the mood for the rigorous theological discussion which is now needed.

The Introduction (p. 4) listed three things 'to applaud' in the ARCIC document:

1. Serious theological concern.
2. Resolve to go beyond (or get behind) outdated controversies.
3. Absence of rancour and the desire, shared by Evangelicals, to eschew emotive polemics.

Unfortunately the writers found this resolve mortally strained by the SCDF 'Observations', to which they proceeded to pay almost as much attention as to the Final Report.

The body of the CEEC pamphlet goes on to repeat the familiar Evangelical objections (the phrase 'totally unacceptable' occurs more than once). To read it along with the 'Observations' is to note a curious family resemblance between the two.

The Conclusion of the Final Report says 'we are well aware of how much we owe to others and of how much we have left for others to do. Our agreement needs to be *tested*.' The 'Assessment' fully accepts this, though not quite in the same sense. The only test that appears clearly is that of *scriptura sola*. (The account of the authority of Scripture given in FR, p. 52 is particularly disliked: 'Assessment', p. 9.) From opposite sides it is fallen on by both 'Assessment' and 'Observations'.

The CEEC is eager with suggestions for the new commission. It hopes 'that *several* evangelical churchmen will be invited to join it' and offers many suggestions for its agenda (italics mine):

1. Clarify the status of 'observations'.
2. Reaffirm the goal of substantial agreement but 'thoroughly and consistently' (i.e. include the things we think are substantial).
3. Review and *re-work* ARCIC I's report so as to
   (a) eliminate ambiguities (as 'Observations' says);
   (b) fuse the statements with their elucidations;[4]
   (c) pay more attention to the classical formularies of both Churches.
4. See whether there is any way forward without resorting to ambiguity.
5. Add some fresh doctrines to the agenda, e.g. justification. (This was the first thing ARCIC II did.)
6. Tackle contemporary social and ethical problems (of which a formidable list is proposed).

A different type of examination of the ARCIC documents was given in the *Modern Churchman*[5] by Professor S. W. Sykes. The main object of his interest was the statements on Authority, which he had already, in an earlier paper following on the FOAG comments, described as 'for Anglicans the most important ecumenical documents of this century'. Professor Sykes declared his intention to concentrate on the theological issues raised by ARCIC's 'authority papers' but at the same moment to argue that

> while the Anglicans ought broadly to welcome the documents as 'consonant in substance with the faith of Anglicans' there remains a considerable problem with the implication of such agreement and thus with any further stage of implementation.

Sykes begins by recalling, that Anglicanism, having been busy de-confessionalizing itself for 150 years (partly perhaps as a result of reading more and more German Protestant theology), now with 'the ARCIC movement' looks like re-confessionalizing itself – not however on the basis of the Prayer Book, the Articles and the Homilies, but on that of Vatican I and Vatican II.

> In particular, if the Anglican Communion were to accept ARCIC's argument for a universal primacy, would the nature of that primacy be expounded in the particular definitions and declarations of the Roman Catholic Church of the past?

ARCIC acknowledged that the search for unity is an integral part of the process of renewal. Renewal means recognizing and putting right faults and recovering what you have lost or neglected. Sykes implied that ecumenical obstacles lie not just in the head but also in the pit of the stomach, where they are usually harder to shift.

When Professor Sykes asks whether Anglicans would be expected to accept a primacy as expounded *in the past*, he is either ignoring or dismissing one of the basic principles of ecumenical dialogue – that you must be not only *self*-critical and prepared for self-reform but give the other side credit for the same dispositions.

If you are discussing (seriously) the possibility of unity coming about between two Churches one of which has a universal primate, the other having been born largely out of dispensing with him, a distinction between the ideal and the actual seems hardly avoidable. Vatican II did something to modify the actual in accordance with the ideal. 'How does agreement about an ideal help if there is residual dissatisfaction about the actual?' asks Sykes. Professor Nicholas Lash (having been courteously given space to comment in the next issue of *Modern Churchman*) said neatly:

> The answer, I should have thought, is that it sets the agenda for a programme of reform to be undertaken by both the parties which have reached agreement on the goal.

Another of Professor Sykes' apprehensions about Anglican–Roman Catholic rapprochement was that it was 'a diplomatic coup which leaves the whole matter of Anglican responsibility towards the so-called non-episcopal Churches in a most unsatisfactory state', because 'the Anglican understanding of the episcopate[6] has become extraordinarily puzzling'.

If the Anglicans were to *wait* as Sykes advises until the primacy is reformed to the universal and entire satisfaction, the mind boggles at how long it would take and at what the resultant marriage might look like. The Roman Catholic Church has not found this problem so formidable as to inhibit dialogue with the non-episcopal Churches. This has proceeded happily with mutual edification and profit for a quarter of a century.

International reactions

Three national responses to the *Final Report* from widely separated parts of the world seem to me important to mention. They are predominantly favourable but with significant differences.

The Roman Catholic United States Episcopal Conference entrusted its evaluation to an *ad hoc* committee of six bishops and one consultant. The group acknowledged help from the United States Anglican–Roman Catholic Commission (a body somewhat older than ARCIC) and from the Roman Catholic National Association of Diocesan Ecumenical Officers. Here was one way of taking reception seriously. Each part of the Final Report was carefully examined. A few criticisms emerged which were recommended for examination to ARCIC II.

In 1982 the provincial synod of the Anglican province of South Africa received the Final Report 'with gratitude to God', commending it to the dioceses for study, and asked the province's Theological Commission to make its comments available.

There was a natural tendency to pay more attention to reactions coming from countries in which Anglicans and Roman Catholics lived side by side in considerable numbers. But this was not always a favourable factor. A detached approach when combined with intelligence and sympathy could be more profitable. This was demonstrated by a 'Reaction of the German Episcopal Conference' (32 pages) sent to the SPCU. Beginning with aperceptive summary of the Commission's method, it went on to examine the whole report. Having given two pages to the obstinate problems of reception, it concludes 'It is to be regretted that the Commission was not able to classify completely the complex of problems associated with reception'.

NOTES

1. As early as its November 1978, the SPCU felt the time ripe to devote its plenary meeting to a stock-taking on existing bilateral dialogues, most of which had been in progress for twelve years. This was no exercise in self-congratulation.

   The Secretariat noted with reserve the tendency in discussion to assimilate reception of dialogue results to the historic problem of the reception of the findings of ecumenical councils: there is an analogy, but obvious important differences. The SPCU described the dialogues as *facta ecclesiae*, but also resolved to 'encourage reflection on the historical and theological *novelty*' which the fact represents in the life of the Church as a whole.

   It insisted too (prompted by a firm speech from the new Pope, addressing the plenary for the first time) that 'In the process of reception of the dialogues, theological faculties should play a primary role'. At the same time the faculties should be introducing the future theologians to the dialogues, their problems and results.
2. Perhaps 'community' here is a misprint for 'communion'.
3. In *The Tablet* (7 and 14 January 1984).
4. The same suggestion was made both by the SCDF's 'Observations' and by the excellent 'Reaction' of the German Episcopal Conference.

5.   *Modern Churchman*, new series, vol. 25, no. 11.
6.   To which he has now been elected, at the venerable see of Ely.

24

Marriage

Background

The Common Declaration signed by Pope Paul VI and Archbishop Ramsey at Rome on 24 March 1966 said that the 'serious dialogue' to which they pledged their two Churches should include, besides theological matters, 'matters of practical difficulty felt on either side'. There was little doubt that the chief of these lay in the dissatisfaction, even resentment, felt by most Anglicans about the Roman Catholic Church's regulations concerning 'mixed' marriages. The subject was raised in para. 16 of the Malta Report:

> The increasing number of mixed marriages point to the need for a thorough investigation of the doctrine of marriage in its sacramental dimension, its ethical demands, its canonical status, and its pastoral implications. It is hoped that the work of the Joint Commission on Marriage will be promptly initiated and vigorously pursued, and that its recommendations will help to alleviate some of the difficulties caused by mixed marriages, to indicate acceptable changes in Church regulations, and to provide safeguards against the dangers which threaten to undermine family life in our time.

It will be seen at once that this proposal does not recommend mere bargaining about the 'practical difficulty'. There were fundamental questions about the theology of marriage which were a necessary basis for discussing regulations.

Until 1857 there was no substantial difference between Anglican canon law and practice and those of the Roman Catholic Church in the matter of divorce and re-marriage. In that year a Matrimonial Causes Act set up a special *civil* court empowered to dissolve marriages *a vinculo* (i.e., to decree divorces in the proper sense). Church reaction to it revealed differences of opinion even at the highest levels in the Church and highlighted the problems arising from the relation of the Church of England to the state.[1]

At the beginning of the present century, the Church of England was beginning to feel the tension between the principle of indissolubility and the increasing pastoral problems presented by the spread of divorce.

The 'Herbert Act' of 1937, besides widening the grounds for divorce, left clergy free in law to solemnize or not the marriage of divorced persons, but most of the bishops and clergy refused to exercise this legal right.

The Lambeth resolutions from 1888 to 1958 reflect growing concern over the increase in broken marriages and divorce and continue to affirm the principle of indissolubility. We find also concern for trends in civil legislation in some provinces of the Communion. Resolution 94 of Lambeth 1948 shows a new element:

> The conference affirms that the marriage of one whose former partner is still living may not be celebrated according to the rites of the Church *unless it has been established that there exists no marriage bond recognised by the Church.*

When Geoffrey Fisher visited Pope John XXIII in 1960, the Church of England, and in varying degrees other provinces of the Anglican Communion, was in the midst of a long phase of reflection and discussion about the problems of Christian marriage. Fisher himself in 1955 had published *Problems of Marriage and Divorce*, which insisted that the Church could not solemnize the marriage of divorced persons with a partner still living without ceasing to bear witness to what Christ affirmed marriage to be. On the other hand he defended the Church of England practice of admitting the divorced to the sacraments of the Church, as following the example of Christ in seeking and saving the lost.

In Rome, he was unlikely to have had occasion to discuss this. It is not even clear that he raised the question of Roman regulations about mixed marriages, though Anglican dissatisfaction with these was well known.

During the 1950s and early 1960s there had been attempts in Parliament to provide for divorce after seven years of separation, vigorously resisted by Fisher and later (1963) by the principal Christian leaders jointly. In 1964 Archbishop Ramsey appointed a group (mainly but not entirely Anglican) to examine the *law of the land* to see whether it could be altered to ensure better marital stability and happiness without prejudicing the approach to marriage as a lifelong covenant. The group reported in 1966 in a document called *Putting Asunder* and made the radical recommendation of abandoning matrimonial offence as the ground for divorce and substituting 'irretrievable breakdown', to be determined not by the parties but by the court. The report was submitted to the examination of the Law Commissioners and also met criticism and discussion outside, but the central proposal was endorsed by the Church Assembly in February 1967. Archbishop Ramsey and a number of other critics remained seriously dissatisfied with the proposal. Nevertheless in 1969 a Divorce Reform Act was passed and came into force on 1 January 1971, laying down that 'the sole ground on which a petition for divorce may be presented . . . shall be that the marriage has broken down irretrievably'.

Though the Archbishop's Group had been motivated by Christian principles in drawing up *Putting Asunder*, the whole history of the document and the divided opinions about the significance for Christian marriage of the new legislation had increased the conviction that the time was ripe for a formal re-examination of the Church's own doctrine of marriage and divorce. It was not long before a commission was appointed for the purpose under the chairmanship of Professor Howard Root, of Southampton University.

Lambeth and Rome

In 1958 the Lambeth Conference met and devoted a long committee report (no. 5) to 'the family in contemporary society'.[2] The bulk of the report, though cast in a much less imperative mood than Roman Catholics were used to, could have been endorsed by Catholics and indeed by all men of good will. It placed less emphasis on procreation as the primary end of marriage, though it declared that 'the responsible procreation of children *is* a primary obligation'. But this was no more and no less than the Vatican Council was to say seven years later (*Gaudium et Spes*, para. 50).[3]

Even when the report went on to assert the right of married couples to make their own responsible choices about contraception, it added that this does not 'take away from the beauty and strength of abstinence mutually accepted'.

The Vatican Council, in its much-discussed *Pastoral Constitution on the Church in the Modern World* had set out to stress 'solidarity' with 'the men of our time' and their problems. This naturally called for a chapter on marriage and the family. Of the general principles set out, the one most emphasized and attracting most attention was 'the dignity of the human person'.[4] This logically led, in the treatment of marriage, to a more 'personalist' approach than had always been detected in ecclesiastical pronouncements.

The core of the matter is well put in the 1978 report of the Church of England Synod's Marriage Commission. Having set out some ideas and ideals analogous to those implicit in the current Roman Catholic phrase describing the family as 'a domestic Church', it goes on:

> If marriage is to fulfil these high expectations, the relationship
> between husband and wife, no longer buttressed by clear-cut social
> rules, strong extended family networks and economic pressures which
> often made the splitting up of the marital home unthinkable,
> demands a great deal of them. The institution of marriage now stands
> or falls on the quality of the interpersonal relationship between the
> couple. The potential for richness of personal fulfilment may be
> greater – the risk is certainly greater and the price of failure may be
> high. Marriage breakdown may mean not only the loss of a sexual
> partner and companion but the destruction of a shared universe of
> meaning and understanding.

On the very day the Lambeth Conference (1968) opened, the papal encyclical *Humanae Vitae* appeared and was debated for two days (see above, Chapter 13). The 1968 resolution recognized the positive elements shared by the 1958 resolution and *Humanae Vitae* and recorded 'appreciation of the Pope's deep concern for the institution of marriage and the integrity of married life', but, it continued, the conference 'finds itself unable to agree that all methods of conception control other than abstinence from sexual intercourse or its confinement to the periods of infertility are contrary to the order established by God'. More strongly, it rejected the contention that conception control necessarily leads to moral degradation.

Humanae Vitae and the very considerable disturbance in Roman Catholic church life which it occasioned were not much reflected either in the Anglican document *Marriage, Divorce and the Church* or in the Anglican–Roman Catholic report. In MDC the encyclical is referred to only once. More surprisingly, the encyclical is not referred to at all in the Anglican–Roman Catholic report.

To be sure the report was mainly concerned with the problems of mixed marriages and with what it called the 'relevant theology'. But it is hard to see how, after 1968, the question of birth control and the differing Anglican and Roman Catholic attitudes to it could fail to be matters of primary concern to those serious Anglicans and Catholics at whom the report was levelled.

ARCM

We have so far been occupied with sketching (very much the right word) the history of the state of affairs in which Anglican–Roman Catholic dialogue on Marriage and Mixed Marriages began. It was also a state of affairs which prompted and affected internal dialogue in the Church of England as well as other provinces, issuing in MDC. Only one person was a member of both commissions – Professor Gordon Dunstan, then F. D. Maurice Professor of moral and social theology at King's College, London. It would be impossible to over-estimate the contribution he made, of learning, sympathy and dedication, to the discussions which issued in the Anglican–Roman Catholic Commission on Mixed Marriages report, of which he was a co-drafter. One other member of the Root Commission which produced the MDC report, Lady Oppenheimer, graced one of the most important meetings of ARCM, the fourth (1973).

Like ARCIC itself, ARCM was instituted as an international commission, between the Roman Catholic Church and the Anglican Communion, in whose 26 provinces both the ecumenical problem and the problem of marriage and divorce gradually presented themselves differently and developed at different paces.[5]

The report is divided into four main sections:

A. Proceedings of the Commission
B. The relevant theology
C. Defective marital situations
D. Mixed marriages.

Section A is purely descriptive of the progress of the dialogue through its six sessions, though it does enunciate 'Three fundamental theological principles' which have governed our deliberations:

1. That Holy Baptism itself confers Christian status and is the indestructible bond of union between all Christians and Christ, and so of Christians with one another. This baptismal unity remains firm despite all ecclesiastical division.
2. That in Christian marriage the man and the woman themselves make the covenant whereby they enter into marriage as instituted and ordained by God; this new unity, the unity of marriage, is sacramental in virtue of their Christian baptism and is the work of God in Christ.
3. That this marriage once made possesses a unity given by God to respect which is a primary duty; this duty creates secondary obligations for the Church in both its pastoral and its legislative capacity. One is the obligation to discourage marriages in which the unity would be so strained or so lacking in vitality as to be both a source of danger to the parties themselves and to be a disfigured sign of or a defective witness to the unity of Christ with his Church. Another is the obligation to concert its pastoral care and legislative provisions to support the unity of the marriage once it is made and to ensure as best it can that these provisions be not even unwittingly divisive.

ARCM, para. 21 turned to the question whether marriage is a 'sacrament'. The stance at this stage was clear enough:

The Anglican doctrine, given formal expression in its liturgy, conceives marriage as God's ordinance, in the order of creation *taken by Christ and the Church into the sacramental order* as representing the covenanted unity of Christ and the Church and *signifying effectively the sanctifying* of the marriage and its partners within the communion of Christ and the Church.

When ARCM returned to the subject in Section B ('The relevant theology') it began:

on marriage itself the Commission finds no fundamental difference of doctrine between the two Churches as regards what marriage of its nature is or the ends which it is ordained to serve.

Gaudium et Spes is cited as entirely at one with the Anglican liturgies in preferring the term covenant (*pactum, foedus*) to contract. The sacramental nature of marriage is also affirmed, says the text, and uses the expression 'made by Christ into an effective sign of grace'. It concludes with the assertion that 'this substantial convergence in doctrine, despite differences in the language used to express it, is a welcome fact of our time'. Neither of the Anglican documents, *Marriage, Divorce and the Church* (MDC) or *Marriage and the Church's Task* (MCT), takes such an irenic view of this 'convergence' on sacramentality, but neither of them is an official statement, though they obviously express serious views held within the Church of England and elsewhere in the Anglican Communion.

On the Catholic side an important speech was made to the Synod of Bishops at Rome in 1980. The Synod's theme was 'The Christian family', and Cardinal Willebrands spoke to it about the works of the two joint commissions, the Anglican–Roman Catholic and the Roman Catholic–Lutheran Reformed. From their reports, he said, 'it is clear that these Churches are already in agreement with us on many elements of the fundamental doctrine concerning marriage and the Christian Family' and

> In particular it is clear that, although these Churches do not call matrimony a sacrament of the New Law, they do acknowledge it to be a sacred reality, a state instituted by the Creator and renewed in Christ as a mystery of the New Covenant in Christ with the Church; indeed they admit that it is promised a special grace by Christ. They certainly do not regard matrimony as a merely civil matter.
> (SPCU Information Service no. 44, p. 116)

Section C of ARCM (pp. 14ff.) was given the slightly clumsy title 'Defective marital situations', to cover both defects in the original covenant, which could give rise to a plea for *nullity* and *breakdown* in the marriage relationship which could occasion a petition for divorce.

That marriage may be null because of a '*diriment* nullifying *impediment*' has always of course been recognized by both Churches. A declaration of nullity is *not* a divorce but a recognition that the 'marriage' concerned has never been a marriage; there is no *vinculum* (bond) and hence the question of indissolubility does not arise.[6]

Nullity procedures were never popular or frequent among Anglicans in England, while for Rome they were the only regular way of escape from a ratified and consecrated marriage tie.[7]

Catholics were not very pleased when, as late as 1971, the MDC report treated the matter under the heading 'Medieval views of indissolubility' (paras 124–126) with little suggestion that 'medieval abuses' were not still the regular thing.

Marriage and the Church's task

By the time ARCM met, both Churches were faced with a problem increasingly grave as divorces grew in number: how to go on witnessing to the Christian principles of marriage and at the same time take pastoral care of those whose marriages had broken down and ended in divorce. By 1978 the MCT report was saying that most of the Commission found the doctrine of indissolubility untenable (para. 158). From other parts of the report, e.g. p. 108, para. 38, it is clear that what the Commission rejects is what Roman canon law calls *intrinsic* indissolubility:

> In short we are all agreed in affirming that indissolubility is characteristic of marriage as it should and can be. There is something radically wrong when a marriage does break down. Marriages ought to be indissoluble. However, most of us reject the doctrine that marriage cannot by definition be dissolved. It is only too possible for men and women in particular cases to break the bond which God, in principle and in general, wills to be unbreakable, and to put asunder what God, in his original purpose, has joined together. Therein lies the measure of human failure and sin.

It was clearly recognized that here the Commission did not speak for all Anglicans. The Anglican–Roman Catholic report had said:

> The introduction of the possibility of divorce and re-marriage by civil process, in the mid-nineteenth century, enabled these 'exceptive indissolubilists' to authorise action in accordance with their conviction. The general tendency in modern Anglicanism however, until the last two decades, has been towards a full indissolubilist position, and resolutions of Lambeth Conferences have declared this unequivocally. At the same time however, Anglicans found themselves increasingly unable to live with the logical consequences of their own affirmed position: they began to develop expedients to mitigate its rigour. (ARCM, p. 18, para. 42)

In other words, the pastoral problems of re-marriage after divorce existed only for those who continued to hold marriage indissoluble.

An approach to the dilemma which seems common to both of the Church of England reports is that of redefining indissolubility. This approach is less direct and searching in the 1971 report but is brilliantly and fairly expounded in Lady Oppenheimer's small book, *The Marriage Bond* (1976).

The problem, we remember, is not one of words but very practical. What should be done by the Church about people who have been divorced but wish to re-marry in Church? The Roman Catholic answer, in the then Canon Law, was simple and harshly expressed.

There were at least three Anglican views. The first was more or less identical with the Roman one. The second accepted indissolubility but with the Matthean exception – allowing divorce for *porneia*, which was incorrectly translated 'adultery'. The third view (strongly influencing the 1971 report) was based on a different interpretation of 'indissolubility'. What was the bond (*vinculum*) which made Christian marriage indissoluble and thus excluded re-marriage after divorce? Was the idea of this bond incompatible with the notion of 'irretrievable breakdown' which was now, in England, the ground for divorce?

The Joint Report

These were the terms of the problem when the ARCM Joint Commission turned its attention to it. The Commission was strongly reinforced with consultants either attending or contributing papers. The question at issue seemed to be 'Does "indissoluble" mean *cannot* be dissolved, or does it mean *ought not* to be dissolved?' Everybody present accepted the second meaning, which does not of course imply the first. *Ought* states a moral obligation, *cannot* says something which corresponds to the canon lawyers' view. The Code of 1917 says indissolubility is an essential property of marriage and acquires in Christian marriage distinctive firmness by reason of the sacrament. The report, however, comes down firmly on the side of unqualified solemnization of marriage in Church after divorce – unless the clause 'by use of one or other of the existing permitted orders for the solemnization of marriage *with the addition of an appropriate invariable Preface*' be a qualification of the sort recommended in the MDC.

How much does the Joint Report show? The Joint Commission was aware of MDC and often cited it, but did not consider itself bound by it.[8]

Paying more attention to each Church's established doctrine and practice, it could claim (para. 49):

> Each Church, Anglican and Roman Catholic, can accept the assurance of the other that it maintains, and has a settled will to maintain the full Christian doctrine of marriage, and that in each Church an intention to accept marriage as a permanent and exclusive union is and will be required of all who seek marriage according to the Church's rites.

There was agreement about the tension of the pastor, aware at once of a responsibility to Christ and the Gospel – a responsibility for integrity of witness – and of a responsibility to the people of God to enable them to bear their burdens and to live the Christian life in the conditions in which they find themselves.

These agreements about principle, limited though they were, aimed to provide a foundation for the last section of the report, Section D, entitled 'Mixed marriages'. The last papal legislation on the matter was the Motu Proprio *Matrimonia Mixta*, the delayed appearance of which (1970) had held up the ARCM's third meeting.

At the time of Vatican II, marriages curiously named *mixtae religionis* (i.e., between a Catholic and a baptized non-Catholic) were governed by canon 1060 of the 1917 Code.

The second ruling about mixed marriages concerned the *form* of the marriage (canon 1099). It laid down that a Catholic could only be married (whomever he married – whether a baptized person or a non-Christian) before an authorized person and two witnesses.

The *Instructio*, a document of the SCDF, attered matters very slightly: 'The excommunication incurred, according to canon 2319, para. 1, no. 1, by those who marry before a non-Catholic minister is now abolished. The effects of this abolition are retroactive' (Flannery, *Vatican Council Documents*, p. 478). The only concessions on canonical form were these: firstly, that if difficulties should arise, the ordinary (bishop) should refer the matter to the Holy See outlining all the circumstances; and secondly, that mixed marriages were no longer to be relegated to the sacristy or similar place, but could be conducted in church with the usual ceremonies.

In the treatment of the promises about the upbringing of children there was a slight change. The language was more courteous. The non-Catholic party was to be *informed* on this matter with *due delicacy* and *invited* to promise at least not to impede the Catholic in his or her duty (italics mine). If he still had conscientious objections, the matter could be referred to the Holy See. The promises were ordinarily to be given in writing but the local bishop could now decide whether or not to waive this and allow oral promises.

ARCM had delayed its third meeting hoping that the second report might be considered by those who were preparing the new document *Matrimonia Mixta*, which appeared in 1970. It was not, but on the other hand there were signs of movement which encouraged the Commission to press on.

There are explicit allusions to the Council Decrees on Ecumenism, and the Declaration on Religious Liberty, to the Synod of Bishops of 1967, and even more importantly, to the fact that a new Code of Canon Law was already in preparation. In this connection one of the most important sentences in the preamble to *Matrimonia Mixta* is:

> no one will be really surprised to find that even the canonical
> discipline in mixed marriages cannot be uniform and that it must be
> adapted to the various cases.

The principal changes in discipline were as follows: to marry a *baptized* non-Catholic, a Catholic still needed a dispensation. Without it, the marriage was against Church law but *not* invalid. To marry a *non-baptized* person without dispensation (*disparitatis cultus*) was not even valid. From both impediments however the Church was prepared to dispense *for a just cause*.

The most notable general feature of the new document was that it gave more latitude to bishops and bishops' conferences in interpreting and applying the rules. This was seen by Anglicans as a mixed blessing. It guarded against insensitive and ill-informed centralization. It also opened the door to very unequal interpretation and application of the rules.

The rational way for episcopal conferences to use their new initiative was to prepare a new set of dispositions of their own; the ecumenical way was to do so in consultation with the non-Roman-Catholic authorities. Many did this.

'Mixed marriages'

The joint commission ARCM had its own work to do. Its concern was with what some liked to call inter-Church marriages, that is, those in which the Catholic and the Anglican is equally serious in his or her Church allegiance. The *practical* problem of which Church the children of such a marriage should be brought up in could never be wholly disposed of except in a united Church. The Anglicans felt that the solution should be left to the partners to work out for themselves. This reflected a view of the nature and authority of the Church different from the Catholic one, as ARCM pointed out early on (paras 26–27).

Was Roman Catholic insistence on a promise an invasion of religious liberty? *Matrimonia Mixta* seemed to go some way towards acknowledging this. It required only that the non-Roman-Catholic party should be made aware of the Catholic party's 'promise and obligation'. These last words were important. The promise, however unwelcome, does not *create* the Catholic's obligation. The obligation is integral to his Catholic conscience. But is it an absolute promise? In the solemn, sacramental covenant of marriage he or she acquires other grave obligations. These may conflict with the obligation about the children. An impasse may come about which endangers the marriage. The ARCM report discusses the pros and cons of this at some length (paras 65–70). The authors of *Matrimonia Mixta* had not ignored it, and it induced them to introduce an important qualification. The Catholic is called upon to promise to *do all in his (or her) power* to have all the children baptized and brought up in the Roman Catholic Church. This qualifying phrase is not a very precise one. But it has no sense at all except on the assumption that some things are *not* in his (or her) power.

From this the Commission goes on to ask

> Is there an alternative to the promise, a course by which the Roman Catholic Church can do what its doctrine requires of it in a way which encounters less objection? In the opinion of a majority of the Commission there is. It would be for the Church to require of the Roman Catholic priest responsible for the marriage a written assurance to his bishop that he had duly put the Roman Catholic partner in mind of his obligations concerning the baptism and upbringing of the children, and, according, to opportunity, satisfied himself that the other partner knew what these obligations were ... The bishop, if satisfied in other respects, might then issue a dispensation for the marriage on the strength of this assurance. ... This procedure is offered in an earnest attempt to make possible a real step forward in charitable relations between two Churches.

On *canonical form* the Commission's recommendations for change were that the scope of canonical form should be enlarged to include marriage before an Anglican minister, all other requirements, joint preparation and so on, having been fulfilled. This would accord with the regulation for Roman Catholic–Orthodox marriages given in the decree *Crescens Matrimoniorum* of 22 February 1967.

This proposal met little difficulty in the Commission and was presented to those who were drafting *Matrimonia Mixta* but had no influence either in that document or the revised Canon Law of 1983.

Changes in Church and society

The Church's task – what justifies her in intervening in marriage – is *sacramental*. In an institution which has so much power for good or ill she must be seen to be concerned above all with the salvation of souls, with the spiritual good, but also with the peace and happiness of those who marry and produce families. Legislators too are concerned with the good of society and the individual. One of the first acts of John XXIII's reign, some time before he convoked the Council, was to announce a full-scale reform of the Code of 1917. It was hoped that the work of ARCM would be reflected in the new Code, and steps were taken to bring the ARCM report directly to the attention of those in charge of the revision.

The new Code deals with mixed marriage in Book IV, Part I, chapter 6, in eight canons.[9] The chief interest in this short chapter lies in the economy of treatment and the considerable latitude given to episcopal conferences and diocesan bishops.

In the twenty years or more since the Roman Catholics and Anglicans began to talk about mixed marriages, the focus of anxiety has moved elsewhere. Where one marriage in three is likely to fail, nightmares about the institution are inevitably less specialized. Ecumenical concern is with what are now called inter-church marriages – those in which the two partners are actively committed each to his own Church. But in considering these marriages, ARCM could not ignore the situation, the crisis of marriage as a whole, the changing conception of the marriage bond.

In addressing representatives of other Christian Churches in Madagascar on 29 April 1989, the Pope said:

> I should like here at least to mention the life of those families of
> mixed marriages where at the very centre of conjugal love the drama

of disunity of Christians is encountered. These families, despite what they suffer, and sometimes because of what they suffer, can be builders of unity of Christians. For this to happen they must have pastoral help that takes account of the particular difficulties inherent in the relationships between husband and wife with regard to respect for religious freedom; this freedom could be violated either by undue pressure to make the partner change his or her beliefs or by placing obstacles in the way of the free expression of these beliefs by religious practice. (Exhortation *Familiaris Consortio* 78)[10]

NOTES

1. Gordon Crosse wrote in 1912 'The effect of the Act was to separate the laws of Church and State on an essential point of morals and divine revelation': Ollard and Cross, *Dictionary of English Church History*, p. 359.
2. It was published, with certain other material from 1948 to 1968, in *What the Bishops Have Said About Marriage* (SPCK, 1968).
3. Cf. *Church and Nullity*, p. 194.
4. This was the leading idea behind the Declaration on Religious Freedom.
5. An excellent summary down to 1968 is in Winnett, *The Church and Divorce* (Mowbray, 1968), chapters 3 and 4.
6. The age-old habit of talking of Henry VIII's 'divorce' from Catherine of Aragon has perpetuated confusion here.
7. The only regular way, the 'Pauline privilege', is an interpretation of 1 Corinthians 7:12–17 and is not found convincing by Anglicans. Still less is the *privilegium fidei* by which the Pope can dissolve a marriage involving at least one unbaptized person – even if the impediment has been dispensed (see ARCM, no. 58).
8. It should be remembered that ARCM was an international commission with the Anglican *Communion*, which was represented by an Irishman, an American and a Canadian.
9. English translation (London: Collins, 1983) pp. 199–200.
10. John Paul II had said much the same at York, 1 June 1982.

25

The ordination of women priests

Anglican moves

In 1920 and 1930 the Lambeth Conference occupied itself much with how Anglican women might have better opportunities to serve the Church and with revitalizing, not very successfully, the order of deaconesses. The Conference also said:

We have had before us from various quarters an urgent plea for the admission of women to the priesthood.

The majority of the sub-commission considering the matter thought there were 'insuperable theological objections' (a very strong phrase for Anglicans to use). Others rather saw grave practical difficulties. The Ministry Commission as a whole did not think that

new conditions demand a departure from the universal custom of the Catholic Church and therefore we cannot encourage in any way those who press for the priesthood for women.

World War II prevented the conference meeting again until 1948 and also changed the terms of the problem. In 1944 the Japanese occupied the island of Macao and refused to let clergy go there. This persuaded Bishop Hall of Hong Kong to ordain Deaconess Florence Li Tim Oi as a priest.

In 1946 the bishops of the Anglican Church in China regretted this uncanonical action and requested Hall to accept Miss Li's resignation, which he did 'for the sake of harmony'.

In 1948 a proposal came before the Lambeth Conference from the South China diocese for a twenty-year experiment in ordaining deaconesses to the priesthood. The Conference disapproved.

The 1958 Conference had a good deal to say about the problems of ministry; shortage of manpower, of facilities and funds for training, but only a short paragraph on the ministry of women.

In 1962 (the year in which Vatican II began) the English Church Assembly passed a resolution urging the Archbishop to set up a commission to enquire into 'Women in Holy Orders'. This was done: a distinguished membership (fourteen) under the chairmanship of Bishop G. A. Ellison,[1] including a doctor and a lecturer in psychiatry.

In fourteen years, what could be described collectively as the non-theological factors in the matter had increased in number and complexity. Recognizing this, the commission described its aim as 'to set out the issues as succinctly as possible for all to see' and to attach the papers supplied to it.

It disclaimed any intention of advising for or against. When the commission reported in 1966,[2] it was seen to support the wisdom of this intention. The general conclusion was that 'the existing evidence can support different conclusions'.

When the report was debated in the Spring and Summer sessions of the Church Assembly it was simply commended to the consideration of the Church.

In this book we are concerned only with the ecumenical problem.

When the Lambeth Conference met again in 1968, a decade had passed in which the Vatican Council was the central event. It concerned itself much with the Christian mission and ministry and with the role of the laity. Those who, in Rome, followed the Council know that these concerns were more intense and varied than is reflected in the Council documents, but the idea of women priests hardly loomed large.

At Lambeth in 1968, in Section II, on 'Renewal in ministry', the Conference at last had a sub-committee, no. 21, assigned to 'Women in the priesthood'. It had eleven members, four from England, three from the USA and one each from Ireland, Canada, West Africa and the Jerusalem archbishopric (Sudan). The matter was also debated on the Council floor where the chief speaker on either side was an evangelical Archbishop,

Dr Coggan of York (in favour) and Marcus Loane of Sydney (powerfully opposed). A preparatory essay by the Dean of York (Alan Richardson) concluded that 'the fundamental question concerns the theological propriety of an innovation within one branch of the historic Church, lacking the consensus of the whole Church'.

The Conference adopted four resolutions (nos 34–37). The first affirmed that theological arguments were inconclusive. The second called for careful study throughout the Communion, the findings of which should be reported to the Anglican Consultative Council.[3] The third requested consultations with other Churches, both those which did and those which did not ordain women. The fourth recommendation was that no final decision be taken without advice from the ACC. Three things became evident here:

1. The movement for ordaining women was gathering strength.
2. Theological reflection on grounds for it was not advancing at the same rate.
3. Any pan-Anglican consensus on the matter was a far-off prospect, not strictly required and not universally wished for.

Here was a matter which greatly strengthened the case for the Anglican Consultative Council, which was born at Lambeth 1968 (resolution no. 69).[4] It had of course as the name implies no executive powers but if it developed *esprit de corps* (delegates were eventually elected for six years) it could become a strong pressure group.

The ordination of women became one of its two most tense topics (the other and the more dramatic was pressure for action to support the World Council of Churches anti-racist programme).

The diocese of Hong Kong had clearly not thrown in the sponge after the rebuff of 1946. Its synod had again approved ordination of women to the priesthood and now 'sought advice' as recommended by Lambeth '68. Following a debate which seemed relatively calm after that on the anti-racist motion, the meeting resolved (no. 28)

to advise the Bishop of Hong Kong and *any other bishop of the Anglican Communion* acting with the approval of his Province, that if he decides to ordain women to the priesthood, his action will be acceptable to this Council, and that this Council will use its good offices to encourage all Provinces of the Anglican Communion to continue in communion with these dioceses.

The underlined words were an amendment to the original motion and came from the USA. The resolution was carried by 24 votes to 22.

There was much perplexity about this: it seemed hard to reconcile with the fact that so far only eight dioceses had set about studying the question (as recommended by Lambeth '68) and none had reported. The president, Archbishop Ramsey, was visibly unhappy and considered that the infant Council had 'overstepped the mark'. (As we filed from the room he said to the present writer 'Well, I believe that in twenty years' time your Church will be doing it'.)

In December of that year (1971) the Bishop ordained two women priests in Hong Kong.

In June 1971 the Church of England General Synod commissioned a 'survey of the present state of opinion on the ordination of women' from Miss Christian Howard. A first draft of this was produced, in consultation with the Dean of York, Alan Richardson, the Revd Donald Allchin and the Revd Roger Beckwith, in May 1972 and eventually published in October by the Advisory Council for the Church's Ministry.

Its thirteen chapters in 87 pages do much more than 'survey opinion' in the ordinary sense of that phrase. They range widely in very articulate fashion over almost every aspect of the question – biblical, historical, traditional, theological, sacred, ecumenical and (for England) legal – but conclude (p. 84):

> we must then admit that there exists among us a fundamental
> difference as to what may properly be used as evidence.

The report says (p. 48):

> It is a mistake to equate pressure for the ordination of women with a
> campaign for the rights of women (a sort of ecclesiastical 'women's
> Lib').

Equate? No. But to deny all connection between them is naïve, as has often been painfully demonstrated.

The Roman Catholic position was fairly described. It was pointed out that the Roman Catholic Church is in dialogue at world and regional levels with several confessions which have already accepted women's ordination. To this it must be answered that not all dialogues are alike in progress and commitment, nor have they all equally explicit aims. Nor, above all, do those involved have the same ideas of what a priest is.

Though this report was published as a 'consultative document' to provide background information in convenient form for the Synod and not to anticipate an answer to questions which the Church itself must decide, it remained at the heart of the Church of England deliberations.

The Anglican Consultative Council met for the second time in Dublin, 17–27 July 1973. The Ordination of Women was the subject of a rather more prickly debate in which the sense of the Council as a useful locus for pressure had increased. The word 'resolution' was avoided and replaced by 'statements of the Council'. The first of them merely repeated Limuru about not breaking communion. The third asked for further responses. The second declared that ecumenical repercussions were important, to be taken into account, but not decisive. The Churches of the Anglican Communion must make their own decisions.

There was no hint that taking ecumenical repercussions into account might include dialogue,[5] though earlier (p. 8) the report was repeating the usual 'satisfaction and welcome' for the work of ARCIC. In fairness it should be said that ARCIC had shown no sign of concerning itself with the matter and was later (1979) to insist that it was beyond its brief.

The ACC did not meet again until 1976 and things hotted up meantime.

1. On 29 July 1974, three retired US bishops and the diocesan bishop of Costa Rica ordained eleven women deacons (ages ranging from 21 to 79) to the priesthood at a ceremony in Pennsylvania.
2. In November 1974, the November/December number of the *Ecumenist* published a 'Roman Catholic statement on the ordination of Women' signed by over a hundred theologians.
3. On 1 January 1975 a women's association in the USA addressed a manifesto to each US bishop.
4. On 16 January 1975, a short memorandum was addressed to the SPCU by the Bishops' Commission for Ecumenical and Interreligious Affairs, and delivered personally by Bishop Helmsing. It referred to incidents 2 and 3 above.
5. In the March number of the Anglican periodical *Theology* the archdeacon of Bloemfontein, J. A. King, who had just visited Rome, wrote:

Enquiry spread over a number of Vatican offices including the SPCU confirmed that the ecumenical implications are seen as very serious and that should the Anglicans in particular take precipitate or unilateral action in the matter, this could make for a great setback in unity negotiations.

6. On 6 March 1975, Dr Smythe of the Rome Anglican Centre came to the SPCU offices and reported that he had discussed the question with Archbishop Coggan while in England for the latter's enthronement. At the Lambeth Conference of 1968 the Archbishop had been the leading advocate for the ordination of women, but now as President of the Anglican Communion seemed to think a more cautious attitude appropriate. Dr Smythe came away convinced that some statement from Rome would elicit from the Archbishop an overture inviting discussion, and appealed to the SPCU to make it.

A few days later the Council for Foreign Relations at Lambeth took steps to second Dr Smythe's overture. They confessed concern about 'Anglican ignorance of the ecumenical implications of the question' and said that an intimation from the SPCU that it would welcome discussion would strengthen the hands of those who opposed unilateral action.

When the Church of England General Synod met at the beginning of July 1975, it passed the following motion:

> That this Synod, not wishing to prejudice improving relationships with the Roman Catholic and Orthodox Churches by removing without consultation with them the legal and other barriers to the ordination of women in the Church of England, requests the Presidents to
>
> (a) inform the appropriate authorities in those Churches of its belief that there are no fundamental objections to such ordination: and
> (b) invite those authorities to share in an urgent re-examination of the theological grounds for including women in the Order of Priesthood, with particular attention to the doctrine of Man and the doctrine of Creation.

Archbishop Coggan wrote to Paul VI informing him of the steady growth of consensus of opinion within the Anglican Communion that there are no fundamental objections in principle to the ordination of women to the priesthood. He went on:

> At the same time we are aware that action on this matter would be an obstacle to further progress along the path of unity Christ wills for the Church. The central authorities of the Anglican Communion therefore have called for common counsel on this matter, as has the General Synod of the Church of England.

The papal reply to the Archbishop did not mature until 30 November, but before that a beginning of 'common counsel' was made in the shape of 'informal talks' organized by Bishop Howe with the SPCU. This was hardly the occasion for doing justice to the second part of the Church of England's General Synod's motion but plans were sketched for a joint consultation on the question whether sacramental communion was possible between a Church which ordained women and one which did not or would not.

On 11 November Paul VI replied to Archbishop Coggan's letter of 9 July. He combined a firm rejection of the ordination of women with renewed 'commitment to a search for reconciliation' though adding that this was now faced with 'an element of grave difficulty'. He learned with satisfaction of a first informal discussion of the questions. The Archbishop replied on 10 February 1976, echoing the Pope's commitment to further dialogue, particularly raising the question whether legitimate diversity in unity might be involved here. This letter was personally conveyed to the Pope by Bishop Howe, the Secretary General of the Anglican Consultative Council, who was somewhat taken aback by Paul VI's vehemence on the subject. He left the audience chamber saying 'What a man!'

The Pope answered the Archbishop's letter on 23 March, the very day that the ACC was due to meet in Trinidad. There was no vehemence in the Pope's letter. He spoke of the tenth anniversary of Michael Ramsey's visit and the progress of those years. This was a central passage:

In such a spirit of candour and trust you allude in your letter of greeting to a problem which has recently loomed large; the likelihood, already very strong it seems in some places, that the Anglican Church will proceed to admit women to the ordained priesthood ... Our affection for the Anglican Communion has for many years been strong, and we have always nourished and often expressed the ardent hope that the Holy Spirit would lead us, in love and in obedience to God's will, along the path of reconciliation. This must be the measure of the sadness with which we encounter so grave a new obstacle and threat on that path.

The Anglican Consultative Council's report dealt with women priests only in a few dry statistics. One more ordained in Hong Kong. Eight provinces have accepted the *principle*. Seven have taken 'some positive action'. Four have decided against. There was no mention whatsoever of the USA's 'unconstitutional' ordinations.

The following September (1977) the ECUSA General Convention met at Minneapolis. The United States Anglican–Roman Catholic Dialogue had eleven months earlier taken an initiative and set an example of dialogue with its usual thoroughness. At Erlanger in Kentucky on 21–24 October 1977 it had met to discuss the ordination of women under several aspects – reinforced by work it had commissioned from a number of experts from either side in various disciplines.[6] The US Anglican–Roman Catholic statement arrived at no definite conclusion except that 'difference' would not lead to ARC's termination or the abandonment of its declared goal.

Eleven months later the General Convention of ECUSA, meeting at Minneapolis, passed canonical legislation making clear that 'The provision of these canons for the admission of candidates to the three Orders, Bishops, Priests and Deacons, shall be equally applicable to men and women'.

William Norgren, then associate ecumenical officer of ECUSA, was an early advocate of what has come to be called the Gamaliel principle (Acts 2:38–39):[7]

Neither Episcopalians nor the Christian world is obliged to assume that, because the Geneva Convention took a decision on the ordination of women, it has the automatic ratification of the Holy Spirit.

Insisting that consultation must go on, he adds:

We will learn if this change in ministry is of the Holy Spirit by the testing of experience.

Whether coincidentally or not, the Sacred Congregation for the Doctrine of the Faith presented to the Pope a *Declaration on the Question of the Admission of Women to the Ministerial Priesthood*. The date was 15 October, the feast of St Teresa of Avila, a saintly and powerful woman in the history of the Roman Catholic Church. The Declaration begins in a positive way, acknowledging the increasing role of women in contemporary life, and also pointing out the part they have long played in the history of the Roman Catholic Church, played more widely since Vatican II. It then turns to the movement for women in 'the pastoral office on a par with men' (already an accomplished fact in some Reformation communities) and admits that some Catholic theologians have argued for it. It firmly states, however, that

> ... the SCDF judges it necessary to recall that the Church, in fidelity to the example of the Lord, does not consider herself authorized to admit women to priestly ordination.

The Declaration then moves on to reasons. The essential argument is the example of Christ. It shows that this cannot be explained by 'anti-feminism'. Christ attached an importance to women which was conspicuously not Jewish. The practice of the apostles remained faithful to Jesus both in the Jewish milieu and when they moved into the Hellenistic world. The Declaration then asks 'Could the Church today depart from this attitude of Jesus and the apostles?' and glances at some of the current arguments for doing so.

1. Christ and the Apostles simply accepted the milieu of the age.
   Answer   In many ways they went counter to this milieu.
2. St Paul seems inconsistent on this subject.
   Answer   He does not oppose the right of women to prophesy in the assembly (1 Cor 11:5) but only to exercise the official function of teaching (1 Cor 14:34–35; 1 Tim 2:12).
3. The Church has shown her power over the sacraments by changing the discipline.
   Answer   She has disclaimed power over the substance of sacraments.

The Declaration next discusses the ministerial priesthood illustrated by the Mystery of the Church. These sections are the most serious attempt to provide a strictly theological support for rejecting the ordination of women.

> The Declaration therefore suggests that it is by analysing the nature of Order and its character that we will find the explanation of the exclusive call of men to the priesthood and episcopate. This analysis can be outlined in three propositions:
> (a) in administering the sacraments that demand the character of ordination the priest does not act in his own name (*in persona propria*) but in the person of Christ (*in persona Christi*);
> (b) this formula, as understood by tradition, implies that the priest is a

sign in the sense in which this term is understood in sacramental theology;

(c) it is precisely because the priest is a sign of Christ the Saviour that he must be a man and not a woman.

For Anglicans, the 1978 Lambeth Conference was not far off and the authorities feared a clash.

An Anglican–Roman Catholic consultation was arranged to take place at Versailles on 27 February–3 March (*not* in the Hall of Mirrors) on 'The ecumenical consequences of the ordination of women priests'. It had the marks of a slightly desperate attempt at window-dressing, in which the participants deserved much sympathy. Their brief was seemingly simply stated: 'To consider to what extent and in what ways Churches with women priests and Churches without can be reconciled in sacramental fellowship.'

The simplicity was deceptive. It was artificial to isolate the question from the whole vast field of debate which was being opened up. It was at least as much an inter-Anglican debate as an Anglican–Roman one. Everybody at Versailles knew this, though it was not exactly harped upon in discussion. The advocates of ordaining women were hoping that the meeting would do something to diminish the complaints of unilateral action. For this it was too little and too late. It could be no more than a token.

Two things may be seen as ground for hope. First there is the fact that those Anglican churches which have proceeded to ordain women to the presbyterate have done so in the conviction that they have not departed from the traditional understanding of apostolic ministry (expressed for example in the ARCIC Canterbury Statement). In the second place there is the fact that the recent Roman Declaration does not affirm explicitly that this matter is *de jure divino*. These facts would seem not to exclude the possibility of future developments. (Para. 6)

This paragraph sent the balloon up in Rome. It was seen as implying that the promptings of the Holy Spirit were an Anglican monopoly, and the hesitation was just another example of Roman rigidity.

In the end it was agreed that the senior Roman Catholic observer, Bishop Cahal Daly (afterwards Cardinal Archbishop of Armagh), should make an official statement to the Lambeth Conference on behalf of the SPCU, of which he was a member.

The organizers of the Lambeth Conference were not, as we have seen, anxious for it to be dominated by the women priests theme. Their aim was to avoid confrontation. The meetings of the sub-commission on the subject might have been expected to be a no-holds-barred affair. They turned out to be more of an *agape*. Credit for this was mainly due to the masterly chairmanship of the Bishop of Derby, Cyril Bowles, who also introduced the later debate. His fellow peacemaker was Professor John Macquarrie. Their appeal was essentially to Anglican comprehensiveness, the Anglican inheritance, the holding together of diversity within a unity of faith and worship. Professor Macquarrie believed this possible, being convinced that the question of Ordination of Women Priests belongs to the 'outer grey peripheral area' of the hierarchy of truths. 'It is certainly not, I would say, a question by which the Christian faith stands or falls.' Essentially both speakers were appealing for forbearance and under-standing, for the preserving of communion and for the continuance of ecumenical rapprochement. The Resolution was adopted by 316 votes to 37 with 12 abstentions.[8]

Less than three months after the Lambeth Conference the General Synod of the Church of England met and on its third morning the Bishop of Birmingham, Hugh Montefiore, was to move:

> that this Synod asks the Standing Committee to prepare and bring forward legislation to remove the barriers to Ordination of Women Priests and their consecration to the episcopate.

He quickly summed up the pros, identifying them with 'the truth' for which he bore a banner. The cons he listed as ten and swept them aside in as many short paragraphs. None of the ten was a strictly theological objection; they were nearly all concerned with what other people, including opponents of the Church of England, would think.

For our purpose, the most relevant was objection 3: 'Ordaining women will destroy our chances of union with Rome'. 'I just do not believe it', said the Bishop. He supported this incredulity with an assortment of argu-ments. He offered an unusual definition of ecumenism:

> ... it does not mean prevaricating over what you know is right in case you upset other Churches.

It means doing what you know to be right and trusting that other Churches which think differently will accept you in love and truth.

He added, 'Remember Gamaliel; if this be of God, it will prosper'.

But if you are *already sure* that you have the truth from the Spirit, is it necessary to invoke the Gamaliel principle? In spite of this impassioned eloquence, most succeeding speakers were in favour of thinking a bit more and consulting a bit more and the motion was lost. The vote was:

	Ayes	*Noes*
House of Bishops	32	17
House of Clergy	94	149
House of Laity	120	106

NOTES

1. He was then Bishop of Chester – later of London.
2. *Women and Holy Orders* (CIO, London)
3. Cf. *Women and Holy Orders*.
4. The Anglican Consultative Council met first at Limuru, Kenya.
5. If a Church makes a decision so difficult to go back on as this, without previous ecumenical consultation, it is not clear how ecumenical repercussions can have been *taken into account* at all.
6. Produced as *Pros and Cons on the Ordination of Women* (1975) by Seabury Profession Services, 815 Second Avenue, New York. I owe my copy to the good offices of William Norgren.
7. Archbishop Runcie was still invoking the Gamaliel principle as 'in the end the true Christian response' at a lecture in the USA in January 1988 (printed in *Authority in Crisis*, SCM Press, 1988, p. 48). Dame Betty Ridley, who had written in favour of the ordination of women 48 years earlier, said at the C of E Synod in 1975 'I cannot be sure that it is the will of God that our Church should be torn apart by going ahead now'.
8. The whole question, report and resolutions and the two speeches in the Appendix, takes up less than ten pages out of 124.

CHAPTER 26

What now?

A community of reconciliation

When Archbishop Ramsey and Paul VI signed in Rome in 1966 the Common Declaration which launched the Anglican–Roman Catholic enterprise on its official and world-wide scale, they declared themselves 'of one mind in their determination to strive in common to find solutions for *all* the great problems that face those who believe in Christ in the world of today' (italics mine).

When the Joint Preparatory Commission did its work in 1967 it had not wholly lost sight of this Grand Design. Even the practical recommendations made for the future ARCIC still showed traces of it (FR, pp. 111–13). The new commission was to be one of 'oversight and co-ordination' of future work undertaken 'by our two communions'.

The JPC regarded its own work as the first stage of growing together. In its Part II, nos 8–16, it launched into a list of practical proposals. These were all concerned with Church life and worship. They began at the top (para. 8):

In every region where each communion has a hierarchy, we propose an annual meeting of either the whole or some considerable representation of the two hierarchies.

Closely connected with this was (para. 14):

We believe that joint or parallel statements from our Church leaders at international, national and local levels on urgent issues can provide a valuable form of Christian witness.

There were more practical recommendations about sharing resources: churches and other buildings, educational facilities and research projects, liturgical revision, exchange of preachers, mission strategy. The Christian Church was intended and founded as a community of reconciliation. For warring Christian communities to preach this reconciliation was a mockery. Missioners in pagan lands had this anomaly brought home to them because their hearers with no history of confessional quarrels were nonplussed when it was forced upon them.

As for the 'civilized' world, the more secularized it became, the more the obstacle of Christian divisions weakened Christian witness there too.

A brave step towards breaching the barriers was made by the Anglican Communion at the Lambeth Conference of 1920. It numbered among its resolutions 'An appeal to all Christian peoples'.[1] One sentence from para. 8 has become famous chiefly in connection with the discussion of Anglican Orders:

We believe that for all, the truly equitable approach to union is by the way of mutual deference to one another's consciences. To this end, we who send forth this appeal would say that if the authorities of other Communions should so desire, we are persuaded that, terms of union having been otherwise satisfactorily adjusted, bishops and clergy of our Communion would willingly accept from these authorities a form of commission or recognition which would commend our ministry to their congregations, as having its place in the one family life.

The bishops were writing just after the First World War and writing deeply under its influence. As they said clearly:

For four terrible years the loss of international fellowship emphasised its values ... But fellowship with God is the indispensable condition of human fellowship.

This lesson from recent history they saw as changing the approach to Christian reunion.

Another often quoted passage comes from the report of the sub-committee on Relations and Reunion with Episcopal Churches (op. cit., p. 128). It was taken from the Lambeth 1908 report:

> there can be no fulfilment of the Divine purpose in any scheme of reunion which does not ultimately include the great Latin Church of the West with which our history has been so closely associated in the past and to which we are still bound by many ties of common faith and tradition. But ... any advance in this direction is at present barred by differences which we have not ourselves created.

But they saw encouraging signs, particularly in the universities

Post-war developments

The Second World War began in very different circumstances. The German–Italian axis made for coolness and suspicion towards Rome, not lessened by the utterances of some Italian clergy. The robust patriotism of Cardinal Hinsley inspired the origin of the Sword of the Spirit movement (cf. p. 4). The careful account given by Michael Walsh[2] of the Sword of the Spirit and the succeeding Religion and Life down to 1947 can only sadden us today as we take seriously the Churches' commitment to the search for unity.

The difficulties of the Sword of the Spirit merely illustrated the survival at official levels of old attitudes which the experience of war was to shake profoundly not in colleges, seminaries and curial offices but in field and camp and factory.

Whether the surprise of the Second Vatican Council was complete and unwelcome or not in 1962, by 1965 the effect was impossible to ignore. It was a theological effect, and some of that theology met the sharpest resistance, but it was very much more. The whole experience illustrated how theology can be the least academic of subjects.

ARCIC I

The Trinity Institute in New York, founded in 1967 by the Anglican parish of Trinity Church, offered an annual seminar for bishops on contemporary theology. In 1970 this was conducted *jointly* by the Cardinal Archbishop of Malines–Brussels, Leo Joseph Suenens, and the Archbishop of Canterbury, Michael Ramsey. The title was 'The future of the Christian Church'.[3] Seventy-six bishops were there – half of the active bishops of the Episcopal Church in the USA. The director of the Institute, Robert Terwilliger, explained that the title did not announce an exercise in crystal-gazing but was an affirmation of faith and hope. Suenens said at the end that it was another of the 'surprises of the holy Spirit'. These had been crowding on each other for a decade. Ramsey said 'I think it is daft – absolutely daft – that we should have to belong to separate ecclesiastical establishments'.

It was the moment when the ARCIC dialogue was only just getting under way. The joint seminar was not a dialogue in the ordinary sense. Both prelates said memorable things but more remarkable was the sense of harmony, of two heads of Churches walking together to confront the Church's future. It was perhaps the first great response to the primary practical recommendations of Malta (FR, p. 111, para. 8ff.).[4]

In his lecture 'Towards unity' Archbishop Ramsey said:

> The unity for which our Lord prayed embraces aspects of human life
> more numerous than those which belong to the limited realm of
> eccelsiastical concerns. Through the unity of the *ecclesia* all people and
> all things are destined to become one in Christ . . . Every breaking
> down of barriers which divide humanity – social, racial, economic,
> cultural – is a part of the ecumenical task. The ecclesiastical aspects of
> ecumenism must be seen in this larger context. When they are so seen
> it is apparent that ecumenism is no hobby for church-minded people;
> it is a task of divine and human reconciliation in which every
> Christian, man, woman and child, can have a share.

The corresponding lecture by the Cardinal added:

> We have often been led to consider doctrine as one part of existence
> and living as another part, but the doctrine of Christ is like the sun, you
> cannot separate its light from its warmth . . . it must be at the same time
> something that warms the heart and soul and heals human wounds.

The decade of Anglican–Roman Catholic relationship which followed, which saw the bulk of ARCIC I's work and reached its peak in the papal visit to Canterbury and yet another Common Declaration, was dominated by theological dialogue.

The Introduction to the Final Report of ARCIC was, as introductions often are, the last thing to be written. It drew threads together. It showed that the three prescribed themes (Eucharist, Ministry and Authority) were not chosen at random as three historic matters of contention: they 'all relate to the true nature of the Church'. Fundamental is the concept of *koinonia*, 'communion' (FR, pp. 4–8). 'Union with God in Christ Jesus through the Spirit is the heart of Christian *koinonia*', but by the same token 'we are also bound to *one another* in a completely new relationship'. The *koinonia* is a *sign* that God's purpose in Christ's salvation is being realized. It is also an *instrument* for the accomplishment of this purpose inasmuch as it *proclaims* the truth of the Gospel and *witnesses* to it by its life, thus entering more deeply into the mystery of the Kingdom. The community thus announces what it is called to become (para. 7). 'The *koinonia* is grounded in the *word* of God *preached*, *believed*, and *obeyed*.'

In this account I have italicized several words because they all deal with various aspects of communicating. This verb and the cognate nouns, 'communication' and 'community', are very prominent in our lives today. We are in a sea of communication, not so much keeping our noses above water as abiding in it like fish.

The ARCIC passage just quoted insists that the *koinonia* of the Christian Church is *sui generis*. In the deepest sense it is not of this world because it originates in and is sustained by the Trinity. It is a sign and instrument of an eternal purpose. Yet it is not separate from this world, because it binds the *people* of God together, though in a completely new relationship.

The weakness for differing persists, raising the problem of authoritative discrimination. ARCIC (FR, p. 70) speaks of 'a combination of permanence in the revealed truth and continuous exploration of its meaning' as 'what is meant by Christian Tradition'.

Beyond Rome and Canterbury

As ARCIC I's Final Report appeared, the two communions were, as we have seen, challenged to respond to it, to say whether it provided a sufficient basis for a restoration of communion.

From the early 1960s there was a rapid growth of 'bilateral conversations'.

The Anglican–Roman Catholic was one of the earliest of these. The impact of Vatican II was decisive. The Roman Catholic relationship with the World Council of Churches was close from the earliest days of the Secretariat for Promoting Christian Unity, but the Roman Catholic Church was never a member. This emphasized the fact that bilateral dialogue raised questions about Roman Catholic relationship with the WCC. If there was one ecumenical movement, where did they fit in? How did they modify the concept of unity? The WCC was not a Church, but it was there to promote the unity of Churches – not, as had at one time seemed the aim to suspicious people, a Protestant-dominated unity. The steadily increasing Roman Catholic involvement in its work was especially evident in the field of doctrine: the Faith and Order Commission had Roman Catholic theologians as full members.

The outstanding achievement of the Faith and Order Commission has been the document on *Baptism, Eucharist and Ministry* (Faith and Order Papers no. 111; Geneva, 1982). The document is also called the Lima Document because it was in that city in January 1982, at a meeting of more than a hundred theologians, that the final text was approved.

Its status needs to be carefully understood. During the 1970s, as the BEM document was maturing in successive Faith and Order meetings, this commission felt the need to know of the works and progress of bilateral dialogues – indeed the exercise would have been pointless without a comparative study of them.

A first step was documentary – a survey and analysis of bilateral dialogues made by Nils Ehrenstrom and Gunther Gassmann under the title *Confessions in Dialogue*. A similar compilation, a *Continuing Bibliography*, was begun by the Atonement Fathers at the Centro Pro Unione in Rome. This led to the formation of an unofficial Forum on Bilateral Conversations agreed on between Faith and Order and the Conference of Secretaries of World Confessional Families (later re-christened Christian World Communions).

The co-operation of these two bodies, with the choice of the title Forum, was intended to dispel the ancient apprehension of a 'WCC takeover'. The first meeting at Bossey, 2–7 April 1978, did not for various reasons wholly succeed in doing so, but by the third meeting at Glion (October 1980) the Forum had settled on the increasingly intricate theme of reception, by this time meaning mainly the reception of dialogue results.

At Glion the Forum distinguished two forms of this reception – the stricter, which means the formal decision of the respective Church *authorities*, and the wider, which 'includes all phases and aspects of the process by which a *Church* makes the result of such a dialogue its own'. The relation between these two processes is not simple and is not the same in every Church.

In the Roman Catholic Church four centuries of history had inclined us to think much more of the first, stricter form: doctrinal statements which were judged by the Pope with the assistance of a small number of officials and theologians, by a summary process.

Agreements made with other Churches could hardly be treated in exactly this way. They were a new kind of statement, made by officially appointed commissions, based on Vatican II's recognition of some 'ecclesial reality' in these other Churches and its commitment to seek Christian unity in association with them. It was therefore unthinkable that agreed statements could be simply treated with traditional Roman procedures.

The second kind of reception distinguished by the Forum at Glion speaks of 'all phases and aspects by which a church makes the results of such a dialogue its own'. The process of mutual reception, whether we call it growing together or convergence or reconciliation, is a movement on several fronts. On some of these fronts it is quicker, on some slower, on some there can be halting or even retreat. The doctrinal front is central, manned by a *corps d'élite*, but can move so quickly as to be cut off.

Getting to know each other

Though ARCIC I was almost exclusively concerned with the doctrinal front, it also alluded several times to unity by stages, which it did not see as merely a matter of theology. The Lambeth Conference of 1988, the first to be held after the Final Report had been completed and was in the hands of the Church authorities, said:

> The idea of growth into unity by stages is important because it shows that progress towards full, visible unity does not have to wait for complete agreement on every aspect of faith and order. Each level of such agreement can be expressed in a corresponding growth in relationship and co-operation.

The vast majority of Christians today have little time and, in truth, not much more inclination, to concern themselves with theology. But the conditions of living encourage them – if they take notice of religion at all – to have feelings about it, passionate in proportion as religion is mixed up with other more devouring concerns.

Speaking in Rome on his last visit, Archbishop Runcie found a telling passage in one of Newman's letters:

> Men must have chronic familiarity to understand each other, for truth slowly sinks into the mind ... Paper argument is most disappointing. No theological arguments suffice unless we know each other no longer as strangers but as friends.

On 11 March 1980 a pamphlet was published in the United States called *Tale of Three Cities*. It was a brief account of the establishment and growth of three Anglican–Roman Catholic Covenants. It was not merely a report, with statistics from the three cities concerned, but the result of a serious visit of some days made to each of the cities concerned by a joint standing committee of the two Churches. The covenant is a formal written agreement, witnessed by the respective diocesan bishops. The agreements vary but their common element is a commitment to co-operate in living their Christian life and sharing their resources to the fullest extent sanctioned by the respective authorities.

The practical aspects were worked out with careful attention to the conditions of each of the three localities, marked by the sort of contrasts found at their most striking in the United States.

Tale of Three Cities repays study. It is not a burst of uncritical enthusiasm and the experiments it describes are not shown as such. The approach is realistic, both in the preparation for the covenants, in their regular exercise and in the periodic reassessment of them from within and from without. Without any attempt to ape full communion or to exaggerate what is achieved, the impression given is that the relationship intensifies the commitment to the faith of both partners.

Such arrangements often depend for their origin and their achievement on the character of the clergy concerned, but it is striking how often they survive changes of personnel.

We have already seen an example of one, happily exceptional, difficulty in Church relations in England – the occasion of Cardinal Willebrands' visit to Liverpool Anglican Cathedral in 1971 (Chapter 16). Here was a distinguished ecumenical occasion which a handful of bigots tried to disrupt, to the great distress especially of the Anglican hosts. The disturbance positively turned out advantageous but it was a grim reminder of a long heritage of bitterness which was a burden for all the Churches – but only one of many challenges to their mission. The problems collected under the label 'inner city' dominated all else.

Within a short time in the mid-1970s Liverpool received a new Anglican Bishop and a new Catholic Archbishop. They are still there in 1995, their relationship and joint work a unique example of what can be done. They were both southerners, strangers to Liverpool. They were only a little acquainted with each other, though they knew that they shared interests and concerns which made them the right men for their new task. They made a prompt decision to face the task together in prayer, in thinking, in action and tenacity.

In 1988 they published jointly a book on their thirteen years of co-operation. They called it *Better Together*, a thought-provoking title with several possible shades of interpretation, all valid. The subtitle is 'Christian partnership in a hurt city'. There is no substitute for reading the book – except perhaps living in Liverpool. Here I am merely exploiting the story, first as a spectacular illustration of the value of Newman's 'chronic familiarity', secondly as showing the impossibility of isolating what the WCC calls 'Life and Work' from what it calls 'Faith and Order'.

Of course the WCC does not isolate them – it merely separates them for administrative purposes. Paul VI coined the phrase 'dialogue of charity' to describe the first phase of Roman Catholic–Orthodox rapprochement which for good historical and other reasons had to go before the theological dialogue.

To talk of either separation or precedence between the two in Liverpool was pointless. The authors of *Better Together* say

> The lessons we offer our readers have not been learned in the serenity of a lecture room or on an ecclesiastical commission.

The book, and knowledge of the writers, dispels the idea that this is a 'superior' remark. They organize study courses for clergy and laity, especially of ecumenical documents. But this side of their work gets, I suppose, little publicity compared with what they get when their pastoral care prompts them to stand up to local councils and Members of Parliament.

Two other points emerge strongly from *Better Together*. One is that firm theological bases for such remarkable common witness can co-exist with clearly held differences. For instance, the co-authors discuss sensibly the ordination of women, on which they differ (pp. 108–13). For this they follow the example of Pope John Paul II and Archbishop Runcie.

The second point is that they are not simply a duo hogging the Liverpool stage. They take all reasonable opportunities to collaborate with other Churches. There are many issues or which there can be no substantial disagreement among any who adhere to Christ. The effect of mass unemployment and bad housing on families and marriages is an obvious example.

National Pastoral Congress, 1980

It was in Liverpool in 1980 that the Catholic Church of England and Wales held a National Pastoral Congress. This was carefully prepared over two years. No such gathering of Catholics had taken place in England before. None could have taken place before the Second Vatican Council. No one could have thought of such a thing happening in Liverpool – and with generous non-Catholic participation and interest.

Certainly in the 1950s some would have seen it as a giant display of Roman Catholic clannishness and triumphalism and it would have provoked appropriate reactions. 1950, the centenary of the restoration of the Roman Catholic hierarchy, had been a moment for historical reflection and thankful memories of the heroic work and sacrifices made by ancestors, of thanksgiving to God for his blessings. But self-criticism, questioning about our relations with the world at large and with other Christians, had been a minor theme, if there at all.

In 1980, when the bishops sent out their message from the Congress, they looked back over *two* hundred years and borrowed a phrase of Bishop Richard Challoner, from the days of Catholic depression – a prophetic phrase, 'The New People'. It was prophetic because it looked forward in hope to Catholic expansion, with no very visible grounds. To borrow the phrase in 1980 was to give it a new, deeply theological meaning: to cling to hope of advancement in the face of obstacles hardly to be dreamt of in 1780 or even in 1880, obstacles consciously shared by every Christian witness.

Lambeth 1988

Eight years after the Liverpool Congress, the twelfth Lambeth Conference of the Anglican Communion took place in Canterbury. As well as 518 bishops (compared with 76 at the first) there were 59 consultants, 29 observers from other churches and a very large number of assistants of every kind.

The conference divided into four sections:

- Mission and Ministry
- Dogmatic and Pastoral Concerns
- Ecumenical Relations
- Christianity and the Social Order.

This was a matter of division of labour, not an illusion that here were four water-tight compartments.

The vice-chairman of Section 1 was no less than David Sheppard of Liverpool. This section's report on 'The arena of mission' was even sharper than that of the Liverpool National Catholic Congress. Noting the danger of 'introverted preoccupation with ecclesiastical concerns', it went on:

The arena of mission is the whole world – a hungry world, an unjust world, an angry world, a fearful world. A world that has been polluted and is in danger of irreparable damage. A world that is governed by many false gods and pays little heed to the God and Father of our Lord Jesus Christ. It is also a world of beauty and hope in which goodness and love abound. A world which struggles for justice, integrity and peace. A world which belongs to God.[5]

I have moved in the last few pages between the local, the national and the universal. Nowadays all questions of human relationships, religious or not, do this. The WCC uses the phrase 'all in each place'. The very title 'Roman Catholic Church' is a title which insists on the 'both . . . and', not the 'either . . . or'. The bishop's ministry is to his own diocese but is also a co-responsibility for the world-wide Church (cf. Vatican II's *Christus Dominus, passim*). The Bishop of Rome and the Archbishop of Canterbury in their different ways have this double charge.

Archbishop Runcie's courage needs no advertisment. He could hardly have shown it more, after Lambeth '88, than by visiting the Pope whose earlier life at most of its stages had taught him to practise and appreciate courage. The Archbishop had already shown courage enough to stir up controversy – in his opening speech at the Conference. The stark question, he said, was: did they really *want* unity in the Anglican Communion? He referred to earlier slogans like 'Mutual responsibility and interdependence' (1963) and 'Partners in mission' – which were now inadequate to present problems like the ordination of women.

They did not throw much light either on the questions raised by ARCIC about Primacy. Anglicans did not want an alternative papacy but

> would rather continue to deal with the structures of the existing Petrine ministry and hopefully help in its continuous development and *reform* as a ministry of unity for all Christians.

Reform was the key word here, and he applied it to bishops and synods as well, but he was careful to warn against an ecumenical idealism which

> prefers to wait around until episcopacy, synods or popes are exactly as we would have them. Renewal then would become an excuse for inaction, a retreat from committing ourselves to each other as we are. It would be like a perpetual engagement in which marriage was for ever being postponed until the partners were perfect. No, the way to perfect your partner is to enter a new and more intimate relationship so that mutual change comes by intrinsic desire rather than extrinsic demand.

This was very much what ARCIC I had in mind in the last paragraph of Authority II (FR, p. 98) – a statement which the Conference was to accept by an overwhelming majority.

But it was also to pass a Resolution (by 423 votes to 28 with 19 abstentions) accepting the ordination of women. Jean Tillard OP, one of the most dedicated and resourceful members of ARCIC, later[6] ascribed this to 'the Anglican ethos', which, he said 'is comfortable with roads which go forward by a number of detours like someone walking in a mist', whereas 'the Roman ethos likes to go forward in a straight line only under a full sun'.

The visit

It was a year or more after the Lambeth Conference of 1988 that Archbishop Runcie came to the Vatican. He said crisply that he was going to Rome 'to block the way back'. A long road had been travelled since

1960. Grave obstacles can induce retreat. But in these years too much had been achieved to be tossed aside and forgotten. Runcie was the fourth Archbishop to come to Rome. His visit had its own character and needed its particular approach. Those who planned it did well.

Again the Archbishop lodged at the English College. His first appearance at the Vatican was not in the 'majestic halls' but in the gardens of the Casino of Pius IV. It was an inspired choice for what amounted to an English garden party to which the weather was kind. It was simply a warm welcome for the Archbishop and his party from Cardinal Willebrands and the Roman Curia.

On the morning after this cheerful gathering, 30 September 1989, the Archbishop and his party were received by the Pope. As usual, only the two formal addresses and the exchange of gifts was reported, but a month later the Archbishop, presiding at the Church of England General Synod, devoted his presidential address entirely to his visit to Rome, and said a good deal about his private discussions with the Pope. His first points were as follows: He was returning the visit made by the Pope to Canterbury in 1982. With the agreement of the Anglican primates, he was representing the Anglican Communion. 'Contrary to some reports', he had received 'the warmest possible welcome' from the Pope and the Curia, and had valuable discussions. He singled out Cardinal Ratzinger. At lunch the Pope had said that 'eating and drinking together represented a very high degree of communion'. At the Papal Mass in the square he exchanged the kiss of peace with John Paul II.

When the Pope and he talked privately, they 'chiefly focused on the need for the common presentation of the Gospel to the World'. 'We talked a good deal about how our two Churches face the same problems': secularization lessening the impact of the institutional Church; the multiplication of sects; the difficulty for central authority to do more than provide a 'strategic framework' for the tasks of the local churches in presenting the Gospel; the concept of ecumenical primacy (on which they scarcely set out from identical premisses). Runcie raised the subject of Rome's delay in responding to ARCIC. 'He [the Pope] has now himself called for procedures to expedite their official responses.'

'The sensitive issue of the Ordination of Women Priests did not dominate our discussions ... we were able to locate the issue in its proper place ... the debate about authority, communion and the Church ... about how the Churches judge development in the tradition.' 'It is simply not correct', Runcie told the Synod, 'to suggest that the Ordination of Women Priests is the only obstacle to unity; nor that all obstacles come from the Anglican side.'

Nevertheless, 'the actual difference of *practice* makes it very difficult to see how the reconciliation of ministries could be effected as things now stand'.

On 30 September the Bishop of Rome and the Archbishop of Canterbury came to the church of St Gregory to pray and preach together publicly to a crowded congregation. Both looked at the daunting Gospel tasks of today.

> If men and women are to know the peace of Christ, if they are to be
> reconciled in him who alone can bring peace to the world, then
> Christians must be seen to be a community that is both reconciled
> and reconciling

said the Pope.

> In my own country I long for Anglicans and Roman Catholics
> together with other Christians to work together much more closely.
> I long for them to bring the Gospel afresh to a society in which
> religious language has largely lost its meaning.

Thus Archbishop Runcie.

The encounter issued, as earlier ones had done, in a common declaration. Its theme is found in the middle:

> we urge ARCIC and all others engaged in prayer and work for
> visible unity not to minimize these differences. At the same time we
> also urge them not to abandon either their hope or work for unity.

This exhortation was boosted by two reminiscences bestriding a millennium and a half of history. When Augustine's company set out for England in 597 they did not know what to expect; what they got (Gregory claimed in a letter to Eulogius of Alexandria) was miracles. When the Joint Preparatory Commission set out for Gazzada in 1966 they did not know what to expect: what they got was not exactly miracles but, first, a very heartening result for some hard work and second, stealing up on the first, a 'new and grave obstacle'.

Comparisons

What parallels were there between the cases? There were plenty of obvious differences. The Church of Rome and the Church of Canterbury had each had chequered careers (one much longer than the other) and their relations had dramatically changed. But what brought them together in 1989 was a movement for reconciliation, in view of a new movement for evangelization. This was linked logically with the last thought of the declaration – that God's will for unity is not just a cosy concern of Roman Catholics and Anglicans or even for Christians alone.

Such attention as the meeting attracted in the media was often laced with despair and cynicism – one heard Anglicans in particular complain about this.[7] Passages from speeches or declarations which could be wrenched into the idiom of the Great Return (Pope) or the great capitulation (Runcie) were seized upon.

Something of a balancing act was inevitable: what was far from inevitable, and by some unexpected, but clearly prevailing, was a spirit of prayer and resolve.

The last paragraph of the Final Report of ARCIC I (FR, p. 98) says:

> Contemporary discussions of conciliarity and primacy in both communions indicate that we are not dealing with positions destined to remain static. We suggest that some difficulties will not be wholly resolved until a practical initiative has been taken and our two Churches have lived together more visibly in the one *koinonia*.

This is one of several sentences in the last section of the Final Report which cast doubts on its title. Of course the word 'Final' merely indicates that it is the last word of ARCIC I. ARCIC II has been in action for some years.

Authority (the subject on which ARCIC I left off its discussions, very much in a spirit of hope) had been an ecclesiastical concern for a long time. Anglicans (to quote Stephen Sykes in 1987) have been seriously concerned about their claim to authority for some forty years.[8] Roman Catholics had been concerned for rather longer, but in a different way. They had a high conception of Church authority, but a desperate struggle to exercise any against tyrannical regimes.[9]

In 1948 a Lambeth Conference committee of 64 bishops on 'The meaning and unity of the Anglican Communion' combined the two concerns:

> The world is in grievous disorder and needs to be restored to the order which God wills. A perplexed generation is in search of an authority to which to give its allegiance, and easily submits to the appeal of authoritarian systems whether religious or secular in character.
>
> The question is asked 'Is Anglicanism based on a sufficiently coherent form of authority to form the nucleus of a world-wide fellowship of Churches, or does its comprehensiveness conceal internal divisions which may cause its disruption?'

The committee report gave what came to be seen as the classic account of 'dispersed authority'.

Other factors which, in the period with which this book is mainly concerned, have influenced Anglican ideas on authority and made the 'contemporary discussions' persist and even intensify, have been the general ecumenical movement and the Second Vatican Council with its ramifications. Whether Anglicans (and others) understand the nature and depth of the influence of that assembly on Roman Catholics or not, they realize that the total Christian situation is not and probably never will be the same again.

We have seen (Chapter 21) that the elements of that 'dispersed authority' in which Anglicans 'glory' are not something they invented, but 'inherited from the undivided Church of the early centuries of the Christian era'. The Anglican Communion is claiming to be content with asserting the sufficiency of something which has been there all the time. It is also claiming that Anglicanism has preserved the moral and spiritual quality of this ancient authority.

Where this authority of Christ is to be found mediated not in one mode but in several:

> We recognise in this multiplicity God's loving provision against the temptations to tyranny and the dangers of unchecked power.
>
> This authority posseses a suppleness and elasticity in that the emphasis of one element over the others may and does change with the changing conditions of the Church. The variety of the contributing factors gives to it a quality of richness which encourages and releases initiative, trains in fellowship and evokes a free and willing obedience.

It may be said that authority of this kind is much harder to understand and obey than authority of a more imperious character. This is true, and we glory in the appeal which it makes to faith.

From the Roman side Vatican II had said a good deal about how Christ's authority should be mediated – in the Constitution on the Church (especially chapter 3), on Revelation (chapter 2), on the Church in the Modern World (especially Part I, chapter 1) and in the decrees on Religious Freedom (*passim*) and the Office of Bishops (*passim*). These documents profoundly changed the mind of the Church about how authority *should* be administered and exercised. They made possible dialogue with the Anglican Communion which from the beginning aspired to the goal of full communion.

What they did not do was banish all suspicions of 'Roman ways'; there persisted vigilance – eagerness to see whether Rome had really changed her spots. The work of ARCIC I itself developed within the Commission a very high degree of trust, of willingness to think the best even of unwelcome developments – mostly in the exercise of central authority over episcopal appointments and the 'silencing' of academics.

Outside ARCIC there seemed sometimes almost a willingness to think the worst.

The Report on *Doctrine in the Church of England* published in 1938 had the following note on Assent:

The obligation not to teach, as the doctrine of the Church, doctrine which is not in accordance with the Church's mind.
6. If any authorised teacher puts forward personal opinions which diverge (within the limits indicated above) from the traditional teachings of the Church, he should be careful to distinguish between such opinions and the normal teaching which he gives in the Church's name; and so far as possible such divergences should be so put forward as to avoid offending consciences.

This passage combines with some earlier incidents in Anglican history to show that the idea of the Church exercising some control of what was taught *in its name*, as its authentic doctrine, was not strange to Anglicanism. It might dislike (along with Roman Catholics) some *methods* of exercising this control, but hardly abdicates it altogether.[10]

By 1948 any concern for control has disappeared from the Lambeth

Conference section on 'The meaning and unity of the Anglican Communion', though the question of whether Anglicanism is based on a 'sufficiently coherent form of authority' is still there as the section's point of departure.

More than twenty years later, when Anglican–Roman Catholic dialogue had begun under the influence of Vatican II, both partners began to think about the exercise of authority. Those Anglicans who had followed the Council combined traditional aversion to Roman ways with hope that things were going to change. This was reflected in the report of Lambeth '68 (cf. above, p. 118) on 'Episcopacy, Collegiality and the Papacy', and throughout the preparation of the Venice Statement, 'Authority I' (which should be turned back to at this point – above, Chapter 19), there were recurrent references to the *exercise* of the Church's authority on matters of faith.

Para. 18 states:

the Church has the obligation and the competence to make declarations in matters of faith ...

when conflict endangers unity or threatens to distort its gospel, the Church must have effective means for resolving it.

the bishops have a special responsibility for promoting truth and discerning error.

Para. 6:

[the bishop] can require the compliance necessary to maintain faith and charity.

There are agreements here which have been strained in three ways:

1. by the (inconclusive) development of the discussion of primacy in 'Authority II';
2. by certain more recent exercises of Roman primacy;
3. by the exercise of Anglican authority in the matter of the ordination of women to the priesthood and episcopate.

The publication in Canada of a *festschrift* edited by Stephen Sykes in honour of Bishop John Howe, the first Secretary General of the Anglican

Consultative Council, made a considerable contribution to the subject which provided its title, *Authority in the Anglican Communion.* Bishop Sykes in his introductory essay, 'Why authority?', contrasts the 'lofty sentiments' with the reality of Church government, adding:

> If it should be asked where are the essays relating to the actual exercise of authority in Anglicanism, which was the third element of our three-cornered scheme, one is embarrassed. Perhaps it should be admitted that no one really knows whether a given church exercises its authority well or not.

One looks back to that dawn in which it was bliss to be alive, when even sober and eminent people could toy with calculations of how long ARCIC's task would take. One of the lessons that has been learnt is that ecumenical dialogue shares with atomic physics a certain difficulty – nothing stays still long enough. Be still and know ...

Bishop Sykes ends his introduction:

> But it is also certain that a future church will need more than sound theology, good structures and a continuing process of internal reconciliation. It will need also spiritual resources of great depth, if men and women are to be found who will be capable of rising to the religious and ethical challenges of the future of humanity.

This may be compared with something Cardinal Hume told his hearers in Westminster Abbey when, on the day he was installed as Archbishop of Westminster, he moved down the road to the Abbey with 150 Benedictine monks and sang Vespers there at the Dean's invitation.

The contrasting symbols evident in this act needed no underlining and the new Archbishop's words fused commitment with patience and trust:

> Our wounds are ancient: the healing is slow. We shall not respond to Christ's prayer for unity unless our Churches are praying Churches.

NOTES

1. *The Lambeth Conferences 1867–1930* (SPCK, 1948), p. 38.
2. His book *From Swords to Ploughshares* (London, 1980) and two articles.
3. Published in Britain 1971 (SCM Press).

4.   In every region where each Communion has a hierarchy we propose an annual joint meeting of either the whole or some considerable representation of the two hierarchies.

In the same circumstances we further recommend:

(a) Constant consultation between committees concerned with pastoral and evangelistic problems including, where appropriate, the appointment of joint committees.

(b) Agreements for joint use of churches and other ecclesiastical buildings, both existing or to be built, wherever such use is helpful for one or other of the two communions.

(c) Agreements to share facilities for theological education, with the hope that all future priests of each Communion should have attended some course taught by a professor of the other Communion. Arrangements should also be made where possible for temporary exchange of students.

(d) Collaboration in projects and institutions of theological scholarship to be warmly encouraged.

5. Between the Liverpool Congress (1980) and the Lambeth Conference (1988) Archbishop Runcie appointed a commission (1988) to examine Urban Priority Areas. It produced a 400-page report, *Faith in the City*, and also a popular précis. This contained a formidable number of practical recommendations to the Church of England (38) and the government and nation (23). They aroused interest and from politicians some hostility. 'If they evoke a whole-hearted response, they will transform the Church of England', wrote the *Observer* newspaper (a big 'if'). A follow-up report, *Living Faith in the City*, appeared early in 1990. It included a couple of pages on 'Partnership with other denominations', which ended by saying there was scope for much more.

6. In a lecture given at Fribourg University and printed in *One in Christ*.

7. Notable among these was Christopher Hill, Secretary of the Council for Foreign Relations, who accompanied the Archbishop to Rome and so knew what he was talking about.

8. Stephen Sykes, *Authority in the Anglican Communion*, p. 12.

9. In some places Anglicans had had and were to have this struggle, e.g., Uganda, Iran.

10. In 1986 the House of Bishops of the Church of England issued a statement and Exposition of the *Nature of Belief* (Church House Publications). Section E, especially nos 65–74, deals with individual and collegial responsibility of Bishops for the faith of the Church.

Bibliography

Official documents

For *Quanta Cura* and the *Syllabus* see ASS 3 (1867–69); DS 2890–2980.

Lambeth Conference *Reports and Resolutions* and other material have been published at intervals since 1867 by SPCK.

Leo XIII, *Providentissimus Deus*: ASS 26 (1893–94), p. 26. Shortened version: DS 3280–3283.

Apostolicae Curae (Latin text): ASS 299 (1896–97), pp. 198ff.; DS 3315–3319. The English text and the answer of the Church of England bishops published by SPCK (1943).

Mortalium Animos: AAS 20 (1928), pp. 13ff.

G. Bell (ed.), *Documents on Christian Unity*, 4 series (Oxford), 1920–57.

Divino Afflante Spiritu: AAS 35 (1943). Shortened version: DS 3825–3831.

Biblical Commission's reply to Cardinal Suhard on the Pentateuch: AAS 40 (1948). French and Latin in DS 3862–3864.

W. Abbott (ed.), *The Documents of Vatican II and Comments by Catholic, Protestant and Orthodox Authorities* (New York: Guild Press, 1966)

A. Flannery OP (ed.), *The Conciliar and Post-Conciliar Documents*, 2 vols (Leominster: Fowler Wright: 1988)

USA

A useful series of volumes of documents is being published by the Paulist Press:

I *Doing the Truth in Charity* (T. Stransky and J. Sheering)
II *Growth in Agreement* (H. Meyer and L. Vischer)
III *Towards Healing of Schism* (J. Sheerin)
IV *Building Unity* (J. Burgess and G. Gross)

The Catholic News Service publishes, usually weekly, a valuable Bulletin, *Origins*, which selects documents, correspondence and comments of immediate importance.

ANGLICAN CONSULTATIVE COUNCIL REPORTS

1. Limuru   1971
2. Dublin   1973
3. Trinidad   1976
4. London, Canada   1979
5. Newcastle upon Tyne   1981
6. Nigeria   1984
7. Singapore   1987

Archives

Both the Secretariat for Promoting Christian Unity (Rome, section 151) and the Council for Foreign Relations, Lambeth, archives are arranged in simple chronological order, some boxes being additionally labelled according to events, e.g., 'Ramsey visit to Rome'.

Exceptions for Rome are

1. Mixed Marriages, which come under the separate general section *Matrimonia*.
2. Documents of the Vatican Council period, which are housed in the Council archives in Piazza Pio XII.

The late Richard Stewart began an inventory of the SPCU archive, but his untimely death interrupted the work.

The ARCIC papers (some 260 of them), numbered serially, exist in several copies, each member having been given one. Sets exist still in the SPCU and in the CFR and in the Anglican Centre, Rome. A few papers have been published individually on the initiative of the author.

The body referred to throughout this book as the Secretariat for Promoting Christian Unity, but known since 1 March 1989 as the Pontifical Council for Promoting Christian Unity, has since 1967 published, usually four times a year, an Information Service. As well as giving accounts of the Council's work in the many areas of ecumenism, this bulletin regularly prints official documents and the utterances of the Pope on the subject.

General

ANGLICAN

J. Atkinson, *Rome and Reformation* (Hodder, 1966)
J. Booty and S. Sykes, *The Study of Anglicanism* (Fortress Press, 1988)
O. Chadwick (ed.), *The Mind of the Oxford Movement* (London: Black, 1960)
O. Chadwick, *The Reformation* (London: Pelican, 1964)

P. Day, *Tomorrow's Church: Catholic, Anglican, Reformed* (New York: Seabury, 1969)
Roger Lloyd, *Church of England 1900–1964* (London: SCM, 1966)
H. McAdoo, *Being an Anglican* (SPCK, 1977)
H. McAdoo, *The Spirit of Anglicanism* (London: Black, 1965)
A. Richardson, *Religion in Contemporary Debate* (London: SCM, 1968)
E. G. Selwyn (ed.), *Essays Catholic and Critical* (SPCK, 1926)
P. Staples, *The Church of England 1961–80* (Utrecht, 1981)
Norman Sykes, *The English Religious Tradition* (London, SCM: 1954)
Norman Sykes, *Old Priest and New Presbyter* (Cambridge, 1957)
G. Tavard, *The Quest for Anglicanism* (Burns & Oates, 1963)
A. R. Vidler, *The Church in an Age of Revolution* (London: Pelican, 1961)
A. Vogel, *The Next Christian Epoch* (New York: Harper Row, 1966)
E. de Waal, *A Life-Giving Way: a Commentary on the Rule of Saint Benedict* (London: Geoffrey Chapman, 1995)
W. Wolf (ed.), *The Spirit of Anglicanism* (Wilton, PCT, 1979)

ROMAN CATHOLIC

Cardinal A. Bea, *Church and Mankind* (Geoffrey Chapman, 1967)
Cardinal A. Bea, *The Unity of Christians* (Herder and Herder, 1963)
S. C. Britten, *The Churches' Unity* (Geoffrey Chapman, 1979)
W. Burghardt and W. F. Lynch, *The Idea of Catholicism* (Burns & Oates, 1960)
Y. Congar, *Chrétiens Désunis* (Paris, 1937)
Y. Congar, *Dialogue between Christians* (Geoffrey Chapman, 1966)
C. Dawson *The Dividing of Christendom* (New York: Sheed & Ward, 1965)
C. Dawson, *Progress and Religion* (London: Sheed & Ward, 1945)
C. Dawson, *The Spirit of the Oxford Movement* (Sheed & Ward, 1933)
C. Dawson, *Understanding Europe* (Sheed & Ward, 1952)
T. Maynard, *The Story of American Catholicism*, 2 vols (New York: Doubleday, 1941)
J. de Bivort de la Saudée, *Anglicains et Catholiques* (Paris, 1948)
F. Sheed, *Society and Sanity* (Sheed & Ward, 1953)
G. Tavard, *Two Centuries of Ecumenism* (Burns & Oates, 1960)
G. Weigel, *The Ecumenical Movement* (London: Geoffrey Chapman, 1958)

OTHERS

E. Digby Balzell, *The Protestant Establishment* (New York: Vintage, 1964)
H. Butterfield, *Christianity and History* (Bell, 1954)
H. Butterfield, *History & Human Relations* (Collins, 1951)
H. Butterfield, *The Whig Interpretation of History*
H. McLeod, *Class and Religion* (Croom Helm, 1974)
David Martin, *Sociology of English Religion* (Heinemann, 1967)
E. Norman, *The English Catholic Church in the Nineteenth Century* (Oxford, 1984)
G. Scott, *The RC's* (Hutchinson, 1967)

E. Wickham, *Church and People in Industrial Society* (Lutterworth Press, 1957)
B. Willey, *Nineteenth Century Studies* (Chatto & Windus, 1949)
B. Willey, *More Nineteenth Century Studies* (Chatto & Windus, 1956)
Bryan Wilson, *Religion in Secular Society* (Pelican, 1966)

ON NEWMAN

Newman continues to attract writers in many fields, more so since Vatican II.

W. Ward, *Life of John Henry Newman* (Longmans, 1912)
O. Chadwick, *From Bossuet to Newman* (Cambridge University Press, 1957)
L. Bouyer, *Newman, His Life and Spirit* (Burns & Oates, 1958)
Meriol Trevor, *Life of Newman*, 2 vols (Macmillan, 1962)
J. Coulson and A.M. Allchin (eds.), *The Rediscovery of Newman: An Oxford Symposium* (Sheed & Ward, 1967)
N. Lash, *Newman and Development* (London, 1975)
Brian Martin, *Newman, His Life and Work* (Chatto & Windus, 1982)
O. Chadwick, *Newman* (Past Masters Series) (OUP, 1983)
I. T. Ker, *John Henry Newman* (OUP, 1988)

Bibliographies by Chapter

3   Fisher's visit to John XXIII

E. Carpenter, *Cantuar: The Archbishops in Their Office* (Oxford: Mowbray, 1971/1988)
Cardinal J. Heenan, *A Crown of Thorns* (London, 1974)
W. Purcell, *Fisher of Lambeth* (London, 1969)
S. Schmidt, *Il Cardinale dell'Unità* (Rome, 1987). pp. 27ff. A monumental biography by Cardinal Bea's faithful secretary. English translation in preparation.

6   Further English conversations

P. Crowe (ed.), *Keele '67: Evangelical Congress* (London: Falcon, 1967)
Nottingham Conference of 1964, *Unity Begins at Home* (London: SCM, 1964)

7 Preparations for the Second Vatican Council

E. E. Y. Hales, *Pope John and His Revolution* (Eyre & Spottiswoode, 1965)
B. Häring, *The Johannine Council* (Dublin: Gill, 1963)
P. Hebblethwaite, *Pope John XXIII* (London: Geoffrey Chapman, 1984)
Lorenz Jaeger, *The Ecumenical Council* (from German; London: Geoffrey Chapman, 1961)
H. Küng, *The Council and Reunion* (Sheed & Ward, 1961)
J. S. J. Levie, *The Bible – Word of God and Words of Men* (London: Geoffrey Chapman, 1961)
B. Pawley, *Looking at the Vatican Council* (SCM Press, 1962)
W. A. Purdy, *Church on the Move* (Hollis & Carter, 1966)
S. Schmidt, *Il Cardinale dell'Unità* (Rome, 1987)

8 First session: death of John XXIII

DOCUMENTS

(See also entries under Chapter 18)

W. Abbott, *Constitution on Sacred Liturgy* (April 1964)
Instructio Pont. Comm. de re Biblica: AAS 56 (1964) and DS 3999
A. Flannery, *Constitution on Sacred Liturgy*, vol. 1, pp. 1–38. Vols 1 and 2 contain many, mostly practical, Instructions down to 1981.
Pius XII, Encyclical *Mediator Dei*: AAS 19 (1947); DS 3840–55

OTHER WORKS

Olivier Beguin, *Roman Catholicism and the Bible* (Lutterworth Press, 1963)
P. Bradshaw and R. Jasper, *Companion to the Alternative Service Book* (SPCK, 1978)
Bernard Cooke, *Ministry to Word and Sacraments* (New York: Fortress, 1976)
J. D. Crichton, *Christian Celebration* (3 vols; Geoffrey Chapman, new edn 1993)
G. J. Cuming, *A History of Anglican Liturgy* (Macmillan, 1969)
J. G. Davies, *A New Dictionary of Liturgy and Worship* (SCM Press, 1986)
G. Dix, *The Shape of the Liturgy* (Black: Dacre Press, 1978)
C. Jones, G. Wainwright and E. Yarnold, *The Study of Liturgy* (SPCK, 1978)
R. Kaiser, *Inside the Council* (Burns & Oates, 1963)
K. E. Kirk, *The Vision of God* (Longmans Green, 1934)
X. Rynne, *The First Session* (Faber & Faber, 1963)
G. Tavard, *Holy Word or Holy Church* (London, 1959)
J. M. R. Tillard, 'Liturgical reform and unity', *One in Christ* (1983)
H. Winstone and J. Ainslie, *English Catholic Worship* (Geoffrey Chapman, 1979)

9 Session II: Decree on Ecumenism

and

10 The Council's last phase

B. Leeming, *The Vatican Council and Christian Unity* (New York: Harper Row, 1966)

J. R. H. Moorman, *The Vatican Observed* (London, 1967)

B. Pawley (ed.), *The Second Vatican Council: Studies by Eight Anglican Observers* (OUP, 1969)

A. Stacpoole, *Vatican II by Those Who Were There* (Geoffrey Chapman, 1986)

T. Stransky, *Decree on Ecumenism* (Paulist Press, 1966). Lists many articles on the subject and includes valuable appendices. This is among the best of the Paulist Press series of short books on Vatican II documents.

S. Stuber and G. Nelson, *Implementing Vatican II in Your Community* (New York: Guild Press, 1967)

J. Tillard, 'Did we receive Vatican II?', *One in Christ* (1984/5), pp. 276–7

H. Vorgrimler, *Commentary on Documents of Vatican II* (Herder, 1969)

12 Anglican–Roman Catholic Joint Preparatory Commission

Alan Clark and Colin Davey, *Anglican–Roman Catholic Dialogues: The Work of the JPC* (OUP, 1974)

13 Lambeth Conference 1968

Preparatory Essays by various authors are published by SPCK, as are the *Reports & Resolutions* of the Conference.

Catholic Observers' Impressions (SPCU Information Service no. 6)

J. B. Simpson and E. M. Story, *The Long Shadows of Lambeth X* (New York, 1969)

Humanae Vitae (25 July 1968) in Flannery II, pp. 397ff.

15 ARCIC at Windsor I

Papers in ARCIC series

Reports in SPCU Information Service no. 11, pp. 16–17.

16 Cardinal Willebrands in England

The Cambridge sermon and (in part) the Liverpool one are in SPCU Information Service no. 11, pp. 10–15.

17 Windsor Meeting II: The Eucharist

Baptism, Eucharist and Ministry: The Statement; Faith and Order Paper 111 (Geneva: WCC, 1982)
F. Clark, *Eucharist Sacrifice and the Reformation* (DLT, 1960)
J. G. Cumming, *A History of Anglican Liturgy* (Macmillan, 1969)
Doctrine in the Church of England, republished with Preface by G. Lampe (1982)
E. Echlin, *Anglican Eucharist and Ecumenical Perspective* (Seabury Press, 1967)
M. Green, *Christ's Sacrifice and Ours* (in the 'Guidelines' series; London: Falcon Press, 1967)
M. J. Hatchett, *A Commentary on the American Prayer Book* (New York: Seabury, 1981)
P. Hinchcliff, *The South African Liturgy* (Cape Town: OUP, 1959)
M. Hurley (ed.), *Church and Eucharist: An Ecumenical Symposium* (Dublin: Gill, 1966)
J. Lawrence (ed.), *A Critique of The Alternative Service Book* (SPCK, 1980)
W. Lazareth, *Growing Together in BEM (Study Guide)* (Faith and Order Paper 114; Geneva: WCC, 1982)
H. McAdoo (ed.), *Modern Eucharistic Agreement* (SPCK, 1973)
E. Mascall, *Corpus Christi* (Longmans, 1965)
Max Thurian (ed.), *Ecumenical Perspectives on BEM* (Faith and Order Paper 116; Geneva: WCC, 1983)
J. Tillard, 'Terminology in the Eucharist', *One in Christ* (1981/2)
A. Vogel, *Is the Last Supper Finished?*

18 Ministry

J. Charley, *Agreement on the Doctrine of Ministry* (Nottingham, 1973)
Constitutio Apostolica Sacramentum Ordinis: AAS 40 (1948); shortened in DS 3857–3861.
P. Cross, *The Influence of Recent Ecumenical Dialogue on the Anglican Theory of the Historic Episcopate*, PUG thesis (Rome, 1983)
M. Fahey (ed.), *Catholic Perspectives on BEM* (University Press of the USA, 1986)
Faith and Order BEM documents as under previous chapter.
J. Griffiths, *Church Ministry and Unity* (Blackwell, 1983)
J. J. Hughes, *Stewards of the Lord* (Sheed & Ward, 1970)
J. McQuarrie, *Theology Church and Ministry* (London: SCM, 1986)
Synod of Bishops, Rome, *Ultimis Temporibus*; English trans. 'On the Ministerial Priesthood' in Flannery II, p. 672.

A. Stacpoole, unpublished Oxford DPhil thesis
J. Tillard, 'Ministry and Apostolic Tradition', *One in Christ* (1989/1)

19 Authority I: Venice

M. Bévenot, 'Primacy and development', *Heythrop Journal* (1968)
The *Books of Homilies* 'prescribed for the use of disaffected and unlearned clergy'.
     Though unsuitable for modern use they retain a measure of authority in
     view of Article 35 (q.v.). See *Oxford Dictionary of Christian Church*. The
     Homilies were published by SPCK, 1914. I have found no later edition.
C. Butler, 'Authority in the Church', *The Tablet*, no. 231 (1977)
The Canons of the Church of England (SPCK, 1969). This was the work of a
     commission begun in 1947. 'Introduction' by E. W. Kemp (Hodder &
     Stoughton, 1957) and by E. Garth Moore (Oxford, 1967). Both these throw
     much light on an extremely complicated section of legal history.
H. Chadwick, *The Status of Ecumenical Councils in Anglican Thought* (PUG:
     Rome, 1973)
A. Dulles, *A Church to Believe In* (New York: Crossroads, 1983)
J. Hamer, *The Church Is A Communion* [French original, 1962] (London: Geoffrey
     Chapman, 1964)
The Revised Catechism of the Church of England (SPCK, 1963)
J. Stott, *Jesus Christ our Leader and Lord: Towards Solving the Problem of
     Authority* (Evangelical Guidelines; Falcon Press, 1967)
S. Sykes (ed.), *Authority in the Anglican Communion: Essays in Honour of John
     Howe* (Toronto, 1987)
J. Todd (ed.), *Problems of Authority*, Downside Symposium (London: DLT, 1962)
E. Yarnold and H. Chadwick, *Truth and Authority: A Commentary* (SPCK/CTS,
     1977)

20 Archbishop Coggan in Rome

The 'Common Declaration' is in Flannery II, p. 183 and the SPCU Information
     Service no. 34 (1977/2), p. 34.

21 Lambeth Conference 1978: Authority II

M. Dudley, 'Waiting on the common mind: authority in Anglicanism', *One in Christ*
     (1984)
A. Dulles, 'Jus Divinum as an ecumenical problem', *Theological Studies* (1977)
A. Dulles, 'The Papacy – bond or barrier?', *Catholic Mind* 1285 (1974)
C. Dumont, *Analysis of ARCIC on Authority* (SPCU Information Service no. 32,
     1976)

A. Farrer *et al.*, *Infallibility in the Church*, Birmingham symposium (London: DLT, 1968)

J. Heft, 'Pope, infallibility and Marian dogmas', *One in Christ*, vol. 18, no. 4 (1982), pp. 309–40

Eric Jay, 'To Canadian ARC' (June 1976)

H. Küng, *Infallible?* (Collins, 1971)

P. McLeod (ed.) *A Pope for All Christians?* (New York: Paulist Press/London: SPCK, 1976)

J. M. Miller, 'The divine right of the Papacy in recent ecumenical theology', *Analecta Gregoriana* (Rome, 1980)

T. Murphy (ed.), *Papal Primacy and the Universal Church* (Minneapolis, 1974)

R. Stewart, *The Pope and the Church* (London: CTS, 1982)

F. S. Sullivan, *Magisterium – Teaching Authority in the Church* (Paulist Press, 1985)

G. Sweeney, 'The small print of Vatican I', *Clergy Review* no. 54 (1974)

J. Tillard, *The Bishop of Rome* (SPCK, 1983)

J. Tillard, 'The horizons of the primacy of the Bishop of Rome', *One in Christ* (1976)

22 The Pope in Great Britain

'Common Declaration' in Canterbury 29 May 1982: in Flannery II, p. 187.

The Pope in Britain. The Complete Texts (London: CTS, 1982)

'Runcie to General Synod before visit', *One in Christ* (1982)

A. Webster (Dean of St Paul's), *Theology* (May 1982)

G. H. Williams, *The Mind of John Paul II* (New York: Seabury Press, 1981)

Church Times Leader, 28 May 1982. (The *Church Times* anticipated the visit with cordiality, Webster mainly with liberal-theological reservations. After the visit the *Church Times* (11 June) was still cordial: *Theology* had nothing to say)

23 Reactions to ARCIC Final Report

(cf. also Chapters 19 and 21)

H. Chadwick, 'Lima, ARCIC and the Church of England', *One in Christ* (1984/1)

Church of England Evangelical Council, *ARCIC: An Open Letter*

C. Davey, 'The ideal and the actual', *One in Christ* (1986/2)

English ARC, *A Study Guide to the Final Report* (CTS/SPCK, 1982)

English and Welsh Bishops (RC), 'Reactions to the Final Report', *One in Christ* (1985/2); also published as a CTS pamphlet.

H. Montefiore, *So Near and Yet so Far* (SCM Press, 1986)

A. Nichols, OP, *The Theology of Joseph Ratzinger: An Introductory Study* (Edinburgh, 1988)

D. Papandreou (ed.), *Les Dialogues Ecuméniques hier et aujourd'hui*, Lectures in French, German and English (Chambesy, 1986)

R. Runcie, *Authority in Crisis: An Anglican Response* (SCM Press, 1988)
M. Santer (ed.), *Their Lord and Ours* (SPCK, 1982)
J. Tillard, 'The RCC and bilateral dialogue: lecture at Chevetogne', *One in Christ* (1983/4); French in *Irénikon* (1983/1).
Towards Unity in Truth: Westminster Lent Lectures (Leominster, 1981)
E. Yarnold and H. Chadwick, *An ARCIC Catechism* (CTS, 1983)
J. Zizioulas and R. Steward, 'Reception: Centro pro Unione lectures', *One in Christ* (1985/2)

24   Marriage

Archbishop's Group, *Putting Asunder* (SPCK, 1966)
ARCIC/M, *Anglican–Roman Catholic Marriage* (CIO, 1975) 'French pastoral recommendations', *One in Christ* (1981)
G. Bell, *Mixed Marriages* (SPCK)
Familiaris Consortio, nov. 1981, in Flannery II, p. 15.
Marriage and the Church's Task; 95 Commission Report (c10, 1978)
J. Hotchkin, '*Familiaris Consortio*: New light on mixed marriage', *One in Christ*, vol. 23 (1986), pp. 73–9
K. Kirk, *Marriage and Divorce* (Hodder & Stoughton, 1948)
P. O'Mahony (ed.), *Catholics and Divorce* (Nelson, 1959)
J. Marshall (ed.), *The Future of Christian Marriage* (Geoffrey Chapman, 1969)
Pius XI, *Casti Connubii*: AAS (1930), pp. 540ff.; shortened in DS 3700–3734.
Marriage, Divorce and the Church, Root Report (SPCK, 1971)
E. Schillebeeckx, *Marriage: Human Reality and Saving Mystery* (Sheed and Ward, 1965)

25   The ordination of women priests

SCDF *Inter Insigniores*, 15 October 1976: in Flannery I, p. 351.

26   What now?

J. Charley, *Rome, Canterbury and the Future* (Nottingham, 1982)
The Easter People: The National Pastoral Congress (Slough, 1980)
Cardinal J. Koenig, *Chiese, Dove Vai?* (1985)
H. Ryan and J. R. Wright (eds), *Episcopalians and Roman Catholics: Can They Ever Get Together?* (Denville, NJ, 1972)
T. Ryan, 'Eleven highlights of Runcie's visit to Rome', *One in Christ* (1989/3)
'Westminster celebrations of the 25th Anniversary of the Decree on Ecumenism', *One in Christ* (1989/3)
E. Yarnold, *In Search of Unity* (Slough, 1989)

Index